The Last Free Man

Also By Dayton O. Hyde

SANDY: *The True Story of a Rare Sandhill Crane Who Joined Our Family*

YAMSI: *A Heartwarming Journal of One Year on a Wilderness Ranch*

The Last Free Man

The True Story Behind the Massacre
of Shoshone Mike and His Band of Indians in 1911

Dayton O. Hyde

THE DIAL PRESS
NEW YORK
1973

Library of Congress Cataloging in Publication Data

Hyde, Dayton O   1925–
  The last free man.

  1. Daggett, Mike, ca. 1845–1911. 2. Bannock
Indians. I. Title. II. Title: Shoshone Mike and
his band of Indians in 1911.
E99.B33D34   979.6'37   73-7784

To the lucky ones—the lonely ones

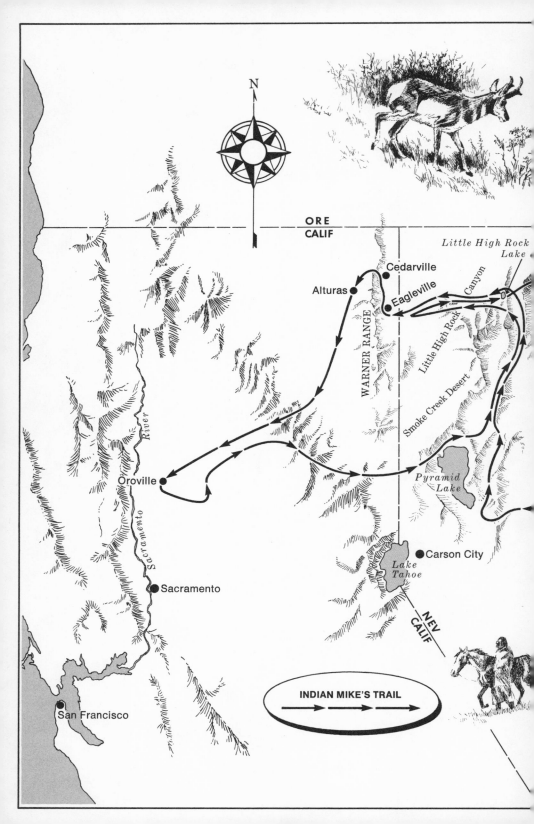

N

ORE
CALIF

Little High Rock Lake

Cedarville

Alturas

Eagleville

Canyon

Little High Rock

WARNER RANGE

Smoke Creek Desert

River

Oroville

Pyramid Lake

Sacramento

Carson City

Lake Tahoe

NEV
CALIF

San Francisco

INDIAN MIKE'S TRAIL

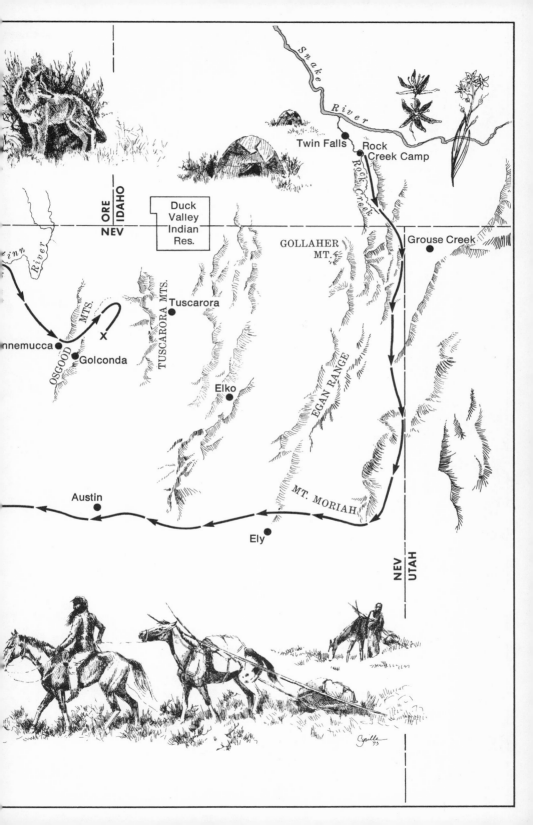

Snake River

Twin Falls

Rock Creek Camp

Rock Creek

ORE | IDAHO

NEV

Duck Valley Indian Res.

GOLLAHER MT.

Grouse Creek

inn River

TUSCARORA MTS.

Tuscarora

nnemucca

OSGOOD MTS.

Golconda

X

EGAN RANGE

Elko

Austin

MT. MORIAH

Ely

NEV | UTAH

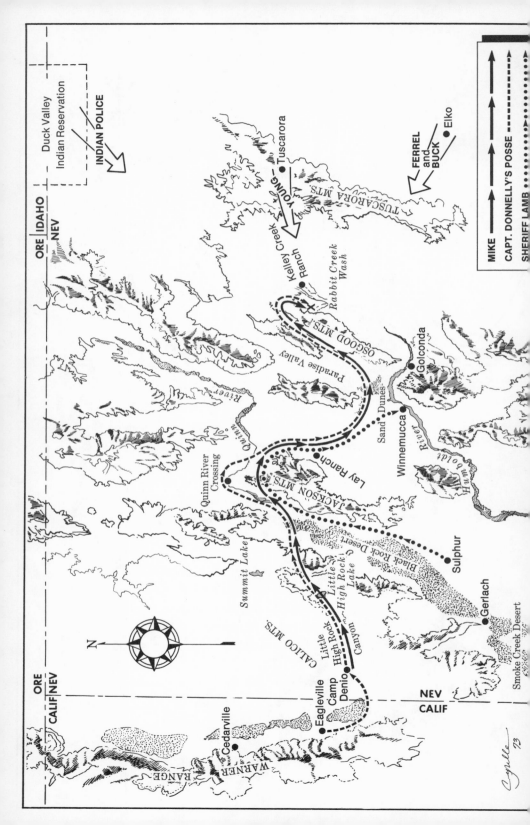

ORE | IDAHO

NEV

Duck Valley
Indian Reservation

INDIAN POLICE

Tuscarora

YOUNG

Kelley Creek
Ranch

Rabbit Creek
Wash

OSGOOD MTS

Paradise Valley

FERREL
and
BUCK

Elko

TUSCARORA MTS

Golconda

Quinn River

River

Sand
Dunes

Quinn River
Crossing

Winnemucca

Humboldt
River

Lay Ranch

JACKSON MTS

Summit Lake

Black Rock Desert

N

Little
High Rock
Canyon

Little
High Rock
Lake

Sulphur

CALICO MTS

Eagleville

Camp
Denio

Gerlach

Cedarville

WARNER
RANGE

NEV

CALIF

Smoke Creek Desert

ORE

CALIF | NEV

MIKE ▬▬▶

CAPT. DONNELLY'S POSSE ▬ ▬ ▶

SHERIFF LAMB •••••▶

Cyrille
73

1

Ask any bartender in the little northeastern California towns of Eagleville, Cedarville, or Fort Bidwell about "Shoshone Mike" and the massacre at Little High Rock Canyon, and he'll forget there's another customer, pour you drinks on the house till you're blind, take up your evening, and meet you for breakfast with a tale worn smooth in the telling of the last Indian massacre in history. Incredibly, it happened as late as 1911, but you won't find it in the history books, preoccupied as they are with big-name stars like Crazy Horse, Sitting Bull, and General Custer.

Chances are you were a stranger when the barkeep started the tale, but suddenly you've got friends pushing along the bar at each elbow, chiming in to tell you that one of their kinfolk, God rest his soul, was among those murdered, or else went along ahorseback through record northern Nevada snows on the last great Indian chase.

"Hey, did you know that when the bodies of Cambron,

Erramouspe, Indiano, and Laxague thawed out in the church at Eagleville, the bloodstains in the wood floor were visible for nigh onto half a century? Or that when Harry Cambron's body was found, his brother, Ben, vowed to wear his white shirt and tie until his death was avenged?

"You didn't? Well, let me tell you something else. When the men failed to show, the youngest man in the search party was a kid named Warren Fruits. Fruits was stumbling along in the snow at the bottom of Little High Rock Canyon, sinking shin-deep with every step, when the frozen hand of one of the dead men grabbed him right by the ankle! Man, little Fruits like to died!"

Back in the bar the next evening, a stranger comes in, and suddenly you're right there at the guy's elbow, helping the bartender along as if you were a native, as though it were your own story instead of his, making sure he doesn't leave out one tiny detail.

Depending on the rate of flow of new listeners into the three towns since 1911, over sixty years ago, the story has probably averaged a telling a week, and thus been told close to ten thousand times. Now and then a new reporter transfers to the area. If he's a drinking man, he'll have the story in a day, if a teetotaler, it may take him two. Caught up in the excitement any newsman feels at discovering a new tale, unaware that the story has thrilled many a newsman before, he usually rushes it out as his first big Sunday feature.

Think of it! Wild Indians massacring poor innocent whites, and as late as 1911. In the same year an astonishing primitive Yana Indian, Ishi, was discovered scavenging offal at an Oroville, California, slaughterhouse.

I first heard a tantalizing snatch of the massacre story from Mustang Smith, then the oldest, feeblest quarter of the population of a Nevada desert town named Denio. You can bet I was excited. The story was exclusively mine until I hit Cedarville a few nights later to discover it was public domain, and I was so shattered I tried to drop it the way you drop a round-heeled woman who's been passed around like a Saturday-night bottle outside a dance hall.

I'd dropped in on Mustang to ask if there wasn't a historic yarn in the old Dufferina place, just across the Oregon border, a picturesque, red flagstone ranch house, surrounded by willow-brush corrals, resting lonely in a sea of sagebrush, its windows vandalized and gaping and its people with their stories gone who knows where.

"Nope," Mustang said stubbornly. "Ebbling built that house way before the government bought the land for an antelope refuge. Nothin' ever did happen there except one time I stopped for dinner and old lady Ebbling tried to poison my dog. Ebbling, a rough, homely bachelor, dreamed up that house just to attract a wife, but if any woman came to look the situation over, the sight of his face, the loneliness of the land, and that mean old mother of his all conspired to run her back to town.

"Like I said," Mustang Smith went on, "there wasn't much story there. What you should really write about is Shoshone Mike. Back in 1910, I saw them Indians up by Virgin Valley. They was wild as wolves, that bunch. I had orders for a thousand head of geldings and dry mares for delivery to E. Stewart at the Western Horse Market, Tenth and Bryant, in San Francisco at seventy-five dollars a round. I'd been breaking colts for Charlie Demmick, the buckaroo boss for Miller and Lux, Black Rock Division, but I couldn't resist runnin' mustangs. I rode into that Indian camp looking for some horses I could buy cheap. Wasn't a soul in sight, but I could feel somebody watchin' and the hairs on my neck began to crawl like lice on a Paiute. Then I spotted a couple of big young braves slippin' down the ridge on pinto mustangs like they was aimin' to cut me off, so I spooked and run. Year after that, when they done what they done, didn't surprise me none. Always figured they was bad Injuns."

"About the Dufferina house," I said, only to be ignored.

"Killed off Harry Cambron and him about to marry Billy Denio's wife's sister, Laura Murphy, the comin' Satidy. When Harry didn't show up for the weddin', well, naturally, folks went to lookin'."

I sat back then and listened as the old man got all steamed up in the telling, and I drank it all in open-mouthed, until his daughter looked in the door, saw the flush on the old man's face, and asked me would I come back another time. I never saw him again. A few days later, I read in a newspaper that Mustang Smith was dead. He took his memories with him.

That year I crowded the story to the back of my mind but it wouldn't stay. I was half in the notion of becoming a writer and wandered around a lot on the desert, looking for things to write about, watching coyotes stalk black-tailed jackrabbits, buzzards drying their morning wings atop the rimrocks, antelopes muzzling their kids to secret napping places in the sage, rattlesnakes hunting noon-time shade.

Often I'd look up and imagine I saw Indians watching me from the rims. Sometimes way out there alone I'd feel them slipping so close behind me, I'd spook and run for the safety of my car, but always it was only the desert wind laughing on my tail.

My next taste of the story came just across the Nevada line, in the Cedarville, California, bar, as I've said, but I kept the story loose in my head, trying maybe to reject it, yet thinking about it on long horseback rides across the desert, tasting it, savoring it as one prolongs a lipful of rare wine.

Every now and then I'd hear the tale from a different source, and, though it was like meeting an old friend, I marveled at how time and the memory of man had distorted the facts in the telling. One thing was ever constant. The murdered men were always good; the Indians were always bad. By then I knew a few things myself about old Mike that made me wonder if the old Indian hadn't taken a bum rap to his grave.

Every now and then on my travels I'd stumble on parts of the story that hadn't been told—little bits here that made a snug fit with little bits there, fragmented maybe, and sometimes contradictory, but not without value. I came to realize that folks were looking at some events of history through too small a window. A story was being perpetuated that, however fascinating, was probably only the buffalo side of the nickel.

"Drop it!" I'd tell myself as I tried to sleep, and maybe I'd doze, only to wake up in the middle of the night with the smell of sagebrush and willow smoke strong in the room, and the sound of mustangs running, and the feeling the old Indian was trying to get through to me. "You want to talk, Mike, let's talk," I'd say. I never heard his voice, but maybe there were other ways he got to me.

I'd been raised with Indians, and loved some of them. I found myself trying to understand Mike in terms of other Indians I'd known personally. Through the years he came to have bones, flesh, a spirit. Instead of fleeing his shadow, I now could build my campfire in one of his lonely strongholds among desert rims, a hundred miles from anywhere or anyone, sit in the half darkness of a sagebrush fire, totally immersed in the past, waiting for Mike to stride in out of the nighttime that is history.

Why me, Mike? What was I to you—or you to me—when first our trails crossed? How deeply I could sleep then! Why didn't I accept you as history has recorded you? The cowboys from Eagleville beat their leather chests and said, "They were no-good Indians, so we killed them." The truth might better have been said, "We killed them, so they were no-good Indians." We whites are on trial here, Mike, even though we stand as judge, jury, and the accused. The Indian wars are different now from in your time, but, in far more subtle ways, we fight them still. Hopefully the end will come not through defeat but understanding.

As I write this I am living at Yamsi, the family cattle ranch in southern Oregon, built of a series of allotments my late uncle bought from Indians. My children are the first white children to grow up here. Surrounded by what was once the Klamath Indian Reservation, this is pine country. Westward I see the shining summer snowfields of the Cascades; eastward, jackrabbits and sagelands are only a few miles away.

As if symbolic of something, today, the very day I began to write Mike's story, I saw a white goose in a flock of normal gray-and-black Canadas. Neither snow goose nor bastard cross of one species with another, but a rare mutation, far lovelier than its brothers, though its beauty serves no function. Apparently, the other geese place no such value on him as I. Geese have their own social hangups, stratifications, and peck orders. Solely because of its color, the white goose suffers abuse, feeds at the periphery of the flock, and must fly the turbulent air in the last slot of the formation. Often alone, he flies an evening circle above my valley, seeking to better his lot, calling for acceptance to flocks feeding below, but, in the end, finding only rejection as before.

My wife raised herself on one elbow as I entered the bedroom. It was two o'clock in the morning and I had just come home from my session with Mustang Smith. Her eyes had trouble focusing. "How was Nevada?" she asked by way of greeting, then collapsed, intending to sleep.

But I wasn't about to let that happen. "Guess what?" I said. "I got myself an Indian."

She sat bolt upright. "You mean you shot one?"

"What I mean is I stumbled across a great Indian story to write about. Something with meaning. No more stalking about the desert trying to catch a couple of bobcats mating."

She gave me her "for this you wake me up" look and folded.

But I was off and running, telling her Mike's story, daring to think I knew Mike's story. Slowly she surrendered, came awake, and her eyes grew wide as I paced the room.

"Great yarn, isn't it?" I suggested. "I can see that you are absolutely spellbound, either by the tale itself or by my skill as raconteur."

Her eyes were china-doll big but sad. "I was just thinking I've never seen you excited like this—at our wedding, or even when the children were born. I think—I think I've lost you to that Indian, and I hate his guts."

From that moment, Mike came to be very much my own secret friend. Into my marriage came long silences, and often I would catch my wife gazing at me sadly. How could I tell her that I was trailing my new friend back into the past, a little-known Indian whose true story had been written years before on desert sands and, but for the faintest trace, erased by the relentless winds of time.

2

I am suspended in time. I have trailed Mike back into his past,
seeking to understand the old Indian, his family, and their
times. I have sought out not the rocky, sagebrushed desolation
of the alien desert upon which he died, but a magic, mountain-
ous loneliness in southern Idaho, the very heartland of his
being. Most likely he was born near there in the 1840s, and
there also he grew to warriorhood, forming an attachment for
his range that was to keep him stable and nearly local for the
greatest share of his days.

High above the fertile plain of the Snake River I sit on the
edge of the rimrock, dangling my feet over the abyss and
watching the white-throated swifts skitter from the rock chimneys to wheel and turn far over the greening checkerboards
of awakening fields, then return to their nests among the
fluted cliffs.

Far beneath me, a broad highway follows the valley, its
stream of hurtling automobiles looking no larger than a col-

umn of foraging ants. Jet contrails on the northern horizon plume the peaks into volcanos gently smoking. Looking down from unaccustomed heights, I see the back of a red-tailed hawk hunting short-tailed ground squirrels, and the back of a red-tailed crop-duster airplane spewing chlorinated hydrocarbons on a billion billion sucking, chewing alfalfa aphids. To distant horizons the land is covered with a pall of smoke. Whereas it once came from a thousand Bannock and Shoshone lodges, now it comes from factories, refineries, field burning, and household furnaces of a host of habitations stretching in a band from Boise on the west to Pocatello on the east.

Born in the 1880s, Pocatello is now a thriving city, though once it struggled for survival in the midst of the Fort Hall Indian Reservation. The white man made demands and the Indian gave and gave. From a mixed group of Bannock and Shoshone, the Utah Northern Railroad pleaded a right-of-way, promised the Indians five hundred head of good stock cows, built their railroad, then forgot to pay. White men drifted in, squatted along the right-of-way, then needed more land, which the Indian was wheedled into giving. Pocatello Station grew and grew, a pernicious cancer spreading out over the reservation and devouring it acre by acre. The Indian had been given a block of land as a reserve for all time in exchange for vast areas of his former hunting grounds; now the whites were slowly gaining it back from him.

Perhaps through that infant city of Pocatello, Mike wandered once with his family and spat with derision into the dust churned up by wagon wheels, staring in helpless wonder and dismay at the wood and stone houses springing up in the midst of Indian hunting grounds. He must have seen that the white man's treaties were no good, that the whites seemed not to honor them. It must have been obvious that the promises the white man made to lure him into trading his life in the hills for one on the reservation was like trading a prime stallion for

9

a blind, spavined, jill-flirted old mare. But, though many Indians fell for promises, Mike kept to his own ancient ways.

Somewhere, if only I knew where, Mike's trail lies before me, crossing and recrossing the land below. Here his band traveled down the Snake to catch salmon below the great falls. There his family drifted north with the spring melt to catch the first blooms of camas blossoms turning the wet meadows into the blue of mountain lakes. At Camas Prairie they spent a happy time healing up from winter, gathering and roasting the sweet, succulent bulbs, socializing with a host of other Indians, horse racing, swapping, and gambling. Here Mike's band struck southward, each travois laden with buckskin sacks of camas bulbs, for rendezvous with other Bannock and Shoshone families; then, protected by such numbers from Blackfoot reprisal, they pushed eastward as a group, over the mountains to the country of the buffalo. There Mike's path stretches southward toward pinion forests, where he gathered pine nuts for roasting, or westward toward the jackrabbit heavens of Nevada.

As I close my eyes, the scene leaps before me with startling clarity. I can see his band starting out on a journey—children running, boys teasing girls, endlessly pranking and eager to be under way, men riding and chatting, women leading up the travois horses in the rear. Infants ride strapped to their mothers' backs; nestled soft in diapers of shredded sagebrush bark, they peer black-eyed at the wondrous world around. Every soul seems tired of living close neighbors with starvation, moving with one real thought and purpose: to fill their winter-shrunken bellies with food.

I see a false bravado about them. Whatever their eagerness, life will not be easy. So disastrous has been the effect of the white man upon the land that even an Indian steeped in techniques of desert survival must struggle hard for existence.

But there is warmth too in the vision. I see a little boy

scampering through the sage, overtaking the leaders. Mike, the wiry gray-haired brave in the lead, thin-faced, golden-skinned, with hair chopped off shoulder length, reins his horse about as the lad trots toward him. He leans toward the child, grins to the other men, swings the lad up behind him in the saddle, then resumes his journey. The little boy's arms clasp tight around the chief's waist; he will be quiet as a mouse for fear Mike will remember he is there and send him back with the squaws.

The sonic boom of a jet plane high above the desert jars me back to the present and sends a whistling marmot scurrying to his palace of rocks beneath my perch. The vision of Mike and his family is gone, and I am more alone than ever. There is a limit to what any man can piece together from history. For the moment, I must rest content to stare out at the panorama before me, trying to understand Mike by understanding his land. I can be certain only that I am viewing lands Mike knew first nearly a century before.

Even before the coming of the whites, life on those arid lands was at best precarious. At times, cyclic buildups of jack-rabbit populations made the living easy for Indian and predator alike. The Indians wove long nets of fiber, staged drives, and netted great quantities of white-tailed jackrabbits. These they stripped of their white pelts for blankets, broiled their succulent flesh over willow fires for immediate consumption, or hung them for the desert sun and wind to dry. Later they would pound the metal-hard carcasses with stones on their flat rock metates into a powder for soup.

But the white-tailed jack was doomed. Year by year the white man's cattle, sheep, and horses covered the land in incredible numbers, cropping the grass into the dirt. No longer did the seed grass wave its tiny flags in the winds. While the Indian muttered about the white man's stock, he could not have known the more insidious results of overgrazing.

Sagebrush and rabbit brush were always present, but the plants were small and scattered, held in check by competition with the grasses. But with overgrazing, inedible brush took over millions of acres of once productive grassland, and soon grass existed in quantity only on the bottoms too wet for sage.

The white-tailed jackrabbit was a large varying hare related to the snowshoe hare, its young born with fur and with eyes open. A most important staple in the diet of the Indian, it preferred grassland to sage, and when the brush took over, the white-tailed jacks lost out to huge populations of the black-tailed jack, a small, scrawny, tough, inferior, and prolific denizen of the desert sage. The blacktails multiplied to incredible numbers, but as is inevitable with cyclic buildups of rodents in nature, sudden mass die-offs occurred until it seemed that there were no rabbits left of any sort, and then populations once more began to rebuild.

With the cyclic buildups of jacks came a corresponding increase of predators, desert bobcats, prairie wolves, coyotes, fox, eagles, hawks, and owls, whose own increase boomed with the supply of food. Predatory animals are geared by nature to adjust. In a situation where food supplies are on the upswing, the coyote, for instance, has more pups per litter, less when the supply dwindles.

The die-offs hit the rabbit population first, and the predators, including primitive man, competed fiercely for what was left.

Being omnivorous and mobile, man had the best chance for survival, but as predators turned to populations of deer, antelope, ground squirrels, sage grouse, and marmots, these too became depleted in number. Starvation ruled the land until, through lack of production or die-offs, predators adjusted their number to the supply of food. Along the rimrocks, fledgling eagles died in the nest; bobcats deserted their young to starve or sought other territories. Owls and hawks migrated hundreds of miles to better hunting grounds. The prairie wolf grew gaunt and lean; bitches coupled as usual, but if they conceived at all had only a pup or two, and perhaps these died when the starving bitch gave no milk. Winter storms weeded out the weak and genetic losers until populations were once more in balance.

Insects too came in cycles. One year the land would be denuded by grasshoppers, traveling in clouds, and wildlife got fat on the surplus; the next year there might be none. One year the pinion pines would be loaded with cones filled with nutritious pine nuts; the next year there would be pitifully few, and before the Indians had half a chance to beat the cones off the trees with cone poles, the rodents and pinion jays would have stolen them away.

Generally, with ample predators, game cycles were slowed, but the white man also wrought havoc on predator populations. The sheep man waged war on coyote, wolf, eagle, and lion until nature's system of checks and balances went awry, so that for many species, population boom and bust became more frequent.

If the Indian were lucky, in a year when pine nuts were scarce rabbits might be plentiful, and he could substitute one protein for another and still flourish. But the Indian knew he played a desperate game of roulette with nature. However fervent his love for gambling, the game of chance he played with fluctuations of food supply was too deadly to be enjoyed. Bad years brought scarcities of all foods. Then other species competed so fiercely for what was left that starvation haunted the land. Those were years when the Indian fed upon the carcass of the wolf, and the wolf upon the carcass of the Indian.

In the harvest of most crops, timing was of the essence. Bands of Indians worked feverishly to harvest one short-lived crop before another ripened. The harvest of camas bulbs, a succulent wild lily, lasted only two or three weeks; then the fields of camas that turned the meadows blue turned green again almost overnight as the flowers faded and the grasses overwhelmed the withering stalks.

By climbing ever higher into the mountains, following the retreating snowbanks, Mike's family extended the seasons for some weeks, but the eventual fading of one crop might mean a forced march of a hundred miles to the next harvest. Those who described the Indians as aimless wanderers were wrong. The Indian was generally on his way somewhere with definite harvest in mind. Often he raced against time, for many harvests lasted only a few days before the winds scattered what the insects, birds, and animals had failed to gather.

One of Mike's functions as chief was dispersing his band well for the maximum harvest, when two harvest seasons coincided. Although they all attended salmon runs, some might be harvesting grass seeds or pine nuts while others were picking fruit such as salmonberry, thimbleberry, elderberry, huckleberry, and choke cherry, while still others dug trail potatoes and other roots, such as tule or wild rose. Mobile as the desert winds, if one crop failed they passed on quickly to another. Mike had learned from his parents, and they from theirs, that this system brought the best yield from the stingy land.

There was a time to gather duck eggs along the marshes, a time to gather the developing heads of cattails for candy, new shoots of the tule, seeds from the yellow water lily, a time when the sage grouse were strutting on ancient booming grounds. Mike had to possess a real feeling for the rhythm of nature and the ability to utilize wild crops the way the white farmer had to master the tame. Next week was often too late. The lazy Indian could be seen only on the reservations, where he lived on allotments of rations. In the wild, the lazy Indian was a myth, a figment of the white man's imagination; the Indian had little time to be idle, for the one thing he could count on was that the winter would be long and, under the best of circumstances, that he would be hungry before spring.

For Mike's band, transportation was a very real problem, as was storage. Often the sheer weight of a harvest for even the twelve to fifteen individuals in his band required that the Indians move tons of food down out of summer ranges into winter storage areas, where they buried it in caches or hid it in inaccessible caves.

Practically all the vegetative foods the Indian gathered had to be cooked or prepared before the material was digestible. Grass seed had to be hulled and winnowed, pounded and ground in stone bowls or on flat stone platters into flour, and then baked before being edible.

Pine nuts were roasted either in the cone or out, depending on the taste desired. Often the nuts were ground into flour, which made a delicious paste to be smeared on meat. Acorns had to be ground and the tannic acid leached from the flour before they were edible. Because there was no available refrigeration in summer, meat had to be cured either by smoking or by drying in the sun, or by a combination of the two. Hides had to be tanned with brains and smoke before they became soft enough to use. Fish had to be filleted and smoked, and all foodstuffs had to be protected from weather or they spoiled with the first rain of autumn.

In the days before the white man, with only raiding parties from other tribes to contend with, life was difficult; now Mike had to function in a fast-changing world in which the whites were supreme. But Mike was a wise man and he adjusted well, although he refused to compromise his way of life.

In all likelihood, Mike was born about 1845, just before the great movement of settlers across the plains to Oregon and California, when Fort Hall was still a remote fur-trading post and the West knew whites only as wandering mountain men and explorers. From boyhood he must have seen bitter battles against white invaders as his tribe fought settlers funneling through their lands on both the Oregon and California trails.

Mike was perhaps twenty-five when the Bannocks and Shoshone were herded onto the Fort Hall Reservation in 1869, thirty-five and in his prime as a warrior and hunter during the Bannock War of 1878. He grew up immersed in traditions that placed great emphasis on a man's ability as a warrior or horse thief. The more dangerous the deed, the more important the coup. Revered was the brave who stole into the camp of the enemy and made off with horses tied by the lodge flap.

Mike must have thought those Indians who accepted life on a reservation lazy, depraved people worthy only of his contempt. He himself clung to the old way and subjected his family to its disciplines. If he made concessions to the whites, they were concessions of expediency alone, without which he could not have survived. He was surprisingly adaptable if the compromise meant that he and his family could live the old way in peace.

Each time Mike visited the reservation at Fort Hall, he must have noticed sadly the changes in the Indians, the effect of idleness, their slavery to alcohol and opium,* poverty in the midst of promises, and dilution of Bannock blood with Shoshone, Negro, and even white. Increasingly, his old comrades of buffalo hunts and Indian raids must have talked about things of which he knew little and cared less. Their worlds came to center on the few acres of their allotments as the government tried to make them into farmers.

Each time he saw them, disease had sent more and more old warriors to their graves. Men he had fought beside grew weak and died in their beds of syphilis, measles, scarlet fever, mumps, and tuberculosis. He watched as children were

*Brought in by Chinese laborers.

snatched from parents and sent miles away to boarding schools to be taught all sorts of useless things that would never fill an Indian's belly when it was hollow from winter hunger.

If Mike tried to share with them the freedom he and his family still knew, and talk to them of the old ways—the thrill of being nomad, brother to the winds, the satisfaction he felt seeing his young men grow not fat but strong, able to survive in the manner of one's ancestors—the reservation Indians only looked at him with uncomprehending eyes. They shrugged off his admonitions as though to say, "If the white man is fool enough to feed us, let it be."

Soon Mike no longer made the journey back to Fort Hall. His world became centered on his family, for they alone understood his preachings before the campfire. His range became the mountains south of what is now Twin Falls, Idaho.

But still his way was fraught with danger. If one were to exist, there were concessions to be made with reality. In the language of the whites, "Thievin' redskin" was just one word. If one Indian sinned, the whites took revenge on the race. At times they seemed to persecute Indians who had committed no other crime than being born brown. There was no feeling among them that one individual Indian might possess rare artistic talent or that perhaps a father loved a wife, his daughter, or his son.

Mike's one great compromise, even though he kept to primitive ways, was to attach himself to white ranches in his territory so that he and his family might supplant any inadequacies of the wild harvest with periodic earnings from ranchers. Even though he might have had prior claim to the land at Rock Creek Canyon, on which he settled, Mike could not have owned such property. Somehow he must have realized that his safety and very existence in that valley depended on how much faith his white neighbors kept in him and on their need for him as a neighbor, able and willing to supply seasonal help. Once he acted to arouse white fears or even suspicions, the valley would be lost to him forever.

Inside Mike, the fierce chief must have existed still, but the practical side of the man held sway. In the mountains surrounding Rock Creek Canyon, and south to Gollaher Mountain, lay an Indian heaven where he could live out his life in a reasonable facsimile of the old way. It was his home, his land, birthplace of his children, and their rightful heritage. But in his infinite wisdom, the old Indian knew his only chance to live in harmony with his white neighbors was to be trusted and useful, and to be ever careful to let them think they owned the land.

Mike's campsite on Rock Creek.

3

Few Indians surrendered less to change than Mike, yet his curious canyon backwater stood immediate to a dramatic and historic altering of the environment. From his vantage points, as he hunted the rims and ridges of the south hills, Mike must have paused frequently for a safe but spectacular view of the changing face of the valley of the Snake.

In 1865, near the point where Rock Creek leaves its canyons and ventures out among the rolling hills of the Snake River Valley, one James Bascomb, later killed by Chief Buffalo Horn during the Bannock War, built Rock Creek Station. It was a sod-roofed log cabin, and to this day stands on the historic Stricker ranch south of the town of Hansen, Idaho. Not only was this the first trading post west of Fort Hall, but it served as a pony-express station, a stop for the Ben Halliday Stage Line, and straddled the largest artery of wagon travel in the United States. Farming operations have erased most of the heavy wagon ruts, but names on the rocks at the mouth of Rock Creek stand as monuments to travelers buried there.

Rather than follow the Snake River Gorge and fight the tributary canyons and wheel-busting devil's rock gardens along the rimrocks, caravans held to the foothills, where occasional tumbling mountain streams from melting snows on higher elevations made natural meadows and oases in the arid, dusty land. There exhausted men and animals found temporary havens of rest and plenty.

But eager to push on to the Oregon country before winter, the travelers took little notice of the rolling, sagebrushed plains, and only cursed the chalky dust that churned in clouds from wheel and hoof alike, to coat the travelers with its flour. In time, those same lowly hills and hollows, ditched and irrigated, would become the Magic Valley, one of the richest agricultural areas in the world.

Idaho did not become a state until 1890, but in April of 1874, a rancher named Pat Garrity traveled to Silver City to file on rights to use Rock Creek water for irrigation. Sparks and Harrel, a huge cattle outfit, were next on April 1, 1878, followed by another rancher, Lars Larsen, Sr., on May 1. Between 1874 and 1887, there were nineteen filings on the water draining from the forested canyons and bald rocky hills that made up Mike's world.

For several years a stage ran daily from Boise eastward, carrying fresh produce and other staples. High on the hill above Rock Creek Station, approaching drivers gave their war whoops so the hotel folk could bring the pots to boil. Fast freight came by horses, slow by oxen who seldom averaged more than nine miles a day.

In the 1870s, placer mining had attracted hundreds of prospectors to the area, and these were followed by Chinese, willing to scavenge through what others had overlooked. Even though there was a population to be fed, the main crops were not produce but cattle, grain, and hay. Canyon ranchers raised their families in dirt-floored, sod-roofed houses, fed them on prunes and jackrabbits until the prunes gave out and only rabbits were left.

Slowly a trickle of small farmers drifted in to settle the Snake River Valley. Some of them had been the route to Oregon, grown discouraged, and remembered better lands back along the trail. Mike must have wondered at the huge clouds of dust and smoke rising from the valley floor, turning the sunsets red and brilliant, obscuring the sun as settlers dragged sagebrush out by the roots, raked it into long windrows, and set it afire.

Heavy with oil, it burned readily, filling the air with yellow acrid smoke and fragile gray ash. Average rainfall was only four inches, but, little by little, irrigation canals were scooped by horse-drawn Fresnos, and ditches moved water out over the thirsty land. Acre by acre, year by year, Mike saw the gray green of his jackrabbit and antelope pastures replaced by the emerald green of irrigated crops.

Grazing and hunting pressures pushed game animals back into the mountains. Often in the hills about him, Mike passed riders from the Shoesole outfit, tending thousands of Sparks-Harrel and later Sparks-Tinnan cattle roaming the vast open ranges of northern Nevada and southern Idaho. If Mike muttered Indian curses under his breath, he avoided friction. Sometimes, if the riders were known to him, Mike rode out of the brush to sell them reatas of braided rawhide or neatly made, dove-soft buckskin gloves. More often he remained hidden until strangers passed upon their business without knowing they had been observed.

Any contact with whites involved risk. However peaceful the sleepy white communities may have appeared to Indians watching from vantage points in the surrounding hills, whatever the seeming conviviality of Sunday picnics and church socials, violence, real and raw, simmered close to the surface, making mockery of the white man's pretentious ways.

While Indians had been forced to adopt a life of peace, the whites still lived by the gun, and although they were wont to praise God, law, and the courts for others, they settled their own differences with fists, clubs, knives, and guns.

On July 4, 1880, an emigrant couple named Edwin and Phoebe Crockett arrived at Rock Creek Canyon after a journey of several days from Grouse Creek, Utah. They drove on past small ranches, looking for a place to camp and rest their tired horses.

While their three little sons slept, they explored around them, discovering plenty of unclaimed grass for the horses and the cows tied behind the wagon. There was also plenty of water and firewood, a welcome change from the dry sagebrush camps of the past days. Springs tumbled from hillsides, and Rock Creek chased through natural meadows profuse with lupine, buttercups, daisies, Indian paintbrush, and pentstemon. After endless days on bone-dry reaches of desert, the couple felt this was the promised land. There was plenty of good land to be had for the taking and water for irrigation; the cattle they saw grazing along the bottoms were exceptionally fat and sleek, ample testimonial to the quality of the feed.

The family settled down, hauled logs from up around the bends of the canyon, and soon they had erected a one-room cabin, followed by sheds and corrals for their livestock. Soon they were ready to challenge the winter with a supply of firewood for the stove they had brought with them in the wagon. It was a lonely land, but so busy were they that they did not miss living in town.

Then, one morning in autumn, they looked up to see smoke hanging over the willows just above them in the canyon, and Edwin Crockett felt a chill pass over him as he discovered that the smoke was coming from a primitive hut of willow poles covered with hides and brush. Hanging from the trunk of a giant river birch that spread out over the camp like a roof were war drums, spears decorated with eagle feathers, bows, quivers of arrows, baskets for gathering food, and jackrabbit nets. That night the Crocketts bolted their door, but they could hardly sleep, for soft and muffled through the logs of the cabin wall came ceaseless, toneless chantings and the faint, persistent thunder of Indian drums.

New to the country, the Crocketts had no way of knowing whether or not the Indians were dangerous. Tales of the Bannock War, only two years past, were still on everyone's lips. Folks down at the store had briefed them as they passed through and made it seem like yesterday when Buffalo Horn had passed by Rock Creek with four hundred angry Bannock warriors.

At dawn, Edwin, tired and exhausted from his long night's vigil, slipped to the window. To his horror there were indeed Indians slipping through the willows. Now and then he could catch a glimpse of a brown face or black hair. He thought he heard war cries, but it was only the sound of Rock Creek tumbling its way over stones on its way to join the Snake River. Then suddenly the figures moved into the open, and he saw it was only a group of Indian boys catching their breakfast, calmly fishing the stream the Crocketts had planned to make their very own.

The storekeeper only laughed when the Crocketts told of their experience. "Why, that's only Indian Mike," he chuckled, "back from his summer wanderings. Their camp has been in that bend of the river for years. Better be neighborly. You can't find a better family for neighbors than the Mike Daggetts, and if he moves away, some bad Indian might take his place."

It was the Crockett children who were most impressed. The ranchers down the canyon from them had no children, and soon the Crockett boys and Mike's young sons were constant companions. Although the Indian boys played along the stream, they were too shy to come into the house. One boy about seven was just learning to hunt from his father, and soon he was making Indians out of the Crockett boys, showing them how to shoot with bow and arrow, how to set deadfalls of flat stones for rodents, how to trap fish with willow baskets or set snares in the brush for cottontails and white-tailed jacks.

Soon Phoebe Crockett herself ventured over to the Indian camp with peace offerings of some bread she had baked and some new potatoes she had bought in the Stricker store. At first Mike's shy wife, Jennie, hid in the hut, but soon ventured forth with much giggling but no conversation, for Jennie spoke but few words of English.

Indian Mike was not a tall man. As the Crocketts saw him, he stood well under six feet. He was slender and thin-faced, and his complexion was lighter than Jennie's or that of his round-faced children. He wore his black hair in two short braids, which came to his shoulders. He was a shy man, accustomed to minding his own business, though he had an engaging grin and spoke easily enough in broken English when spoken to.

Providing for their large family was a full-time job, and one in which all but the very young engaged. When Mike was not hunting, he sat about camp, working his rawhide strips, braiding reatas, hackamores, rolled reins and romals, and all manner of equipment useful to cowboys and in demand as trade goods at the local store. One cowboy bought a reata from Mike that measured over ninety feet long.

Jennie made moccasins that came up almost to the knee and handsome beaded gloves with fringed gauntlets that protected the wrists from biting winter winds. She had a regular clientele who used her gloves. She measured a new customer by tying a knot in a piece of string for the length of each finger, and from then on the cowboy could send for a pair of gloves and Jennie would fish in her pack for his finger strings and the gloves would always fit.

All the Rock Creek boys, Indian and white, had ponies of their own, and much time was spent ahorseback, playing games along the meadows or exploring the hundreds of caves in the cathedral rimrocks that watched over the fertile meadows along the canyon bottom. For the Crockett boys, spring was a time of sadness, for suddenly, one day they would look to find the camp deserted, save for the gaunt ribs of the hut from which the hides had been removed. Their playmates had gone with their parents, no one knew where.

It must have irked the Crockett boys that Mike's children did not have to accompany them to the little dirt-roofed cabin. Indian schools existed on the reservation at Fort Hall and Duck Valley, but the children would not have been welcome at the Rock Creek school. All winter long, the white boys rode their horses down the snowy canyon road. Throwing their saddles over the top log of the school corral, turning loose their mounts, they dashed half-frozen for the warmth of the barrel stove in the one-room building.

When the weather was cold, students vied with one another to sit next to the fire, and often the room would reek with the stench of wet, scorched wool as some pupil huddled too close to the sagebrush fire. Trips to the outhouse in the brush were always executed at a run when the weather demanded; at twenty below, no one cared to dally along the way. Sometimes in fall or spring, when it rained steadily or the snow on the dirt roof melted, the ceiling leaked badly, and students jockeyed back and forth to find a drier place to sit. Sometimes, looking out the window of the school, the students saw Mike Daggett and his boys riding across the hills. Often the Indian boys would be waiting in the brush to ride home with them from school.

The summers were busy times for the Crockett boys. As they grew older and stronger, they pitched in to help their father at haying, building fences, branding calves in the spring, or gathering during the fall from their range in the Shoshone Basin to the south. When necessary, they drove the team and buckboard to the store for groceries, worked in the big garden, picked fruit in the orchard, and fell into bed at night like dropped stones.

Sometimes a rider might drop by for the night, and as he sat in the summer twilight, he might mention that he had seen Indian Mike and his family over by Goose Creek to the southeast, or camped by Salmon River to the southwest just over the Nevada line, and the boys would question him eagerly about Mike's boys, Catchum Charlie, and Eat-em-up Jake.

It was a pretty sight in the fall to sit on a rimrock near the eagle's nest above the Crocketts' house and look down upon the huge stacks of loose hay in the stackyards like giant loaves of baked bread, to see the fat cattle grazing on the aftermath pastures with big husky calves at their sides, to see the wood-shed full to bursting with billets of newly split wood, to see the apple trees golden-leaved in the orchard near the house, and to watch the deer tiptoe down from the sagebrushed hillsides to munch on fallen apples or paw the big yellow pumpkins with hard rubber hooves.

And then, quite suddenly, there would be smoke above the willows again and Mike's family camped as though they had never been away; fish split in half and tied tail to tail over racks, smoking over a willow fire; strips of venison hanging from green willow poles; and Mike's boys, of course, bigger and stronger than ever for their summer in the hills.

At first the boys seemed a mite shy, but soon they were wrestling, chattering, and playing tag, as though the friends had never been apart.

There were girls, too—Lizard, Snake, Heney, and Hattie—

who were busy with girl things and didn't bother the boys, though there was much giggling and teasing.

Mike thought a good deal of his children, and by all accounts they were well raised. No one saw him angry, yet the children minded well. One never saw one of Mike's brood with torn or dirty clothes; they were neat, and as clean as anyone living the life they led could be.

They were part of the scene and had been there as long or longer than most of the whites, who took them for granted and would have been shocked at the idea that Mike and his family might not be there forever.

4

Today an asphalt highway wanders south of Hansen, Idaho, past the store where Mike brought buckskin moccasins and gloves to trade for staples, past the Crockett place in Rock Creek Canyon where Mike wintered with his family, past the streams where Mike fished for trout and salmon, past the towering rocks and sagebrushed hillsides where once he hunted and pastured his trail-worn mustangs. Curvey and treacherous for the gasoline birdwatcher, it winds ever higher into the magic mountain vista of what Twin Falls folks refer to as "The South Hills."

The physical aspects of the land have altered little since Mike's day, but changes are there, and, as I drive up the canyon for the first time, mining for history, I become sullen and unreasonable, as though I have a right to expect the canyon to remain a shrine to Mike's memory, standing un-touched through the millennia as Mike left it on his last day there. In Mike's time only a twisting wagon road, braved by an occasional woodcutter hauling his winter fuel, dared the canyon, for in spite of the small, frequent meadows of rich alluvial soils, in most places when the river was not worrying at the hills on one side of the canyon it was assaulting them on the other.

It is a busy road. Cars laden with skiis and snowmobiles drive past herds of sleek, modern cattle, wintering on small ranches along the bottoms. A haze of blue exhaust hangs over the red-barked river birches as car follows car ever higher up the timbered fastness of Rock Creek Canyon toward the gleaming snowfields high above. The drivers hurry onward, on parole from city jobs, with little thought of history, unmindful that from some rocky pinnacle Mike might look down with some astonishment upon his changing land.

With some of the Indian malice toward whites in me, I stop my car to watch a man cranking hard and desperately on the motor of his snowmobile. His face is red from exertion. From his appearance he has an office job in Pocatello, Twin Falls, or Boise. His children wait impatiently beside him, afraid to bug him by asking when the thing will start. They are like bear cubs, trained by parental anger to be wise, knowing that when parents are under stress it is healthier to be undemanding.

On their lips, however, is their impatience. Their heavy sigh says, "Daddy, when is the snowmobile going to start? Hurry up, Daddy. Those people came after us and there they go up the trail." The children show their disgust as yet another machine starts and a family whirls off over the snow. At this point the urchins would trade their father for a better mechanic.

The father wipes his forehead with his sleeve, leaving a streak of black grease. I sit watching him from my car as he struggles. It gets to him. He stands upright as if to challenge me. "You want something?" he asks with a look.

"Ever hear of Mike Daggett?" I ask maliciously.

29

The man glances over, shakes his head, and looks back at his machine. "Mike Daggett? Hell, no. Who's he?"

I am ecstatic. I have exacted tribute for Mike, trapped this utter stranger into pronouncing his name. "He's just the guy who owns these hills," I reply, and drive off before he can protest that this is National Forest land and he has a map to prove it.

Once I have removed the curse of my presence, the snowmobile starts with head-paining racket, and soon he and his children are speeding up over the ridge where the horizon rounds against the sky.

Mike would have tolerated no such nonsense as the snowmobile frightening the winter-weakened animals of the forest or the motorbike disturbing the silence of his land. As I pass a family sitting in a snowbank and wish them all piles, I smirk deliciously as I imagine an indignant tourist complaining loudly to a forest ranger, "What do I do now, mister? An Indian just rose out of the brush and gut-shot my Honda." The people in the snowbank stare at me because I am grinning in an era when people are too harassed to smile.

Inside I am happy. I had come to Rock Creek for the first time half dreading what the land might tell me about my Indian, but now I am relieved. No man who had chosen this incredible land to be his home could be just another Indian. Mike had to be an extraordinary man.

From the road, the canyon walls rise steeply, then shoulder out into a jumbled land of buttes, round rocky domes, hidden valleys, amphitheaters, canyons, tablelands, bald hills, and thick forests. Low country, high country, each plane presenting a varied cheek to the sun, each hillside, each canyon a different microclimate with its own specific environment and flora and fauna, no two alike.

Spelled out in terms of food and security for Mike and his family, here was the perfect land. When the harvest of one

30

slope changed, five minutes took one to a different world. It was a land where lush, watered mountain forest and meadow met rocky sagebrushed desert, each secure in its own niche, each safe from invasion by the other by its own varied climate and condition of moisture.

The higher elevations are covered with a snowpack, but lower elevations and southern exposures are bare. Even in winter, Mike's mustangs could grow sleek and fat, with nary a bite of hay.

There is food in abundance. In the canyon bottoms are rich forests of alpine fir, river birch, willow, red osier dogwood, maple, aspen, cottonwood, juniper, alder, thimbleberry, elderberry, and a host of others. Rose hips stand bright orange against the snow, a vitamin-C-packed picnic ever available for the hungry Indian. A blue grouse explodes from a thicket, scales a hillside, and is lost in the next valley's glades. It would take a man hours to accomplish the grouse's journey of an instant.

From beneath a sagebush, a cottontail rabbit scampers for a new haven up the slope. A flock of sage grouse, large as young turkeys, blending with the hillside like so many weathered lava rocks, stand from where they have been crouched motionless; for a moment the hillside is alive with them; then, when their motions cease, they blend again with their surroundings as though changed suddenly to rocks by an Indian god.

Loping to the safety of the skyline, just one leap away from disappearing, a black-tailed jackrabbit pauses upright on his haunches, nose quivering as he pauses to see what the frightened cottontail has seen. As I move, he spurts forward and is lost over the lip of the sagebrushed hill. A dozen ravens play with unseen thermals at the rimrock edge, tumbling, catapulting downward, only to fling high again. The poet Edgar Allan Poe could never have known a raven or he would have made his literary bird merry, pranking, full of fun and mischief, but never gloomy.

Up to now, I have ignored the scattered ranch houses along Rock Creek, saving them for last. I have spent weeks roaming Mike's hills, trying to know them as he knew them, but now reality dictates that I leave some footsteps around my own ranch for a time, across the deserts in Oregon. Before I go I should at least interview the natives.

I shudder to violate someone's privacy when I place so high a value upon my own, and I pass ranch after ranch until I am nearly out of them. Pausing by a mailbox I make out the faded, sun-beaten letters: Charlotte Crockett. It is like reading the name on an ancient tombstone, and it is part of Mike's history. Would anyone here remember Mike? Or are all the Crocketts who played a part in the old Indian's life long dead and gone, and the children concerned with more important problems than history? "No Trespassing" signs shout at me from the fence posts, and I am well aware of the problems of the rural landowner, but something gives me courage—maybe it's Mike, urging me on.

A plank bridge takes me across the beer-brown swirl of Rock Creek, and the dirt road curves down a fence-bordered lane. Giant cottonwoods and poplars testify to the age of the ranch; apple trees, barrel-trunked and gnarled, speak of the fertility of the alluvial soil stolen from the mountains by the stream. Dogs bark at my arrival, vicious at one end, tails wagging at the other. They are faking, denouncing my violation of their territory, but secretly hoping to be scratched and noticed.

At first the house seems startled by my daring knock. There are long moments of silence, then, somewhere in the interior a chair scrapes, and the aged floor creaks as someone as yet unknown to me moves slowly to my bidding. For the moment I stand waiting, noting the green lawns and flowers, the feeling of peace and tranquillity. The face of an elderly woman takes shape at the curtains, and the door opens in trust. She gives me the quick "Well, he's not from around here" appraisal common to farm wives, then stands expectantly as though to say, "Well, mister, I've opened my door to you. Better speak your business before the bugs get in."

Shyly I explain that I'm a writer, piecing together the story of an Indian named Mike Daggett, who lived hereabouts before 1910.

It is as good as an introduction to a friend. The suspicion fades from her look. "Come inside," she says brightly. "I'm Nora Fear, Charlotte's mother. You must mean Indian Mike. Well, you came to the right place." Shaking with excitement I enter the house, half expecting to see Mike having coffee at her table.

But the table is empty and the trail dims somewhat. "I've heard lots about Mike, of course," she says, "but you should really talk to Carrie Crockett, my daughter's mother-in-law." I wait in silence, expecting to hear that Carrie just died last week and took her memories with her. "She lives just up the valley at the old Crockett place, and if I can find my bonnet and you'll give me a ride in your automobile, we'll just pay her a call."

Carrie Crockett is in her eighties, a bit brittle and fragile, but spry. As with many older people, she has forgotten what she did last week, but memories of olden days are sharply etched. Independent as an owl, she lives alone with her dog and some cats. I arrive with Nora, so there is no thought that I am a stranger. I am so excited I spill scalding tea down my pants leg, and I am forced to sit in pain rather than hop around the room tearing my trousers off in front of the ladies. At last I am in the hallowed presence of someone who actually knew Mike as a person!

"About time someone straightened out the lies they told

33

about Indian Mike," she says. "Nora and I were talking about Mike just the other day," Carrie remarks, easing herself down in a chair. "The Crockett house here was built in 1880. Mike had lived round about for several years before the house was built. He had a lot of big husky boys, Mike did, and my husband and his brothers used to play with them, and learned to fish and hunt in the Indian way. Somehow kids pick up the Indian way lots quicker than they do the white, but the folks were smart enough to want the boys to see something of a vanishing way of life.

"Mike wintered here for just years and years. Camped just above the upper stackyard where Rock Creek makes a frying-pan bend. He was a fixture in our lives, just part of the Crocketts' growing up, and when he left in the spring of 1910 and never came back, well, I reckon something of the flavor of the valley went with him."

Carrie rises from her chair, shuffles across the room to pick up a paper from the floor. She bends carefully from the waist as though she were a rag doll hung over a clothesline to dry and takes moments to straighten up. "A person gets old," she says by way of apology, as she shuffles back to her chair. "Just you wait."

I want to tell her I've had to take my stirrups up a notch myself and the saddle doesn't feel quite the way it did ten years ago, but I am silent, afraid to break the train of her thoughts.

"Yes, Indian Mike was all right," she goes on. "Always paid his bills at the store. Seemed always to have a little money he got from selling things like rawhide reins and reatas to the ranchers. His wife, Jennie, made buckskin gloves, and they used them as trade goods at the store for things like flour, sugar, salt, and coffee, and maybe canned goods when they were real hungry. For most Indians, though, canned goods were too heavy to pack around and they seemed to like wild food better."

"How did he get along with the rest of the ranchers?" I ask.

"Everyone around here liked Mike, and we knew he wouldn't take any of our calves, though he had every chance. I guess Mike's being here close kept stray Indians away, and we were glad to have one here we could get along with."

Now and again, as Carrie rambles on, I glance at Nora Fear, who smiles happily at me as though to say, "You see, I brought you to the right place!"

"Mike's boys were always fishing up and down Rock Creek. There were lots and lots of little trout. In the spring, before all the irrigation and power dams were built, salmon used to run up Rock Creek. Mike and his family used to build willow dams in the stream, leaving holes beneath so fish could pass upstream. Then they would weave willow baskets into the spillway so that when the salmon were frightened back they would go over the dam instead of under and end up in the basket. Then the squaws would fillet them out into halves, tie the two slabs of meat together by the tails, and hang them on willow poles to smoke and cure."

My wet trousers are cold and clammy against my leg. I shift uncomfortably, and I have sudden memories of being sent home from school as a child in similar condition. I have the ridiculous thought that Indian children with their lack of white man's inhibitions seldom had that problem. "What was his hut like?" I inquire.

"It didn't look like much by our standards," she replies. "They sharpened willow poles, stuck them into the ground, bent them in at the top, and tied them with buckskin thongs, then covered them with hides or even brush. When they left in the spring they took the hides along and left the poles standing. They always had a use for anything the Crocketts could spare in the way of scraps of metal or even food. When the folks had extra food about like fruit or spuds, they always gave it to Mike's family."

"Did Mike work at anything?" I put in.

Carrie reflects a moment. "I never really knew Indian Mike to work, though he was usually busy. Mainly he just fished and hunted and made rawhide. The boys helped, breaking horses, gathering cattle off the ranges, branding calves, haying, fencing; they were good hands, though mostly they were gone in the summer when we needed them most."

"What kind of man was Mike?" I ask. "I mean, as a person."

Carrie shrugs her thin shoulders. "He was a little shy, kept just a little bit apart, though goodness knows the boys were friendly enough. Mike thought the world of his family and was good to them. He never seemed to get angry, and, of course, they did things together as a family, something that the whites with our claim to superior ways could take a lesson from.

"Sure as the wild geese migrated in the fall, Mike would appear with his band. No one saw them come—just one morning before Christmas they'd be there with their camp all set up and a hover of smoke from their fire hanging over the birch trees. Then, most likely, we'd see the boys fishing along Rock Creek, not daring to come to the house, yet when they saw the Crockett boys, why, then they'd come running up, faces split into happy grins. It was always fun to see how they'd grown while they were gone.

"They always wintered here, even after the boys grew up and became men. In the spring they'd load up with groceries at the store Tranmer and Robinson had down the valley a ways; then, one day, Mike's family would be gone and the hides stripped again from the willow ribs. And many a time the Crockett boys wished they could go with them. In those times, of course, life was mighty dangerous for the Indians, and we never knew for sure that they would return."

Again Carrie pauses, reflecting on the past. "We never asked them where they spent the summer. They must have come in the seventies and stayed off and on until 1910. After that, we never saw one of them again."

When Carrie had reminisced enough, she sent me outside her old house to look at Mike's campground at the bend of the stream south of her abode. The site is on a secluded, hidden peninsula of level ground, surrounded on three sides by a rushing stream and protected from the curious by thickets of river birch and willow. I am disappointed that the years have erased all trace of his camp. Cattle stare at me from the brush where they are tending to their winter itches. Far up the hillside across Rock Creek, warming themselves in the late afternoon sun, dry cows laze in the sagebrush. A golden eagle, struggling to get airborne with a freshly killed jackrabbit, descends half the hillside to pick up speed, then finally flaps heavily to an inaccessible spire of rock where it can devour its last meal of the day with a view of the surrounding canyon.

When I return to the house, I have only one exposure left in my camera and have to decide whether to photograph Carrie and Nora outside the Crockett house, holding up a large black clay bowl from Mike's camp, or a chickadee hanging upside down from the gate post.

Alone once more, I wander up Rock Creek Canyon, feeling Mike's presence around me as I climb past the great rocky cathedrals that are common in so many of Mike's camps from here to Nevada and California. Each bend of the canyon brings new vistas. Hills screen me from the world; the steep rising earth on all sides protects me in a womb lined with bleached grasses, brush, and lichened rock. So wild is the land that Mike could live here still, and no one would be the wiser.

Carrie Crockett holding an old Indian bowl found at Mike's camp.

5

If the whites in Mike's day, outside of those who knew him, were unduly harsh in judging his value as a human being and his place in history, and failed completely to understand him in the context of his land and times, I too had to be careful that my own romantic nature did not go to the opposite extreme and attribute to him a magnificence he never achieved. Mike's value as a study came partly from the fact that he was not a great and famous chief, and thus more nearly represented the case for many Indians of that day. What happened to Mike could have happened to any Indian who tried to remain free of white domination. Society, then and now, could neither understand nor tolerate an individual who failed both to depend upon it and to follow its rules.

As a judge of Indians I was more ill-equipped than most. I had fallen heir to all the distorted concepts that a public-school education in the Middle West of the 1930s could provide. Growing up as I did in Michigan, a state that had solved her

Indian problems early and could look upon the race without hatred or envy, I was steeped not in the real poverty of the Indian but in his romance. My first Indians were silhouettes cut out for school windows at Thanksgiving and the improbable redskins of Cooper and Longfellow.

I must have been six when the hired man told me he knew for a fact that Indians felled trees by walking round and round the trunk more than a million times until the roots wore through and down came the tree with a crash. I wore out a summer vacation, a new pair of Buster Brown shoes, and the friendship of a terrier named Bim in testing his theory.

Just when I might have become disillusioned about Indians, I ran across Ernest Thompson Seton's *Two Little Savages,* discovering between the pages of that delightful classic a couple of nature-loving boys much like myself, obsessed with living in the woods like Indians. Other boys wanted to be doctors, firemen, aviators, and the like. From then on I had only one goal in life—to be an Indian.

I was further hooked by the story-telling prowess of my mother, who charmed young listeners at her hearth with tales of a childhood romance with Hiawatha. My patient father murmured to me once over a picture of that historical chief, "There but for the grace of God and two hundred years goes your step-father."

I was crushed to learn that contrary to Longfellow's poem, which placed Hiawatha somewhere in my back yard on Lake Superior, he was actually an eastern Indian. A further blow came when I learned that my mother's only real contact with Indians was limited to one atrocity when her confirmation bloomers were stolen off the line by a Chippewa named Tommy Madosh, who counted coup on whites by raiding clotheslines.

Tommy took only half. If there were two petticoats on the line, some innate nobility in the man made him steal only one.

He finally carried off half the double door of a local mansion, and when this bright blue work of art suddenly graced Tommy's tar-paper shack down in the pine woods near the iron works, the law investigated to find the rooms packed almost to the ceilings with stolen ladies' apparel. Warm and comfy atop the whole shebang dwelt Tommy's ancient Chippewa mother.

I might have learned a worthwhile lesson from this about how Indians take good care of their parents, had not the local judge seen matters in a different light and sentenced Tommy to six years in the prison at Marquette.

By the time I came along in the mid-twenties, the only prominent Indian influences left were a monument in the park to a Chief Kabawgam, names of nearby towns such as Ishpeming and Negaunee, a real birch-bark canoe in the rafters of a neighbor's camp, and an Indian cemetery where the graves had been sadly vandalized by artifact hunters. The sense of shame I felt at being a member of a race that could act so callously toward the dead of another made me desire more than ever to change the color of my skin from white to brown.

I tried. My brother John and I spent our summers on a lonely lake not far from Lake Superior. In that northern latitude, we all looked as luminous white as plants imprisoned under rocks or the sprouts of old potatoes rotting forgotten in damp, musty cellars. We spent days lying naked on the woodshed roof, trying to wrest some permanent stain from the weak northern sun, but to little avail. What tan we achieved beyond a pink blush came from grinding red sandstone into paste and applying it liberally to every part of our bodies.

We made spears of hop-hornbeam wands, hardening the tips with fire; bows we shaped from heavy staves of black ash. In our eagerness to finish, the bows were always so thick and clumsy we had to rest after every shot. Only the hired man, a giant Finn named Boris Paajanen, was stout enough to pull the bows to their limits, but he disappeared forever from our lives when he shot a hunting arrow through the Celotex wall of the woodshed and stuck it quivering into a beam only inches away from my grandmother, who was headed for the ice chest with a plate of butter.

We boys continued our masquerade as Indians until one summer evening we pretended the neighbor's foraging milk cows were buffalo. As we stampeded the herd through the woods, my brother inadvertently ended the adventure when his arrow caromed off a stump and struck a big speckled Holstein right in the udder. For the next few years little was heard of our tribe, but the shame had nearly worn off when I folded my tipi to leave Michigan for my uncle's ranch in Oregon. I left a land where Indians were only history for a land where they were part of my daily life. The ranch was a primitive island surrounded by the Klamath Indian Reservation.

I must have looked a sight to my uncle and his cowboys as I stepped off the train, hampered by not one but two long bows slung across my shoulder, just five days out into the world from northern Michigan.

"Jeezuz H. Crow!" old Homer, the foreman exclaimed. "Damned if they didn't send Sitting Bull himself. What we need around this country is one more Indian."

I ignored the comments, but my knees trembled and almost buckled as I took in the scene. Leaning against the station were a couple of reservation Indians in Levis and huge black Stetsons. They stared back at me in astonishment, then thought it better to move back out of bow range. They were having trouble holding each other up, and I thought they were drunk, though now, thirty years later, with new wisdom, I think they were only laughing.

My uncle, Buck Williams, a tall, sparse man, took me in stride as though he found in me some semblance of his own youth. The son of an Episcopal bishop, he had run away from home to live with the Cree Indians in the Northwest Territories. So ferocious was his first winter that the Cree family across the ridge from him lost the husband on the trapline, and the wife kept the children alive by feeding them the grandmother. Ridden by scurvy from a steady diet of beaver meat, in time my uncle drifted southward to Oregon's Klamath Indian Reservation, where he worked at setting up individual Indian allotments of ranch and timber land.

I hadn't been at the ranch two days when Buck introduced me to my first real live Indian. "Watch out he doesn't lift your scalp," he teased as he shoved me out the ranch-house door to meet the Indian boy who'd come to play with me from the deer camp on the adjoining reservation. For such an adventure as this I had come west, but now the dreaming seemed suddenly more attractive than the doing, and I was thirteen-year-old shy.

In the honest light of the mountain sun I suddenly felt cheated. Leaning against the rail fence, with a shock of sandy hair to match mine, skin freckled by fourteen sunny summers and an Irish ancestor, stood my Indian, and if that weren't disappointment enough, this great-grandson of a chief had blue eyes and, instead of buckskins, wore Levis a whole lot newer and cleaner than mine. Since my uncle had arranged the whole thing, I could sense him now, peering with great delight from the window.

"Hi!" the boy said shyly, holding out his hand to shake mine.

But I didn't give in so easily. So carefully had I rehearsed this meeting of the two races, that I was determined not to waste it. "How!" I said, raising my open palm to show him I had no concealed weapon.

His face showed his astonishment. "Hey," he said. "Cut the

Indian stuff. I might be enrolled as a tribal member, but my dad was just as white as yours and my mom was only half. My name is Dan."

"Guess I got carried away," I admitted. I shook hands and gave him my name, all the time wishing I could have a more splendid moniker, like Pretty Weasel or Growling Bear.

"Let's go hunt some ground squirrels," he suggested.

"Oakey-doak with me," I grinned. "I'll go get my bow and some arrows, then we'll go get yours." What I was fishing for was an invitation to visit the encampment.

"Bow and arrows, my foot. There you go playing Injun. Let's play white man. We'll attack the camp when the menfolk are out hunting and kill off the women and children."

Indoctrinated as I was by white school books, I missed his reference to Wounded Knee. A whole lot of steam had gone out of my adventures, but I followed him Indian file across pine-dotted meadows toward the headwaters of the Williamson River. Scavenging some rusty coal oil cans from a dump in the pine trees, we spent a frustrating hour packing water from the spring and pouring it down holes, hoping to flood out some squirrels to keep as pets. But the squirrels had other entrances and scrambled to scold us saucily from a safe distance.

I soon forgot about the project when Dan told me he knew of a snipe's nest with four brown-mottled eggs. As I trailed behind, pretending I was one great warrior slipping up to count coup on another, I could not know that I was to spend years of my life trailing the ghost of an Indian named Mike who had died fourteen years before I was born.

44

6

By the time I entered his world, nearly thirty years after Mike's death, the Indian had pretty well adapted to the reservation system and had adopted such white influences as schools for his children, indoor plumbing, and the automobile. He functioned best, however, when his life style permitted him a return to the woods to seek part of his food. As they had since early times, the hunting and fishing camps remained a great part of the Indian's life. The camps not only assuaged his cravings for independence by permitting him to gather his own food without white help, but the very sociability of the camp life was group therapy for his soul.

If his bloodlines had been contaminated by those of other tribes and races, so had his culture been diluted by the addition of various handy items from the white man's world. As I trailed my friend Dan, my first view of the Indian camp at the head of the Williamson River shocked me into realizing that, if I had expected to see blanket Indians in full color, I had

come along many years too late. The crude hut of their ancestors, with entrance hole in the roof, had been replaced by the
canvas tipi à la Sears and Roebuck; the bow and arrow by the
Remington automatic; and the travois by the Ford pickup,
mounted with a rotating spotlight atop the cab for blinding
deer at night. Instead of being beaded buckskin, their dress
might have been described as modified western cowboy.

But my nose detected a difference between that camp and
any white camps I had been in. Above the general air of hot,
mildewing canvas and the pungence of willow smoke was the
odor of ripening fish and decaying venison. Racks of smoke-
blackened chicken wire held a forest of fish fillets and venison
strips, over a few slumbering fires that tried half-heartedly to
smoke away the hordes of buzzing bluebottle flies and angry
yellowjackets competing with the smoke for the meat. I had
been dying to taste real smoked trout and venison jerky. Now
I filed silently behind my friend Dan, in desperate fear someone might ask me to try a sample.

Tending the fires sat an old lady, hair bound severely with
a faded pink bandana about her forehead. Her skin was withered and furrowed, her bones seemed to rattle like seeds in
the dried pod of her body as she rocked mindlessly on her
heels. Knees drawn up to her chin beneath skirts of faded,
flowered muslin, she stretched out her arthritic hands over the
fire, ignoring the flames. There was only a faint flicker in her
eyes to mirror our passing. Otherwise her flat, blank look
rendered us invisible.

"Don't look at her," Dan hissed. "She'll put a spell on
you!"

His advice came too late, however, for I'd already given her
my best Sunday smile, one that I'd been practicing for days,
just in case in this forest of tents I met up with some shy young
Indian princess. Only the woman's eyes changed as she

adopted the fierce glare of a goshawk and stared me down for my impertinence.

Carrying a bottle of beer the same shade as his hand, a tall, hawk-nosed Indian came out of a tent, hid the bottle as he saw me, decided perhaps that I was too young to testify against him, and gurgled the whole bottle down as though in defiance of the white man and his law.

"Hsst! Dan! That guy's drinking!" The thought that an Indian was contributing to his own downfall and that somewhere a rich bootlegger was driving a fancy car bought and paid for by selling hooch illegally to Indians was too much for my pure, Middle West mind, and I fell over a pile of firewood.

"That's just beer," Dan said in disgust at my innocence. "You should see him when he's on shaving lotion. He goes blind."

The camp extended to my uncle's fence, where, like frozen laundry, several hundred deer hides had dried metal hard on the top wire. At our approach, chattering hordes of black and white magpies, working the hides for tallow, flashed to the haven of the jackpines.

Looking about the camp, I took the Indians to be a lazy bunch. Some latent Yankee scruple rose up within me at the sight of strong men sleeping in the middle of the day, until I realized that the use of spotlights had transformed the Indians into night hunters, and this was their time of rest.

That evening, regular as clockwork, pickup after pickup would taxi out of the camp, headlights standing off the dust from the truck ahead, scattering over the volcanic pumice roads that bifurcated every nook and cranny of the reserve. For the Indian, there was no regulation as to season or method of harvest, no limits as to sex or number harvested. From every pickup, a brilliant Cyclops eye probed the forest glades.

Eyes glowing like beacons, the deer stood vulnerable, helpless and blind, awaiting the sting of death.

Once the deer had fallen to a bullet, the Indians dragged it a few short yards to the road, gutted it out, loaded it into their pickup, and left intestines and head in the road as primitive sign to other Indians that the hunting had been good there.

In the early evening, most of the deer harvested were does, fawns, or small bucks still running with the does. It was only after midnight that the big patriarchs rose from their beds, stretched, and moved cautiously off to drink or graze on bitter-brush, a low green browse growing beneath the ponderosa pines.

If I had expected the Indians to rush to their lodges at my appearance I was mistaken. The sight of a tall, awkward white boy tripping over his feet in their midst seemed not to concern them in the least. They were on home ground here. For them race either did not seem to exist or was not worth considera-tion. Their eyes looked through me as I passed, with none of the impolite stares of intense interest to which I subjected them.

My glance sought out some vestige of olden times, but there were few. Some of the older women wore bandanas, one man wore braids. Hides hung to dry, jerky and fish smoking on racks, but nothing really Indian other than the dark velvet of eyes, duskiness of complexions, the broad flat accent with which many of them spoke, and the laughter and gay sociabil-ity of the group as a whole.

"If I were Indian," I remarked to Dan, "I'd learn how to weave beautiful baskets and do bead work; it must be getting to be a lost art."

Dan only glanced at me in annoyance, not only because the skills I mentioned happened to be squaw's work, but perhaps because once again he suspected me of pushing the Indian thing. I looked about sadly. The agency superintendents committed to controlling Indian uprisings by destroying their culture and making them dependent upon whites had done their work well. What I was seeing in this hunting camp was a culture in transition, a people in jeopardy as an entity, the last gasp of a race on its way to oblivion. Already they were almost white. I could not see that the transition was to a higher form.

I kept close to Dan, talking eagerly to him, mainly to show those watching that I belonged. In reality, I felt ill at ease, out of place, discriminated against. A minority of one among a hundred Indians.

Dan paused near a sagging, tattered tent, where a heavy-set Indian lounged upon the soft duff of a rotting log. His huge, round battered face had the appearance of raw, purple beefsteak. With clumsy fingers, he rolled a cigarette, licked it like a cow licking a new calf, aimed it blindly at the target of his lips, lit a kitchen match with a discolored thumbnail, and set the contraption to smoking. For a moment it looked as though his whole face was going up in smoke. He grinned then with such a huge "Look, I did it!" smile I was afraid the cigarette would fall back out of his mouth, but there it clung, as though glued to his puffy lower lip.

"How'd he get his face so beat up?" I whispered to Dan. "He looks like a prize fighter."

"Rodeos," Dan answered. "He was once a damn fine saddle bronc rider, but the white contestants kept getting him drunk, so all he'd ever win was day money here and there. He got bucked off drunk once and kicked in the face. That was the end of him as an athlete."

The man rose stiffly to his feet as though we were grownups. His eyes squinted hard to see us, but still they retained their twinkle.

"This is my uncle, Henry," Dan explained. I was never introduced. It was as though my visit had been broached to Uncle Henry days before.

49

"So you're Buck's nephew," Henry said. He had a resonant voice and fine diction, without a trace of the broad, flat accents of the others. Somewhere along the way he had picked up an education. "I've known Buck since he first came to this country many years ago." He crippled to the fire, toed a can of beans away from flames licking off the label, then sat down on a block of wood and became part of it.

"What are you going to do," Henry asked me, "work for your uncle?"

"Guess so," I nodded. "Summers at least. When I'm not in school." I didn't know exactly where on his face to look; my glance kept skipping around that battered terrain. If I squinted, his Levis became buckskin, and if I drew a deep breath through my nose, I could smell the smoke of ancient campfires.

"Well, that's good," he said, nodding his large head so affably that his dusty black Stetson slid forward until he disciplined it back with a sweep of a huge wrist. "I used to work for Buck now and then. It ain't a bad outfit to work for. Feed pretty good." He chuckled at a sudden memory.

"Years ago I was helpin' Buck brand calves at the corral on the claim he bought from an old Indian named Kay Davis. Everybody there got drunk except your uncle, and it would have helped if he had too. I got into a fight with a big German they called 'Dutch.' I never did know what his last name was. He called me an Injun, which I was, but I didn't seem to like being called that by a foreigner. He was on one side of a six-foot Page wire fence and I was on the other side, but we were so drunked up neither of us saw it. I'd take a big swing, hit the woven wire with my bare knuckles, and, man, wouldn't the blood fly. Then he'd do the same thing. Then he'd charge me like a bull and just get so far and that wire fence would pick him up like a baby and fling him back. He'd get even madder then cause he'd think I'd done it.

50

"I would have killed myself right there on that fence, except I fell back into the branding fire and burned the seat right out of my britches. Never saw Buck so mad. Fired us both, and Dutch and I went to town and finished our drunk together. Next time I saw Buck in town he said, 'Henry, when are you coming back to work?' "

Henry paused for a moment to stare into the dying embers, and the big grin faded as though he'd suddenly taken stock and realized there were only a few more years left and not the best ones either, that there was a price he must pay now for all the booze and hard knocks. Like most other Indians, he could laugh about being drunk; in all that huge body there wasn't an ounce of shame.

Toward evening, as Dan and I were trudging up the darkened valley toward the ranch house, we met a big, grumbling Hereford bull ambling down out of the forest toward water. Scared, Dan and I both clambered up the same lone pine tree, which happened to be the bull's favorite scratching post.

"I thought Indians were supposed to be brave," I chided Dan.

"They are," he retorted, "but just now I'm having trouble with my white blood." He glared up at me where I was running out of tree to climb. "Listen, Chief Chicken Liver. You want to be a warrior so bad, why don't you count coup by jumping down and leading the bull away?"

The bull decided matters for us both. Bellowing a nervous challenge to another bull already in possession of the distant water hole, he hooked one great horn against our overburdened sapling, dozed it down, scratched his scrotum on our prostrate forms, stepped calmly over us, and meandered into the gloom.

The gentle old bull, of course, hadn't known we existed, but it gave us an experience shared that reached fearful proportions in the telling and built a camaraderie that was to last

61

between us many a summer; it was strained only on those all too frequent occasions when I tried to turn him back into an Indian.

Dan desired to be neither Indian nor white, but just a person. This astonished me, of course, for I would have been so damnably proud to be an Indian. But then, maybe that's easier—to want to be an Indian when you know down deep in your heart that you'll never really have to be one.

7

Perhaps I could have settled down sooner to write about Indian Mike, had not distractions, a plague to most writers, kept me from the task. In the late fifties, I bought the ranch, Yamsi, from my aging uncle. In the sixties I was much preoccupied with raising a family and maintaining a tenuous truce with the banks to keep them from foreclosing on the mortgage. But I had not forgotten Mike and, year by year, I took time out to travel his trails and add missing pieces to the puzzle.

For the Indians about me, these were years of change. From a group of dissident Indians who wanted cash more than land sprang pressures for termination of the reservation lands granted them in 1864.

The Office of Indian Affairs originally intended that the agricultural and timber resources of the reserve be harvested by the Indian as he needed them to exist while he completed the metamorphosis from savage to white culture. To hasten this end, all lingering traditions, religious beliefs, crafts, and native languages were discouraged. Since the Indian had no written language with which to put his heritage on ice for a time, the chain was soon broken and much of the culture that might have kept pride alive in Indian hearts was lost.

The key thought was that the Indians should manage their own resources for themselves, do their own work, harvest their own timber as needed, saw the logs into lumber in a mill owned and run by Indians, build their own houses, and perhaps sell the balance for a profit. Individual agricultural allotments were set up, and the Indians were issued cattle on a loan basis in hopes that many of them would be able to survive as small farmers or ranchers.

But it was naïve of the government to assume that the presence of a huge block of timber and rich agricultural land right in the middle of Klamath County could long remain uncoveted by the whites. The resources of the reservation and those of the county became hopelessly enmeshed.

White farmers decried the fact that Indians were doing little or nothing with their properties. Tax payers grumbled that Indians gained many a benefit from the county but paid no taxes. Mill operators, searching for a steady source of timber for their mills, petitioned Congress to release more and more Indian timber into the market place.

White supervisors were ordered to give job preferences to Indians, but when the Indians showed poor job attendance, whites took their place. In the end, all the Indian got from his vast timber resource was a small per-capita allowance from which management costs had been deducted.

In time, although a few Indians were successful in the cattle business, most of them failed, defeated in part by the very sociability of their nature and their failure to give up traditions of communal living. Ranching is a lonely occupation, and the ranchers spent much time in town, leaving their herds vulnerable. In the eyes of the Indians, cattle issued on loan with the Indian department ID brand belonged to all of them and were to be eaten as needed, with no concern that the government would one day require the Indian to whom they had been issued to repay the cattle loan with a percentage of the calf crop. When that day came, the Indian merely grinned, shrugged his shoulders, and apologized that the cattle must have died. Which was true.

Year by year the white man drove a wedge into the heart of the reservation by purchasing personal Indian allotments of timber or ranchland. If the last right of the Indian was to hunt and fish on his land as he saw fit, that right soon meant little. Often, when the Indian rode to his favorite deer ridge or fishing hole, he found that the white man had been there before him. Chief beneficiaries of the Klamath Reservation were mill owners, car dealers, and bootleggers, not necessarily in that order.

The Indians were an intelligent people, and their ranks eroded constantly as those who made the transition to educated, responsible citizens shunned the spotlight focused upon a minority committed to mayhem at drinking parties and fled to other localities instead of staying to be a source of inspiration and pride to the others.

Indian children who excelled in the early years at school quit trying as they perceived that, however they tried, there was little future for them. The lucrative jobs would go to whites; banks would be chary about lending an Indian money; the best they could hope for was a second-class citizenship. Young girls stared down at their often dumpy bodies and cast heartbroken glances at the school football star carrying the schoolbooks of a willowy blonde, and took their frustrations out against the system by trying to prove they didn't care.

Money was the great social equalizer, and the way to get money and be as good as anyone else was to sell the reservation.

Capitalizing on the discontent of younger Indians, the whites stood idly by and watched the Indians themselves vote to terminate their reservation. It was a battle for territory that had raged quietly for 107 years, and the whites won it without a shot fired in anger.

Although some Indians invested their money wisely, many Indians now admit that the $43,000, their per-capita share, is for the most part only a memory. Inevitably they must face angry questions from the coming generation, who ask their parents, "What have you done with my share? How could you sell land and hunting rights belonging to all Indians for all time?"

As a means for keeping the Indian isolated from society, the reservation system was never destined to stand the assault of time. But the lands should have remained a continuing resource to produce supplementary aid to help the Indian adjust and compete with a white society.

For the Klamaths it is now too late to go back. No longer do the Indians gather in sociable groups to hunt and make jerky; their camps are gone and the summer forests silent. In autumn, hordes of white hunters swarm over the former hunting grounds of the Indian to engage in a desperate shoot-out. Parents would not allow their sons to face such hazards in the name of patriotism as the woods present in deer season.

Into the Indian towns of Sprague River and Chiloquin pour hordes of refugees from California, fleeing earthquakes, smog, congestion, and its handmaidens, zoning and regulation. Many former Indian lands have been subdivided. In the midst of his jackpine thicket, the mule deer is rooted from his bed forever by the engineer staking out a homesite.

My friend Dan too is gone. Once in elaborate ritual we

swore always to be brothers, but somehow in his late teens he did the very thing he had fought against in his childhood, he became an Indian, bitter and disillusioned, and quit trying, without hope for a life of equality. When I saw him in the council house of his people just before termination, I grinned and held out my hand to him, but he looked through me without seeing. Here, in the presence of other Indians, I did not exist for him.

I saw him again only once. I was half-asleep in the anonymity of a barber's chair when he came in the shop, dressed in flashy attire. His clothes said, "I've got my termination money. I'm doing O.K. for myself. You see, I'm just as good as the white man now." He told the barber he'd been traveling, seeing the world. "You know, Frisco, Bakersfield, Phoenix, Denver." He'd just dropped in to say hello. When he left he slipped the barber five bucks, maybe, for old times' sake. Then, turning to the old, arthritic Negro bootblack at the rear of the shop, he threw some change on the floor. "And here's something for you," he said in a patronizing tone, and disappeared from my life. There was a hush of embarrassment in the shop when he had gone.

One by one my Indian friends vanished from the scene. Idleness got them, and frustration with their lot. There were senseless, drunken murders, automobile wrecks. It wasn't that the Indian could hold liquor better or worse than a white man. He enjoyed being drunk, and for him there was no shame. When he drank the frustrations left him and he was as good as any man. He'd fight anybody that said different.

My uncle hired a wild bunch for haying, and I was soon fast friends with a fat, round-faced Indian named Toy Brown. A three-hundred pounder, Toy always had a laugh ready and time to visit when he saw me. Any small joke would split his pumpkin head into a jack-o'-lantern grin, and his huge belly would shiver and shake with laughter. My uncle would ban me from the hayfields because Toy never got any mowing done when I was around.

Toy was a familiar figure at local rodeos, where he served as flank strap tightener for the bucking horses. Depending how Toy liked you, he could set the strap to buck you off or let you ride. When he put you on the ground, the first thing you heard above diminishing hoof beats and the roar of the crowd was Toy's laughter along the chutes.

Once a prima donna of a world-champion bronc rider came to town. Strutting along the chutes, he pushed Toy out of the way, and I saw the old Indian's jaw tighten; then once more the twinkle was there. He winked at me where I sat dreaming on a pile of bronc rigging, and I followed him back behind the chutes, where I helped him steal a gentle children's horse, a dead ringer for the bronc the champion had gotten in the draw. The announcer gave the man a huge buildup, but the gentle old horse came out at a long trot, looking in the stands for his master. The crowd thought it was just part of the clown act, and all the guy got was uproarious laughter.

The cowboy got a re-ride horse, of course, but Toy knew just where to set that flank strap, and the cowboy, still smarting from the laughter, bucked off on his head. I can still see the tears of laughter streaming down Toy's cheeks.

We would be friends still, had not tragedy put an end to our camaraderie. When Toy sold his ranch near the town of Beatty, he used to talk with quiet joy of the good old age he was going to buy with the money. "Hey," he'd say, slapping his huge belly, "no more sitting on a mowing machine all summer long for your uncle, either."

But, according to Toy, his wife and step-daughter spent his money for him and when it was all gone they taunted him, told him he could spend his old age all alone.

"You leave and Toy shoot you," Toy said, and this time he didn't grin.

"You fat old Injun fool, you're scared to shoot anybody," the step-daughter said, and she and her mother began to pack.

Toy proved two things then. One that he wasn't afraid, and two that he was still a pretty good shot with a rifle.

My friend submitted quietly to the law. There was no use explaining Indian justice to the white man, for he'd never understand.

I sent him cigarettes down at the jail, half expecting they would turn the old man loose, since there were many worse than Toy running free. But Toy got life in the penitentiary.

There was no shame to him when I said good-bye, and we shook hands, man and boy, through the steel bars of the jail. "Yesterday's gone," he shrugged. "Toy just took care of to-day, and anyway, for the Indian, tomorrow never comes."

Now only Mike and his band are left for me. Alone with their ghosts, I feel at ease. On my desk lies a curious scattering of relics from Mike's past, his bones dug by scavenging white ghouls from his grave and dropped to bleach white in the desert sun; willow-lodge poles from his camp in the Little High Rock Canyon rims; weathered remnants of his travois poles, deserted as he fled that lonely bastion; a milk can, its top stabbed open by a stone hunting knife. One by one I hold them in my hands. They are my ticket to the past. The odor of crushed sage gathered from his last camp permeates the room.

The spirit of the man is with me as I write. No hatreds there, no suspicion of brown brother for white. Mike is dead, and the dead know all things. He has seen my heart and found nothing but friendship and respect for the Indian. No thirsting lust for his hunting grounds or hunger to take an Indian as trophy. Only a love of the land and a love of the Indian as he was part of its ecology and its history. Only a sadness that the Indian of old, with a culture far older than Christianity, has bled from the scene.

Mike died in 1911. It is now 1972. I feel a sense of urgency as time slips on, and year by year the trail dims and becomes harder to follow. There are days I can write about Mike and days when I must wait for answers to questions, pursue leads back into the fragile memories of old settlers, pour over newspaper accounts already brittle with age, yellowed by time, delve into archives for letters that will shed some light upon the truth I seek.

Often, as I open the door of the ranch house to let in the winds from the meadow, I hear the calling of geese from the meadow, see the white goose sweep over the house as though it were only a clump of pines, and soon, like a single oarsman, stroke toward the shine of distant water. Sometimes I see the misfit fly one last circle before night, plumage rosy with the last pink gleamings of the setting sun.

No more able to be solitary than was the Indian, it makes frequent, pleading queries to the flocks below, but the ganders and hens alike stretch out their necks and hiss like serpents. His landing only triggers a wing-pummeling charge that sends him airborne again to a painful solitude he will never understand.

The bird is a mutation of Moffit's Canada, a subspecies whose range covers that vast area from Utah to California over which Mike hunted. The head and neck of the bird are normal black with a white cheek patch; the rest of the body is of gleaming ivory, mystically translucent. Ancient man would have worshipped such a bird as a god.

A faint trace of rust mars the ivory perfection, as though the bird has purposely dressed its feathers with iron oxide from the marshes to a shade of drab more acceptable to its fellows. Persecution has made the bird wary. Among all the flocks, he is the first the stooping eagle will mark as prey, the victim the incredulous hunter will pick as a trophy from the clamoring multitude.

60

As a lover of nature I wonder about my responsibilities to the bird. Should I attempt somehow to capture him, to keep him safe from inevitable destruction, or leave him alone as nature intended, solitary in his own hostile world to take his chances as they come? To be judged by nature solely on the superiority or inferiority of its mutated genes, judged without sentiment or long wait in the courts? The white man made a similar determination in deciding the fate of the Indian. One way let the Indian genes swim for it in the great genetic pool, to prosper or perish; the other isolated him on reservations rather than let him take his chances, a brown man in a new white world.

Often the white goose seems to beckon me as it glides over my forest and settles like one lingering patch of snow upon the darkening meadow. I could accept its color, cherish it for being different, thrill to being its friend. Only the flying keeps me from fleeing my responsibilities to finish life as a goose. One cannot know the birds who has not tried to fly, to run, arms beating however clumsily, off a rise, and felt the wind slip cool, strong but elusive through one's fingers.

Nor can one know the Indians of old without wearing moccasins, starving, freezing, roasting, subsisting on fare gathered by one's own hands, eaten raw or squirming or cooked over a sagebrush fire. Someday, as I shuffle across the deserts in my moccasins, Mike will rise out of the sagebrush loneliness to beckon me, and I shall follow, never to be seen again.

8

By 1911, if bands of Indians were seen on the wastelands of the West, they were only hunting parties from the reservations. Ishi, the Yana Indian, who was found grubbing for food among slaughterhouse offal near Oroville, in northern California, in 1911, was unique in that he lived a hidden, secretive life without white contacts. The ruggedness of the terrain assured him of a niche little affected by the white man however close he lived to Ishi's brushy canyon hideaway.

The full story of the Yanas may never be known. Although Ishi never again made contact with his people, and was assumed to be the last of the Yanas, ranchers living in the immediate area are insistent that, as late as 1937, Indian arrowheads were sometimes found embedded in the wool of sheep, and butchered deer, hung from the horns and dressed in the Yana manner, were found suspended from trees.

Mike's band was unique in that it was probably the last band of Indians in North America living the old life, in the ancient way. If their lot was a hard one of extremes of weather and fluctuations of food supply, it was theirs by choice, to be preferred over life on reservations. But it was a life fraught with incredible danger, with starvation or even slaughter ever on the horizon.

It was not the world their ancestors had known, but one more difficult. The white man had cut down the pinion pine orchards for firewood and fence posts, blocked and diverted streams so that no longer did fish migrate in number. They deliberately destroyed the buffalo, and through hunting pressure, drove plains species such as elk high into the mountains. Huge flocks of sheep covered the land like a snowfall, chewed the grasses and forbs into the ground. Cattle and horses ranged out all winter long, and in the wet meadows hogs rooted out the big lush camas bulbs.

To the whites this brought some measure of temporary prosperity, but for Mike's nomads, hunger stalked the land. Most dangerous of all to the Indian was a white hysteria fostered by the conviction that the Indian was a subhuman with no more rights than a coyote. In order to protect himself from the Indian the white man set up an elaborate military and police system; what was really needed was an army dedicated to protecting the Indians from the whites. Little by little the last remaining wild Indians sought the reservations, if only as a means of safety. Mike, of course, while shunning reservation life, did compromise with reality by spending at least part of the year near a white settlement.

The original inhabitants of Rock Creek Canyon were Shoshone, headed by Chief Tuanna, but they either died off or opted for the reservation, until in Mike's time only a handful remained.

One of the most popular Indians with the whites was a peace-loving brave known variously as Indian Jim, Rock Creek Jim, or Salmon River Jim, since, like Mike, he often camped along the Salmon River in northern Nevada, a stream now known as Salmon Falls Creek. Settlers knew Rock Creek Jim as early as 1875, and he died in the Twin Falls Hospital in September of 1924.

As closely as possible Jim tried to emulate the whites, living in log cabins instead of the huts Mike preferred. When a wife died, as frequently happened, he would change the door of his cabin so her ghost could not find its way back in. Once, when Jim was coming down off the rimrocks with a load of venison on a borrowed wagon, the wagon tipped over and he had to walk on in to camp. When the owner asked about the wagon, Jim merely shrugged, "Wagon him lay down."

Another Rock Creek Shoshone was Indian Johnnie, who would work only for a rancher named Lawrence Hansen. Johnnie was slow and fat, weighing upwards of two hundred fifty pounds. When a white friend visited him as he lay ill from pneumonia and told him he'd get better soon, Johnnie shook his head. "Good-bye, old man. I see you no more."

He was soon dead and his family dragged him off by tying a rope around his neck to the wagon, heading into the rose briars to bury him. But it proved a wild event. His squaws got to wailing so loud the team ran away, scattering papooses across a mile of sagebrush and rocks. Then, perceiving that the hole for Johnnie's body was too shallow, a terrified woman frightened the rest by wailing, "Hole no deep enough—Pocotello Indian come dig him up and eat him."

At Johnnie's grave they killed his horse and dog, and buried all his possessions except a fine new twelve-dollar sewing machine Johnnie had purchased for sewing gloves. This the squaws smashed into little pieces and tossed into Rock Creek.

While Mike was not outright hostile to the other Indians he did remain aloof. To a much greater degree, they had become civilized, while Mike still sought to live in the manner of his ancestors. Although he had made some compromises along the food line, living in a cabin and owning cattle like Salmon River Jim was just too much.

One loyal supporter in the Rock Creek area was a Dane named John Hansen, for whom the town of Hansen was named. Hansen was born in Copenhagen, Denmark, on March 20, 1853, where he was educated to be a schoolmaster, speaking five languages besides his own native tongue. He emigrated to Indianapolis in 1873, then came west seeking a drier climate for his health.

His was the first white wedding in the Twin Falls area. Married by Judge Tranmer on September 2, 1877, to Anna Petersen, he moved into a sod-roofed, dirt-floored cabin. Since the wedding party was too large for such a small abode, they were served out of doors on a table made by taking the cabin door from its hinges. Since the bride had no oven, she baked her wedding cake down the canyon at the neighbors'.

The couple's first business venture was a cheese factory, but this ended in failure during the Bannock uprising. They fled the marauding Bannocks only to find on their return that their stock had been driven off and their factory destroyed. A leader in community affairs, John Hansen bought the Rock Creek general store in 1900. Generous to the extreme, he often put his own business in jeopardy by his habit of helping the poor and needy.

However much he and his wife had suffered losses during the Bannock War, Hansen became banker and friend to Mike and the rest of the Rock Creek Indians. Through Hansen, Mike found a ready market for gloves, reatas, and moccasins. In return, Hansen supplied Mike with groceries, keeping his accounts in a ledger book, a process that never failed to astonish and delight Mike, who referred to it as "make book talk." When Mike needed cash money, as when he bought a wagon, Hansen recorded the loan on the ledger. Mike's credit was good, and through the years he never failed to pay his bills.

Even though he might have survived on what he earned, Mike bought only staples such as coffee, flour, sugar, and ammunition at the store. The rest of his diet consisted of wild foods gathered in the hills.

In 1886, drought hit Mike's country, and for the first time in memory of man, Rock Creek went dry. One old settler, L.P. Larsen, told me of building a fire in the streambed up at the Iverson place to boil water for coffee.

If the bitter winter of 1889–90, when temperatures reached forty-two below zero, broke the back of the drought, it also broke the back of what was by now the Sparks-Tinnan cattle outfit, which ranged over much of Mike's territory. The land had been badly overgrazed, and now mass starvation hit wildlife and livestock equally hard. Ninety per cent, or about 75,000, Sparks-Tinnan cattle perished on the ranges. Cattle kegged up in fence corners to die, and townspeople forced starving cattle out of their gardens with pitchforks.

At the headquarters near Rock Creek, only 60 calves were found, whereas the year before they had gathered 38,000. By May, the stench of rotting cattle spread as a pestilence across the land, blown to all quarters by all winds; blowflies flew in clouds like autumn blackbirds; buzzards, gorged to flightlessness, grew finicky and feasted only on eyes.

Penniless, Tinnan moved back to the Middle West, but Sparks went back into business with his former partner Harrel, who had assets untouched by the drought. Together they moved 3000 cows back into the area, under John Sparks' management, and within a few years Sparks had recouped his losses.

The drought years were tough on Mike and his family. Accustomed to replenishing his horses from wild, unbranded mustangs, he was forced to make do with what half-starved mounts he had. These had all they could do to survive a day's ride; more adaptable than bovines, they were able to chew out a subsistence on bark and brush, but even browse was in short supply.

During these years of disaster, Mike's bonds with the whites at Rock Creek had firmed considerably, and although the ranchers had little themselves, they were willing to share. Rather than accept charity, however, Mike insisted upon paying his way. In an era when men toiled incessantly with their hands, gloves were an everyday necessity. Mike and a handful of other local Indians had a corner on the glove market, and their handiwork was as good as legal tender in the store. Busy with their ranches, the cattlemen had little time to hunt, and often Mike would bring his friends a welcome gift of deer meat shot in the mountains.

Spending much of their waking day ahorseback, Mike's boys grew up to be accomplished riders, good at breaking colts and gentling them. Eat-em-up Jake broke many horses for ranchers such as L.P. Larsen or James Buchanen Rice, more commonly known as Buck Rice, who had come to the country at eighteen by wagon train from Missouri. If you wanted a tough, spoiled colt broke gentle as a dog, Jake would handle him with his magic ways, and within days the outlaw would be following at the heels of his moccasins. Most Indians pushed a young horse too hard, broke his heart or wind, and brought him back looking as though he'd been drug through a knothole. But Jake loved horses, and during the drought when horses were scarce he had learned how to make a weak horse last upon the trail.

Catchum Charlie too was a good hand and was almost as good a reata man as Mike. They were big-loop ropers, all of them, which took strong arms and immense shoulders to sail such a big loop out against the wind of a running horse to settle gracefully about the quarry, whether wild cow or mustang.

Besides the girls, Lizard, Snake, Heney, and Hattie, there

At the combined post office and general store in Hansen, Idaho, Mike often traded the moccasins, gloves and reatas the band made for canned goods and cash.

was a daughter Mike buried up on a rimrock overlooking the Shoshone basin. Buck Rice asked Mike once what happened to her, and Mike looked sad and shrugged, "Girl, him lay down die."

Whenever any of the Rock Creek Indians died, the family tied a rope around his neck, tied the rope to a saddle horn or the back of a wagon, and dragged the body along the gullies or rimrocks until the body fell in a hole. Then they cut the rope off the wagon and piled rocks on the body. For several years one could see the end of a rotting rope sticking out from Indian Johnnie's grave.

Once a hunter found the bones of a human being in the rocks above the Shoshone basin and brought the skull in to the sheriff, fearing foul play, but before a search party could be formed, Buck Rice informed them they had dug up Mike's daughter, and the incident was soon forgotten.

The numbers of Mike's band varied from time to time, but usually it consisted of Mike; his Ute wife, Jennie; two grown sons, Jack and Jim; and three younger boys: Eat-em-up Jake, whose Indian name was Hoo go zap, Catchum Charlie, whose Indian name was Wo nig, and Cleve. There were three grown daughters, Lizard, Snake, and Heney, and two small girls—Hattie and an infant born about 1910.

Lizard married Lige Harris, a dark Texas Negro, whose brother, Henry, had been brought north as a cook for the Shoesole outfit. Henry, light-skinned and handsome, was quick to work his way out of cooking into buckarooing and was soon made boss of a group of Negro cowboys working on the Boar's Nest Ranch, so called because the cowboys lived in a cave in the hillside.

Eventually, Henry moved up to be buckaroo boss over Negro cowboys and white as well, and was greatly respected for his cow savvy and bronc-riding ability.

When one stands atop Magic Mountain, south of Rock Creek, one can see in the haze of distance, before the horizon limits vision, a great part of Mike's range. Most probably it was more than wanderlust that pushed him south to the hills and deserts in springtime. Perhaps it was the great clouds of gnats or no-see-ums, the deer flies, and the mosquitoes tormenting man and horse alike that drove the Indians out of Rock Creek Canyon to the drier areas around Gollaher Mountain to the south.

With a daughter married to Lige Harris, one of the Shoesole cowboys and a brother to the buckaroo boss, Mike was pretty well accepted on that part of his range and was welcome at the company store, where his credit was as good as it was at Rock Creek. Here the ranches were far more lonely, isolated, and vulnerable to Indian depredation than at Rock Creek, but here too Mike and his family came to be respected, trusted, and even loved.

It was Hattie Weighall Pounds of Twin Falls who gave me my first glimpse of Mike's life on his summer range when he dropped out of sight at Rock Creek.

I had located Hattie Pounds through a column Charlotte Crockett had written in the *Twin Falls Times News,* mentioning that I was in the area looking for information about Indian Mike. As it had been with Carrie Crockett, I thrilled to talk to someone who had actually known my Indian.

"Oh, yes, I remember him well," Hattie reminisced. "I got to know him when Poppa, Sam Weighall, took us to live on a ranch in the middle of the Shoshone Basin; then later, when we moved to the Hubbard Ranch about six miles south of the Vineyard outfit headquarters at San Jacinto, Mike would drop by to see us there."

I could hardly believe my ears as I listened, totally unaware until she invited me in that I was still standing on her front porch talking through the screen. Hattie was a sprightly gray-haired woman, and looking at her one never would have guessed she was a product of the lonely sagebrush desert.

"Mike came quite suddenly into our lives," she went on when I had seated myself on her couch. "One day when Sam was out riding the cattle, Momma was in the kitchen cleaning shelves, when suddenly she looked about to see a stocky, broad-shouldered Indian brave grinning at her from the kitchen door. She was too frightened even to scream, but somehow she ventured to ask what he wanted.

" 'Mike want coffee, sugar, maybe tabac,' he said, still grinning happily.

"At that moment Momma would have given him the ranch. Laying out pieces of brown paper on the kitchen table, she poured out small mounds of sugar, tea, coffee, flour, and dried prunes, and added a box of Poppa's precious tobacco.

"At that moment, Poppa, who was a big, blustering man given to strong language, chose to arrive back at the house, and what a blistering he gave that Indian. It was enough to send most Indians to the brush, but Mike only grinned.

"He pointed to the towel draped over Momma's shoulder, and with his broken English said, 'That how white him woman get when him see big Injun in door.'

"Maybe Poppa had heard of the Daggett family from cowboys roaming the area. Somehow his anger soon cooled, and from that moment on the two men were friends, though Sam was ever one to speak his mind whenever Mike did something to displease him.

"As Mike was about to ride off that day, he asked if there was any way he could repay us.

" 'You ever get any wild meat,' Poppa said, 'You just bring some in.' He didn't know the Indian word for venison, so he stood there making sweeping motions over his head to indicate big antlers.

"Mike stared at him for a moment in doubt, then shrugged, grunted a good-bye, and rode off into the hills. The next day, he rode in not with meat but with a huge rack of deer antlers tied behind him on his mustang.

" 'Why, you knot-headed redskin,' Sam roared. 'I can't eat the horns!' He made chewing motions with his jaws and suddenly, when Mike got the message, both men dissolved in laughter. Two days later Mike brought him enough deer to feed a haying crew."

Now and again, Mike would drift in out of the sage to bring the Weighalls gifts of moccasins, gloves, or even sage hens or venison. One day as Hattie was playing in the front yard he rode up on his mustang. "I had the habit of wandering," Hattie told me, "so the folks kept a big sheep bell tied around my neck so they could locate me out in the sage. As long as the bell tinkled peacefully, there was nothing to be alarmed about, but when the bell clanked loud and steady, it meant I had found a rattlesnake and was coming home on the run."

On this particular day, Hattie was playing close to the house, for she had on a new dress and her face was fresh-scrubbed and clean. For some time the Indian watched her in admiration. "Him pretty little squaw," Mike said to Sam Weighall who had come to the door. "What him name?"

"Why that's Hattie, Mike," Sam explained.

"Hattie," Mike repeated. "Hattie! Him pretty name for him girl. Name my little girl Hattie too!"

And so he did. Hattie Daggett, named after Hattie Weighall, went down in history eventually as one of the four survivors of Mike's band.

One could tell that Hattie had fond memories of the old Indian. For a time she was silent and I watched as she thought back into the past, smiling with the memory.

"Sometimes Mike would be gone for months," she remembered, "then suddenly he would be at the door for a visit or for some food. He wasn't a big man—he weighed maybe a hundred seventy-five or so. He wore buckskin moccasins with high tops and fringes. The children were so shy that when they came with him in his wagon now and then they'd hide under the canvas in back, and one could see only their dark eyes shining.

"Jennie always sat in front of the buckboard while Mike and the older boys came in to eat. They were always fairly neat and clean, and Mike was nice to all his children, as though he really enjoyed them. In his broken English he would take time to tell me the Indian legends of the surrounding land. He was superstitious and claimed that Tuanna John's peak was an old Indian battleground haunted with spirits of the dead. Sometimes he brought me Indian dolls made of sagebrush, sometimes a brush for my hair made of wire-grass roots, dried, cleaned, and tied together with buckskin like a tiny whisk broom.

"I remember one day," Hattie reminisced, "Mike drove his wagon down the lane toward the house just after Poppa had irrigated, and Poppa came along just in time to see Mike's wagon stuck to the axle in mud. Mike and his boys were sitting in the wagon while the squaws were wading knee deep in mud trying to help the balky team of mustangs by pushing on the rims of the big wooden-spoked wheels.

" 'Why, you lazy Injun!' Sam roared. 'Git down off that wagon and give those womenfolk a hand.'

"For a moment, Mike stared at Poppa, but he grinned kind of sheepish like, said a few words in Indian to his astonished boys, and all of them stepped off into the mud to push."

It was always a special event in their lives when guests dropped by; Mike rated even higher than most. While the men ate inside, Mrs. Weighall took food out to the women waiting in the wagon. She always included a big bag of cookies, which Jennie would take from her shyly and put down under the seat for leaner times. Mrs. Weighall always insisted, however, that leaner times were already here and the children needed them immediately. Soon the children came out from under the canvas and forgot to be shy.

But even though Mike socialized with the whites to this extent, when he disappeared over the first hill, once more he became a wild Indian. Even though he had such friends as the Hansens, Crocketts, and Weighalls, there were Indian haters in the land who could not accept the Indian as anything more than an animal to be feared. Incredibly, Mike managed to roam his range for over thirty years and to elude his enemies.

I once asked L.P. Larsen, one of the few alive today who had known Mike well, what kind of an Indian Mike was. L.P. thought a long moment, then replied: "I guess you might say Mike was a pretty smart Indian. He stood way back and watched the white man rather than stand in front and have to look over his shoulder all the time."

9

Whenever a writer trails a person or story back through time into the realm of legend or history, in order to separate fact from fiction, he must set aside the works of previous historians and return as much as possible to original sources.

Even then, he must examine all available material and sometimes make an educated guess as to which of several conflicting reports has the best chance of being correct. Often, with great anguish, he must discard his best story when he finds out the piece he tracked down with meticulous care simply isn't true.

Nor was Mike's case an exception. In putting together pieces of his life and times from newspaper accounts of the day, from records of the Office of Indian Affairs, from museum archives, and from personal conversations with people who actually knew him, my conception of the man, "Shoshone" Mike, began to change. I came to the conclusion that Mike, though of the great Shoshonean family, was tribally not a Shoshone at all but a Bannock, a fact important to the under-standing of the man and the religion he made of clinging to the old wild way.

On the basis of language, A.L. Kroeber, of the University of California, classified the Shoshonean family as follows (adapted from F.W. Hodge, 1912):

I. Hopi

II. Plateau Shoshoneans (a) UTE-CHEMEHUEVI: Che-mehuevi, Kawaiisu, Paiute, Panamint, Ute, and some of the Bannock; (b) SHOSHONE-COMANCHE: Comanche, Gosiute, Shoshone; (c) MONO-PAVIOTSO: Mono, Pavi-otso, part of the Bannock, and the Shoshoneans of eastern Oregon

III. Kern River Shoshoneans

IV. Southern California Shoshoneans

Since Mike's wife, Jennie, was known to have been a Ute woman, Mike may have been of that branch of the Bannocks most closely allied to the Utes, the Ute-Chemehuevi sub-family. The Shoshone were of the Shoshone-Comanche sub-family.

After Mike's death, Nevada authorities, assuming that any Indian called "Shoshone Mike" would be a Shoshone, rushed to interview other Shoshone about Mike and his mysterious band. It was only natural that the Shoshone would have noth-ing good to say about a stray Indian who had caused a wave of anti-Indian sentiment that complicated their lives. Vari-ously, they reported that Mike was a bad Indian who had run away from the Duck Valley Reservation for the life of a rene-gade, and that he had fled eastern Nevada after killing a white boy.

Testimony of some Indians, which was all but ignored, pointed out that Mike was not a Shoshone but a Bannock. Indian interpreters at the Carson Indian School, in Carson City, Nevada, who interviewed Mike's daughter, Heney,

77

placed the language she spoke as a strange mixture of Paiute and Shoshone.

Historically, the Bannocks may have been an offshoot of the northern Paiute, and though they were surrounded by Shoshone in southern Idaho, they maintained their linguistic and tribal individuality. It is likely that the Shoshone had difficulty understanding the girl because she spoke Bannock, perhaps with some Ute words thrown in.

Since Salmon River Jim, who was a Shoshone, shared Rock Creek Canyon with Mike, he presumably knew him, although they rarely mingled. Jim, too, claimed that Mike was a Bannock.

In a statement to reporters of the *Wells Herald,* on March 22, 1911, Harry Preacher, chief and leader of the Shoshone of Elko, stated that Indian Mike and his band were Bannocks, and indicated that he was glad Mike had been killed.

Another indication of Mike's tribal affiliation was the head-dress he wore. Admittedly a primitive affair, crudely crafted out of what was available in the hills, the tail was made of a strip of red blanket decorated with sage hen feathers, though the bonnet itself was of deer hide decorated with eagle plumes. From the crown rose two slender wands split from cow horns. The ends of these were grooved and tassled.

These horns have been erroneously referred to as horns of an ibex, but the long narrow projections resemble those of no wild species. They were split not out of black buffalo horns, which they were meant to simulate, but from horns of domestic cattle.

Use of such head-dresses was borrowed from more eastern tribes, but there is a remarkable resemblance between Mike's head-dress and that of the famous Bannock Chief, Pat Tyhee. The horns are much alike, split of cow horn, grooved, and tassled, and on both the brow bands are hung with tails of small animals like pack rats, while the bonnets themselves are

78

The primitive headdress
Mike wore had been fash-
ioned from deerskin, eagle
feathers and split cow horns.

decorated with eagle plumes. The similarity seems too great to be coincidental.

By nature, too, Mike seemed closer to the Bannock than the Shoshone. The Shoshone very early became the white man's Indians, adopting his dress, his customs, and even his names. The Bannocks, however, fiercely resisted civilizing influences and even into this century gave their children Indian names. Mike's children had both Indian and white names, but the Indian names were used when not actually conversing with a white person.

The fact that there was a tribal difference between Mike and the other Indians in Rock Creek Canyon readily explains why Mike and his family never really mingled with them.

To date, all published accounts of Mike's story—two books and numerous newspaper and magazine articles—refer to the man as Shoshone Mike, and this appellation has persisted for sixty-two years. To my knowledge, however, until after the drama of his death, at which time Mike himself claimed to be Shoshone, the name was never used.

In the prologue of *The Indian Massacre of 1911*, by Effie Mona Mack (1968), the author gives Mike's dying words as "Me Shoshone Mike! Me Shoshone Mike!"

The same book quotes an account of the death scene as given from memory by Mort West, a member of the posse who hunted Mike down. According to West, Cambron had asked Mike, "What kind of an Indian are you?"

"Me Shoshone! Me Shoshone!" Mike had replied, glaring about at his enemies.

O.D. Van Norman, one of the posse members who was also at the death scene, told me the story with only slight variation. "As Ben Cambron stood over Mike as the old Indian was gasping his last, among obscenities, Cambron said, 'What kind of damn Indian are you, anyway?'"

80

And Mike replied, "Me Shoshone! Me Shoshone!"

Van Norman also told me that the old Indian had no chance to say more because Cambron pried open the dying man's mouth with his rifle barrel and said, "Wonder how old he is. Let's have a look at the son-of-a-bitch's teeth." Van Norman had to pull Cambron off Mike's body.

Van Norman was accurate in his accounting, and there is no reason to doubt the testimony indicating that, at that precise moment in his life, Mike did claim to be Shoshone. But I think that Mike lied.

At that time, Shoshone were very much the white man's Indian and partially civilized. They had long before accepted the yoke of reservation life and were more often ridiculed than feared. The Bannocks, however, noted for their stubborn reluctance to have anything to do with the white man's way, remained aloof, keeping as much as possible to the old way. Even before the bloody Bannock War, the term Bannock was synonymous with larcenous, treacherous, and ferocious.

In Mike's predicament he did precisely as any other self-respecting Bannock would do. He lied. In effect what he was saying was, "Hey, lay off me, you guys. I'm Shoshone, one of your good Indians, a friend to you white men." It was no time to claim to be a Bannock.

Most likely the moniker "Shoshone Mike" was inflicted upon that aged primitive by members of the posse telling the story and by writers reporting upon Mike's dramatic end. In truth, no editor would have been happy to print a wild Indian story whose lead character happened to be a redskin named Mike Daggett. The latter name, plus Idaho Mike and Rock Creek Mike, all make the old man sound like an Irish emigrant fleeing the potato famine. "Indian Mike" was too general, "Bannock Mike" would not have fit, since everyone considered him a Shoshone. In the end, "Shoshone Mike" seemed just right. Although it had sprung out of the drama of his death and was nurtured by his growing legend, it was a name Mike himself never heard spoken.

If Mike's Indian name was ever known to the whites, it has been lost in the mists. In that day Bannocks had two or three names during the course of their lifetime, and many Indians kept their names secret. His white name, Mike Daggett, might have been given him by some Indian agent who found his other name hard to spell.

After the hysteria of the Bannock War a white name gave the Indian some protection, as though it suggested that the bearer was no longer hostile to the white civilization. Some Indians took the names of white settlers for whom they worked, or of ranchers who befriended them. Daggett was a common enough name among settlers, though either the Daggetts were not prolific or inclined to wander, for none of them frequent Mike's area now. In Mike's time a man named Daggett was superintendent of the Duck Valley Reservation, and Mike might have known him earlier in his career.

Shoshone were quick to adopt white names to get preferential treatment. But true to form, Bannocks kept their Indian names much longer. Mike had no connection with reservations, so his white title would have meant little to him. Alone with his family, doubtless he used an Indian name.

Through the years, Mike has been referred to as Mike Daggett, Salmon River Mike, Rock Creek Mike, Idaho Mike, Indian Mike, and after his death, Shoshone Mike.

The name "Mike Daggett" was used by the Office of Indian Affairs. Since Indians were wards of the government, that office kept as much contact with Mike as was possible in that lonely land. The name "Salmon River Mike" did not imply that he came from interior Idaho's famed Salmon River country, but that he lived for a time on the Salmon River in northern Nevada, a stream that is now called Salmon Falls Creek.

Those who knew Mike best, his neighbors at Rock Creek, called him "Indian Mike," while those across the mountains on the southern part of his range, near the ranch headquarters of San Jacinto, not far from the present town of Jackpot, Nevada, often called him "Rock Creek Mike" or even "Idaho Mike."

Whether or not Mike was involved in the Bannock War is not known. A letter from G.A. Gutches (District Forester at the Fort Hall Agency, at Rossfork, Idaho) to E.P. Holcombe (Chief Supervisor of the Indian office), written presumably about 1911, states, "Mike Daggett and his family left the Fort Hall Reservation some twenty years ago and settled on a small ranch near Rock Creek, Idaho."

The "small ranch" referred to happened to be the Crockett place. Gutches' testimony would place Mike at Rock Creek about 1890. But Carrie Crockett had Mike well established in the area when the Crockett house was built in 1880. Probably, since Mike lived a solitary life with his family, he did not get caught up by the emotional upheaval that gripped the reservation at Fort Hall. Presumably he kept hidden in the hills until the war was over and carried no lasting hatreds to mar the rapport he kept with his white neighbors, but he must have had deep misgivings, for one does not give up the Bannock traditions all that easily. His earliest memories, of course, and those of his youth must have been steeped in violence.

During the 1840s, shortly before Mike was born, and at the time Fort Hall was built in southeastern Idaho as a center for the fur trade, most of the Indian troubles came from the Blackfeet farther east, who butchered solitary trappers in the mountains as they found them. But since the Bannock territory was bisected by both the Oregon and California trails, it caught a double flow of pioneers and soon frictions developed that led eventually to violence.

Known early for their peaceful, tractable ways, the Shoshone soon became reservation Indians, accepting their lot even when the whites failed their treaty promises to provide sufficient food for winter subsistence.

But the Bannocks were a fierce, restless bunch, and failed to accept domestication. They also rejected starvation and left the reserve yearly during the lean winter months to fend for themselves, scattering over vast areas, much to the dismay of white settlers.

It was fortunate for the remaining Shoshone who shared the reserve that the Bannocks pulled out, for their mass exodus left the remaining rations for them. But there was often little enough for those that stayed, and many a Shoshone huddled trusting on the reserve only to die of starvation or disease.

The Bannocks were never a large tribe. In 1845, there were probably no more than a thousand, and those were practically surrounded by the more numerous Shoshone. When there was need of numerical strength, as when they journeyed east over the mountains into Blackfoot country to hunt buffalo, they teamed with the Shoshone, but they worked at maintaining their individual culture and dialect as long as possible, or until the early 1900s, when intermarriage with Shoshone took its inevitable toll.

Causes of the Bannock War were varied. In 1877, Chief Joseph led his Nez Perce into war, and to prevent neighboring tribes from acting in sympathy authorities confined the Bannocks to Fort Hall Reservation. No longer were they allowed to roam far and wide to hunt, but were forced to subsist on whatever lean provender the government provided. Since Mike had habitually stayed clear of the reservation, his very existence was forgotten by the authorities.

The building of a railroad through the preserve proved vexing to the Indians in that it brought in a flood of whites, and treaties that might have protected the Indian, fed him when hungry, or clothed him when he was freezing were not worth the paper on which they were written. Indeed, some treaties existed for years without ever being ratified by Congress.

It is surprising that, through years of broken promises, the Indian continued to do business with the government in such good faith. In some cases, of course, the government was not entirely to blame, for the treaties were signed by chiefs who either failed to understand what was actually involved or far exceeded their jurisdiction as chief.

In history, whenever the government asked for the return of reservation lands for purpose of right-of-way or unforeseen development, the Indian was the model of cooperation. But in the case of the Fort Hall Reservation, the lands ceded back to the whites were so vast as to be scandalous, and dissension inevitably followed.

Another major sore point was the usurping of Camas Prairie by white farmers, due to a conscious or unconscious misprint in the treaty. Article 2 of the Treaty of Fort Bridger referred to it as "Kansas Prairie," and the whites used this as subterfuge for open settlement.*

Camas Prairie was a vast, productive, and well-watered plain in southern Idaho. In the spring, Indians came from far and wide to dig camas, the large succulent bulb of a wild blue lily that grew in such profusion that a meadow in bloom resembled a mountain lake. Here Indians gathered in numbers, and when the seed was ripe, harvest of the bulbs began. Women and children dug the bulbs with crooked sticks whose tips had been hardened in fire. The bulbs were roasted in pits, each layer covered with grass or branches, and with more ashes and slow coals. After being roasted for twenty-four hours the bulbs were dug, cooled, and husked; then the warm bulbs were mashed between the palms of the hand to resemble

* *The Bannock of Idaho,* Madsen, Caxton, 1958, p. 183.

cookies or macaroons. They tasted like maple sugar, and were stored in sacks for later use. It was only natural that the Indians should value the camas fields above most other things and be willing to go to war to protect them. Throughout history many an intertribal war has been waged solely because one tribe trespassed upon the camas fields of another.

The Indians became understandably enraged when Camas Prairie, theirs by treaty, was invaded by white farmers, whose hogs rooted up the camas and destroyed the stand forever.

Due to unrest, authorities at Fort Hall confiscated Bannock horses and guns. Since 1800 the Bannocks had been a horse culture, and the whites failed to realize just how deeply the love of the horse was ingrained in the Indian's heart. Hatreds long smoldering threatened to flame anew.

The alleged rape of an Indian woman, who was out gathering roots, by two white men may have been the breeze that fanned the tinder into flames. When the girl's brother and a friend avenged the act by killing two whites, authorities gave the Bannocks ten days to turn the guilty Indians over to officials at Fort Hall.

The Bannocks were ready to comply, but after one day's journey out of Fort Hall with their prisoners, they learned from white travelers that the officials planned to confine them all at Fort Hall and kill them. Prisoners and captors alike went on a rampage of killing and plundering across the land.

By June of 1879, marauding bands of Bannocks roamed at will, terrorizing whites and Indians alike throughout southern Idaho. Chief Winnemucca had been encouraging the Bannocks to throw off the white yoke, but when they sought aid from Winnemucca and his northern Paiutes, the chief backed down. At gunpoint, the Bannocks forced Winnemucca and his men to come along. When the Shoshone also refused help, the Bannocks were enraged, and turned against Indians who had formerly been friends.

One promise made by the Bannocks was that when they had destroyed the railways and killed the whites, they would divide up both sides of the world [north and south of the railroad] amongst their friends and kill all the Indians who had not united with them. (Captain Sam's report to Nevada agent A.J. Barnes, *Report of the Commissioner of Indian Affairs,* 1878, p. 105, as reported in *The Bannock of Idaho* by Madsen.)

Indians fled for their lives to reservations at Fort Hall and Duck Valley, not only because they feared the Bannocks, but because they feared the whites might suspect them of being implicated in the uprising and slaughter them.

At Duck Valley Reservation, to the west, panic reigned. For years the reservation Indians had dreaded the Bannocks. Now rumors flew that raiding parties were on their way. The whites too were in an uproar because the Bannocks were led by Buffalo Horn, a noted Indian scout and veteran of many a skirmish under white leadership. He could be expected to know all the battle techniques employed by white officers.

From vast areas surrounding Duck Valley, white ranchers drove their stock down out of the hills and onto the reservation for protection. They had little regard that the hungry, milling animals demolished the Indians' crops, leaving them even more destitute and discouraged. Many of the Indians moved south to escape both the Bannocks and starvation, hiring out as laborers in the mines at Tuscarora and Mountain City, picking up ranch work if they could find it, or begging for scraps at hotel eateries and military posts.

Some took to scavenging the garbage heaps of settlements for edible scraps or sifting the manure outside stables for kernels of undigested grain. For the women, prostitution was often the only means of survival for them and their children. All too often the men bought their product and booted them out without paying. There was no going back to the land, for

vast herds of cattle, sheep, and horses had grazed the grass-
lands into a nothingness of sage. The game had been driven
out of the country, and it was now a major expedition to get
meat. Besides that, they had been in captivity too long; they
had lost the tradition of eking out an existence on the harsh
desert lands. Mike could exist because he had kept his family
schooled to such rigors. He and his band knew the system and
could still survive and prosper where less hardy Indian families would have starved.

Wherever the Indian wandered he was in grave danger of
being mistaken for a hostile man by nervous whites who often
found it safer and easier to shoot the Indian down in cold
blood than to take a chance that he might be a thief or a
murderer. The tensions and hatreds between Indian and Indian, or Indian and white, which mushroomed in the hysteria
of the Bannock War lasted into the following century.

In the West existed a dual system of morality. The white
man made a joke of killing the Indian, but whenever an Indian
killed a white, the whites promptly lost their sense of humor.
This did not mean that a white man could shoot an Indian
down in cold blood in the heart of town. He had to use some
discretion. If he caught an Indian alone without witnesses,
then there was little chance that the murder would ever be
solved.

By treaty, the government was obligated to feed and clothe
the Indians on the reserves until the time when the Indian was
able to fend for himself. Most often the ink was scarcely dry
before the treaty was being broken. Sometimes the agents
were at fault, converting for their own use foodstuffs, clothing,
seed, tools, and blankets. Sometimes the goods, hauled long
distances from the railheads by wagon, were lost through
bungling or sent to wrong destinations.

In many cases the Indians were charged outrageous prices
for what was theirs by treaty; often their requests for breeding

stock or farm implements, items that might have helped them help themselves, were turned down or ignored. Sometimes unscrupulous agents billed the government for credits of food and clothing allegedly extended to certain Indians, when the Indian received only a fraction of what was claimed. Since transactions were carried on in fractured English or makeshift sign language, communication seldom went beyond a certain basic level of understanding. The war only aggravated what was already a tragic situation.

The government had its hands full fighting the war and could do little to get the Indians back on the reservation. The Indians had tried reservation life and found it wanting. There they had been crowded together in abject poverty, unable to understand or communicate, ravaged by hunger and disease, kept from the comforts of native customs or religion, and allowed to starve in the midst of a feast of promises.

Then, too, wrapped in superstition, many Indians feared the white man's schools for their children. It was only natural for parents who loved their children to object when their children were removed by force and sent to distant boarding schools where disease and demoralization took a terrible toll. Although the child, had he stayed at home, might have died anyway, the fact that he died alone in a hostile and foreign environment evoked unanswered questions and suspicions on the part of the parents. Hatreds grew in Indian hearts that only death could erase.

In time the Bannocks, defeated by General O.O. Howard, either returned to the reservation at Fort Hall or were punished by being dispersed to other reservations. Numbers had been reduced by war. Now, surrounded on all sides by the more numerous Shoshone and deprived of the chance to wander over the land during the winter months, they had little chance to retain their culture. Valiantly they fought this one last war, but little by little they lost out as member after member intermarried with other tribes until nothing was left of their ferocity and pride but an ancient reputation.

It is probable that, during the hostilities, Mike took his band far back into the lonely roadless canyons of the Rock Creek mountains, where a moment's journey around the bend of a canyon or a climb over the lip of a rimrock took one into a whole new world, from which an army of soldiers could not have dislodged him.

With the end of the war, whites came flooding back to Idaho in unprecedented numbers. From high in some eagle's eyrie in the mountains, Mike must have watched the dust clouds as white farmers grubbed the sagebrush from the great valley of the Snake. He had existed through a trying moment in history; no reason to brood about the morrow. In all that vast expanse, Mike was the last free man.

10

Are you laughing at me, Mike? Laughing because I am alone in the mountains above Rock Creek, tired and sick, lonesome and hungry, failing miserably to exist in a good time of year when you and your band were able to put on fat like a steer? Can you understand, Mike, what guts it takes to stay on here, when, if I walked a few miles down the canyon, Charlotte Crockett would invite me in for one of her fantastic meals of steak, Idaho potatoes, fresh biscuits and gravy, and home-made ice cream, with maybe a big bowl of raspberries she picked right out of her garden?

Sixty or ninety years ago, Mike, you found excuses to bum from the Crocketts too when you were hungry. Would it be cheating then if, in the name of research, I slipped down for a bath and a meal? Do you appreciate, Mike, that the lizard I bit the head off and swallowed raw was done for you? It wasn't, of course, that I was red-hot for lizard, but I did want to understand the life you led, and what better way than to eat what you ate.

Do you think I am dirty because I enjoy being this way? And those things I found crawling, Mike—oh, God—do I really have lice? And the ticks I've found—do they carry spotted fever?

The rock chuck was delicious, and I thought it was going to be easy, this living off the land, but that was two weeks ago. I heard his whistle taunting me from a tumble of jagged lava stacked against the sky, then I found his burrow and made a deadfall of a heavy rock platter, holding it up with the figure-four arrangement you showed Hoo go zap and Wo nig, and they showed the Crockett boys, and Carrie remembered and told me fifty, no, seventy years after. I baited the trap with succulent grass I packed up, lungs bursting, from the meadow, a thousand feet below. Within minutes he was back acting smart, nibbled the bait, and wham! I had him, cleaned him, built a hot fire, let it die to coals, and roasted him slowly, hide and all. Half a day of anxious waiting, gathering nettles and boiling them for spinach, picking tiny wild onions from the hillsides, and the meat was done. I knocked the charred hide off with a few raps of a stick. It was so delicious I thought I would live on rock chuck from then on, but the next three rocks I lifted had rattlesnakes under them, and, besides, word must have traveled around through the rock-chuck world that I was a gourmet fan and greedy for them, because after that they all went for vacations or spent their days reading in their burrows.

As I was coming down the hill, a black stinkbug cocked his rear end at me, and I pretended not to see, for fear I would remember someone saying you ate them; then I'd have to. The white wood grubs weren't that bad. I closed my eyes and pretended I was eating chocolate cremes until one of the chocolate cremes bit my tongue. I used to think Indians camped along streams in summer, but I soon found that the gnats, mosquitoes, deerflies, and horseflies took more out of me than I was currently putting back in, so I camped far up the hillsides where the morning sun struck my bed hours before it warmed the bottom of the canyon, and my presence didn't keep the wild things away from their waterholes.

I soon figured out that when the seed ripens, the bulb is ready to be harvested and stored. There is not too much that ripens in June. I found quantities of sand grass or rye, but my trouble was that I had no squaw to prepare it.

Gathering huge bundles of sand grass, I set them one by one on an altar of smooth rock and burned them, making sure the fires smoldered slowly. When the grass was burned and the ashes fanned away, I was left with a quantity of hard black seed, which I ground into a dirty gray flour with a crude pestle and mortar that some Indian, years before, had abandoned along the rims. When I was done, the hole in the mortar seemed considerably deeper than when I started, due to wearing away of the rock. When I baked the flour into a cake over the coals of a sagebrush fire, it tasted like a mouthful of dry sand, and I had to swallow without chewing or risk grinding my teeth down to the quick.

Braiding a snare out of wild clematis vines that choked the vegetation in the canyons, I managed to snare several ground squirrels by setting a slip loop around the entrances to their burrows, then jerking it quickly as they stood up like picket pins to see where I was hiding. Shed of their garments they looked like ten little embryos awaiting birth, but I put them into a pot with wild onion, tule roots, and sego lily bulbs that I dug with a mountain mahogany digging stick, its tip sharpened and then hardened with fire.

As it simmered over the hot coals, the stew smelled so good that I gathered roots and bulbs as I found them, adding, as I afterwards found, locoweed, larkspur, and death camas. One

93

or all of these proved both emetic and laxative. By morning I was so weak I couldn't move, my head ached fiercely, and my eyes were swollen shut as though stung by hornets.

I lay in camp for a few days drinking licorice-root tea, or quitchemboo, as the Bannocks called it, which was supposed to be a tonic and to give me a strong voice for singing. To this I added toya bawana, the seed heads from horse mint, which the Bannocks used against cold and as an appetizer.

After that I did not gather much, mainly because I still felt awful and partly because the sharp rocks had cut the soles out of my genuine, store-bought Blackfoot Indian moccasins.

It was the raid on the white settlement, Mike, that saved me. I sat on the rimrocks beating on the war drum I'd made from a beef hide hanging on the Crockett corral. This I soaked in Rock Creek until the hair slipped, then stretched over a bottomless wash tub I found in the Crockett dump.

It was a magnificent sound, so like thunder that, all along the valley, men who were worried about their drying hay crop came out of their ranch houses and glanced at the sky.

As I chanted I prayed to the god of the hunt to give me success, for the antelope to give me meat, and for the buffalo to fall down with my arrow quivering in his ribs. In the morning I felt so strong in heart that I watched from the rimrock until I saw Charlotte and her mother drive off to church, then crept down, down, down the sagebrushed hillside, past the wreck of old wagons and car bodies in the canyon, then cut around the point straight for the chicken house. I had intended to take only eggs, Mike, but the tender breast of the indignant little white hen felt so plump as I reached under her that I thought Charlotte would never miss just one hen.

For the first time, playing Indian was sort of fun. With renewed vigor I dug camas, while the gnats made my neck burn, mosquitoes drank what little blood was left, and the deerflies buzzed, entrapped in my grimy locks. The big and

94

succulent bulbs under the blue flowers were easily dug. I roasted them in layers separated by grass and coals, and when they were done, I cooled them, husked them, and patted them into cookies. The chicken I might have eaten plain, but the temptation to triumph over my environment proved too much and I stuffed the chicken with mushrooms I found in the canyon.

"You look terrible," Charlotte Crockett said as she looked out her door.

"Never felt better in my life," I replied as I collapsed on her doorstep.

A few good meals at the Crocketts' restored body and spirit, and once more I set out to try to understand the forces that had shaped Mike's world.

With few exceptions in history, whenever one culture has attempted to live side by side with another without benefit of an iron curtain of geographic, political, or religious barriers, the weaker culture has been absorbed and all but lost. At best the isolation of the Indian on reservations was a stop-gap measure inevitably doomed to defeat by time. Sadder perhaps than homogenizing of blood was loss of native cultures.

What we gained in the process of assimilation were maize, the turkey, the sweet potato, and other agricultural entities, as well as a treasury of colorful geographic names such as Winnemucca and Pocatello, a national neurosis or guilt springing from our disgraceful handling of the Indian, and some very choice real estate.

What the Indian got from us were venereal disease, tuberculosis, measles, smallpox, diphtheria, a written language, the horse, alcohol, automobiles, television, a feeling of frustration and despair leading often to suicide, and an almost total loss of land and culture.

Some of our gifts were more positive, such as the metal container, the horse, and the written language. The metal container in the form of the rusty can or galvanized bucket made it possible for the Indian to cook right on the fire instead of by the cumbersome process of dropping heated rocks into a waterproofed basket of food. The horse gave him mobility in fighting or gathering food, though in many areas the horse competed disastrously with the Indian for the scant seed supply, as well as displacing whole populations by destroying historic balances—giving the tribe with horses superiority over the tribe without. The written language, though handy for petitioning Washington, came sadly too late to capture much of the Indian's great oral tradition and cultural history, thereby breaking a tradition or chain that all the scientific wizardry of modern times cannot bridge. Mike saw how tradition was being lost from the reservations, and this may have influenced his decision to remain wild and do everything in his power to keep the old traditions alive in his band.

For those in charge of the Indian in those days, under tremendous political pressure to keep the Indian pacified at all costs, reduction of numbers was a most effective means. Since the Indian had no resistance to foreign diseases, introduction of measles and other such diseases was as effective as germ warfare in keeping tribal numbers reduced and the Indian subdued. Often tribes were so reduced as to disappear completely. On a disease basis alone the Indian would have been perfectly justified in turning the white man back at his shores on the ground that he was not only diseased but physically dirty.

As a semi-nomadic Indian, Mike struggled for food constantly. At no moment in his life could he relax in an unguarded camp, for just around the bend of the next canyon could be a white sportsman out to get himself his Indian, a missionary trying to convert him, or a white official trying to steal his children to send them off to government boarding schools. Considering even the everyday forces that opposed him, for an incredible number of years Mike managed not only to survive but to flourish.

Around 1800, the coming of the horse to the Bannocks simplified hunting, food gathering, and transportation, while in addition it made them a strong force in battle. So important did the horse become in the Bannock's mind that he has been horse-poor ever since, since horses eat more than a cow but bring in little income.

To Mike, horses were a way of life, but there were difficulties in maintaining his herd. Often he rode in with his band over long, dry, dusty wastelands only to find that the white man had fenced the water holes to gain control of the ranges and would not let the Indian so much as drink from an oasis his people had used since prehistory. It became harder and harder to find ample pasture. If his stock strayed into a white man's field, often the rancher would shoot the animals and leave them for the buzzards.

The non-reservation Indian such as Mike had little chance but to become assimilated. What land off the reservation the Indian tried to develop for his own use became more desirable to the whites. The better the land, the more the pressure to move the Indian away. In time even the wastelands were lost to him. Lonely canyons echoed to the clank of the miner's hammer. Mining towns sprang up in the midst of solitary nowhere. Piles of toxic spoil from mining choked streams. Fertile hunting grounds became wastelands of boulders or sterile mud flats, littered with rubble.

In Mike's territory, however, the ranches were generally isolated wherever a small stream made a natural meadow of alluvial deposits, soil gleaned through the centuries by the slow wearing away of the hills. Often, far distant from labor supplies, the ranchers welcomed Indians like Mike for seasonal jobs such as haying, cattle gathering, and branding. Many a rancher wondered at the uncanny sense Mike's band had as to when jobs were available.

In reality the hills were seldom so empty as the white man imagined. From one moment's watching from the lonely hills above the ranch, the Indian, trained in observation, knew much of the rancher's business. He had merely to note that the rancher was repairing his hay machinery, that the hay looked almost ripe, or that the corral was full of horses being roached for haying or shod for the fall roundups. Once he had sized up the need for labor, he had his own way of communication through smoke, signal fires, mirrors, or even drums, systems astonishingly simple but effective. Out of the hills came Mike's people to earn a little cash.

Generally, each ranch had its own Indian campground, which in may ways resembled the modern migrant camp, though it was even more primitive. The Indian was, after all, a man of simple needs and a great hand at doing without. Perhaps the camp consisted only of a few brush shelters, an outhouse, plus an available water supply, a pile of rusting cans handy for cooking and not much else.

Some ranchers built shacks for the Indians, but generally they preferred the brush huts of their ancestors. In many such camps, their tipi poles stood year after year, and when the Indians moved on they took only the coverings with them. Usually the camps were at some distance from the ranch house, perhaps around a bend in the canyon where the Indian could live in his own private world, drumming and chanting his evenings away, yet emerging long enough to earn money for such staples as tea, coffee, salt, bacon, ammunition, mirrors, and other items he could not easily duplicate in his wild world. Whenever the ranches butchered, Indians flocked in as inevitably as magpies and carried off the intestines and all else the white man discarded.

The one white disease to which the Indian seemed immune was mining fever, although a handful of Indians throughout the West inadvertently made rich strikes. Many a cowboy or miner tried in vain to trail a drunken Indian back to his source of gold. One old Duck Valley Shoshone, remembering back to Mike's time, told me how he had fought off starvation by selling gold nuggets to miners at five cents apiece.

The Indians of the last century watched curiously as the white man rushed westward for the gold strikes of California, then back to Nevada for a silver craze when gold was almost ignored. Vast fortunes were made on former Indian hunting grounds; huge mining enterprises flourished in once empty hills. Nevada had untold wealth, but functioned as a mining camp for California. Even her historical documents were bled off to that neighboring state.

Once the shallow mineral resources were depleted, boisterous boomtowns died and mine buildings battled the elements, losing out to vandals, winds, rust, and time. But if the white man passed on to new lands, leaving one man where there were ten, those who remained somehow kept control and the Indian never again regained his lost hunting grounds.

Mike and his family gave the deserted towns a wide berth, not quite understanding what pestilence it was that had killed off all the people and caused the white man to move off, leaving his possessions behind.

There was much else he did not understand. The white man preached peace, but to Mike, attempting to live his life in a territory stretching from the south hills of the Snake River Valley southward over the Nevada line to Gollaher Mountain and San Jacinto, the vicious sheep and cattle wars that caught him in their midst must have seemed little different than ancient tribal wars of territory.

Trouble came first with the advent of nomad bands of sheep, which swept across the vast open ranges in succeeding waves, illegal but tolerated, stealing feed from local herds with no regard for the morrow, trampling, churning to dust, chewing all available forage into the ground. To discourage transients, legitimate sheep outfits used systematic overgrazing to create a barren no-man's-land at the periphery of their ranges, and soon valuable native forages were replaced by cheat grass and unpalatable species of brush.

Violence erupted when sheep invaded cattle ranges, fouling the scant water supplies and making trampled bedgrounds of the adjacent meadows. Cattle hated the smell and sought other areas of their range. Cattlemen set up a deadline area through the heart of Mike's territory, across which sheep were not allowed to stray.

But inevitably the sheep scattered and strayed across lines, or herders made a game of trying to steal feed. Soon cattlemen took matters into their own hands.

In 1895, the Shoesole outfit hired a brash braggart of a gunman named Diamondfield Jack Davis to patrol the deadline in the Shoshone Basin between Deep and Goose creeks. Since this was in the heart of Mike's summer range, Mike must have known Jack well.

The nickname "Diamondfield" came from an incident at the Stricker Ranch at Rock Creek when Davis bragged that he intended to find a diamond field and get rich. Having established his reputation as a gunman by parading through towns armed to the teeth and by shooting up sheep camps, in 1896 he was charged with killing a sheepman named Wilson in his camp six and one-half miles south of what is now the village of Rogerson.

The subsequent trial became a battle between sheep and cattle forces. The late Senator William E. Borah of Idaho headed the prosecution. Jack was actually innocent, but he was convicted and sentenced to death. While the battle over his fate went through various appeals, Jack himself seemed more interested in watching construction of the hanging scaffold than in following the political furor over his conviction. Sheepmen still insinuate that Sparks, Diamondfield's employer and owner of the Shoesole, took a little trip with the governor, and when they returned, Davis was set free.

In 1913, he was reported shot by a Mexican firing squad for interfering with the revolution, but Davis appeared in New York shortly after, very much alive, if without funds. That same year he was reported shot and badly wounded in Butte Falls, Montana, in a street brawl. But the colorful Davis did not die until March of 1948, when, at eighty-five years of age, he was run over by a taxi in Las Vegas, leaving no survivors to mourn his passing.

In 1908, Sparks-Harrel sold to the Vineyard Land and Stock Company. Their headquarters remained at San Jacinto, a name Sparks had brought with him from Texas.

South and west of Rock Creek, across the mountains, near Mike's winter range, it consisted of a few ranch buildings and a company store. Today the buildings still mark its existence in a broad expanse of rolling sagebrushed hills and willowed river bottoms.

It was important to Mike's life, since there, as at Rock Creek, he was able to trade his handiwork for the few supplies he needed to supplement a diet garnered by hard, endless work from a harsh, unyielding land.

11

The white goose again. For weeks I had been drifting around Idaho, living the life of an Indian, trailing Mike back into his past, talking to people who had actually known him and remembered him, good responsible citizens such as L.P. Larsen, Sam Weighall's daughters Hattie Pounds and Tillie Ford, as well as Carrie Crockett.

Sons and daughters of pioneers, they had been born in Mike's time and had spent their lifetimes in the country Mike knew and loved. I had spent hours on end in the Twin Falls Public Library, scanning old records and reading periodicals until my hands and face were black with printer's ink and the girls at the desk giggled at the sight of me.

I had inveigled the publisher of the *Times News,* Al Westergren, into letting me prowl through dusty newsrooms, long abandoned, for fragile, yellowed, brittle newspapers missing from his morgue, searching for articles written sixty years before by writers long dead who had done their work in anonymity with nary a by-line. While Carrie Crockett had slippered about her creaking pioneer homestead, the original Crockett house, doing housework or chasing rattlesnakes off her front step, I had sprawled in her armchair engrossed in Charles S. Walgamott's charming *Reminiscences of Early Days* and had caught the flavor of Mike's land and times.

I had talked to ranchers, miners, sheepmen, lawmen, teamsters, bartenders, cooks, and wagon bosses who were tip-toeing past their prime when I was born, some still blessed with a keen grasp of history, others with not much else than brittle bones and fading minds, men and women who had witnessed history at Fort Hall, Grouse Creek, Oakley, Rock Creek, Hansen, Kimberly, Twin Falls, San Jacinto, Tecoma, or the Shoshone Basin more than half a century before.

Because this was the land where Mike had spent nearly half his life, I wanted to be part of the scene, to be more to the Crocketts who had known Mike than just a writer from Oregon hooked on the story of their pet Indian. I wanted them to accept me, to understand that I too was of the ranch tradition, spoke cowboy lingo, could rope a bit, had ridden broncs, eaten trail-drive dust and frying-pan bread, pitched hay from frozen, loose haystacks, driven teams, and run mustangs, and that when I wasn't off trailing Mike I too had a ranch to run.

While Charlotte Crockett and her crew held a bunch of nervous cows crowded in a hillside fence corner, I roped calves for her and dragged them bucking and bawling to the branding fire. I caught each calf with a sense of relief, because to miss a loop in that steep, boulder-strewn hillside meant to lose the calf to the brushy thickets on either side. Astride Charlotte's prize Appaloosa, I was suddenly old Mike himself. Though my shots lacked grace and my nylon had to be stiff and clumsy compared to his limber rawhide reata, it was as though the old Indian himself guided my hand. I was transported back into time, roping calves on the Shoesole outfit for John Sparks and Andrew Harrel. I was Mike; I was Eat-em-up Jake; I was Catchum Charlie.

Sitting astride that Indian pony, trying my damnedest not to miss a loop, pretending I roped that well all the time, I drank in the experience, the sight of the rocky palisades above me, the scudding, dizzying clouds racing over Rock Creek Canyon, the fragrance of hoof-crushed sage, the bawling of cattle, the odor of singed hide, and the yellow smoke of burning calf hair.

Then, suddenly, I saw in the cloud of smoke, moving wraithlike on a cool wind down the canyon, the white goose, and my sudden fear for its safety mounted almost to a frenzy to get home to Yamsi, to my own ranch, to make sure some crass, unthinking poacher hadn't ignored my signs, pushed through my fences, invaded the pristine loneliness of my river valley to end the beauty of my white goose with his gun.

It was then that I decided to trap the white goose, capture him for his own protection and settle him to a reservation life on the ranch pond where he would be safe and well fed for the rest of his days.

Home once more on the ranch, I baited a small marshy ooze along the river, scattering oats, wheat, corn, barley, and milo. Then in the tall, frost-bleached grasses, I anchored a cannon net, artfully concealed, primed with explosive charges to hurtle the leading edge of the net over one goose or a flock.

Exhausted by long journeys from the north, strange Canadas accepted my hospitality, descending by the hundreds to the bait, but, conditioned by persecution, the white goose stood warily aside, refusing to be deceived. Often, as I crouched half-frozen among withered rushes listening to the tick of sleet on brittle rush, lunching on tule roots as Mike might have done, I looked up to see the white goose poised as though to step into the baited area, but always some vague suspicion moved him away.

Days passed. Fearfully I watched the skies for new storms to come scudding over the somber, pine-encrusted ridges to the south, afraid that one more blizzard might send my rare bird winging south over the gun clubs of California. Little by little the sloughs and the river margins froze, locking in what scant food was left with a metal-hard covering of ice.

Flock after flock took to the air. The last large band flew one last circle over my lonely valley, then headed southward. Dejected and alone, the white goose flew the marshes, calling plaintively, but of the few wing-weary northern birds left, none called him down.

Perhaps it was hunger, or the almost Indian sociability of his nature that brought him finally to earth. Snow fell in giant wet flakes, as a small flock of Canadas swam to the bank near the trap and climbed to feed on the few patches of grain protected by grassy hummocks from the storm. It was almost evening and in a few more moments the pines would be shrouded in white, no longer distinguishable from the snowy meadows.

I had almost deserted my blind for the warmth of the ranch-house fire when suddenly I heard, plaintive and mournful, the cry of a lone goose overhead, then the sudden beating of pinions as, ghostlike, a white bird braked his descent. I waited for a few long moments, then detonated the trap.

I listened, heard terrified gabbling, yet no wingbeats of escaping birds. Dashing forward, I saw in the gloom a dozen geese helpless under the cover of the net and there among them, his body almost indistinguishable against the snow, I saw the white goose.

For a long moment as I held him, feeling the sharp edge of his breastbone keel, I paused, tormented by guilt, to reconsider what I had thought to do. But I thought of the hunters who would show the bird no mercy, and then, sadly, I clipped the flight feathers on one wing, rendering him flightless until the stubs moulted and new feathers grew in their place.

The floor of the pickup cab was a new world to the bewildered bird. To immobilize his wings I thrust his head and neck through the sleeve of a sweatshirt, and, as he crouched on the floor, neck swaying like a cobra with the motions of the truck, watching me with dark, angry eyes, he made a strange sight. A university emblem spread emblazoned on his back, and head and neck rose from the floor like an extra gearshift.

Released into his pen, he gave one terrified, agonized honk, then tried to fling himself airborne. For a time in the darkness he paced the wire mesh of his cage; then, as I waited silently, feeling the large wet snowflakes melting down my collar, I heard his feathers ruffle like a deck of cards being shuffled, then, at long last, the rattle of his feed pan as the hungry bird forgot his fears and began to eat.

Soon he was a slave to my handouts and would follow the fat, tame Canadas who frequented my ponds and meadows as they waddled meekly up to beg for corn.

There was a sadness in the appearance of the bird. So much of its beauty had been in the freedom of its flight. Now it knew only the boredom of captivity. His life consisted of swimming first to one end of the long pond, then to the other, or moping on the bank, head tucked beneath one ivory wing.

There were times when I should have been writing when I found myself staring out my study window over the frozen meadows, now the domain of the white goose. Often I would be filled with a sense of shame for what I had done, sensing that a few precarious months of freedom were somehow better for the bird than anything I could possibly offer.

I had assumed that I could let the bird go free simply by allowing the flight feathers to grow out again, but I was wrong. The truth was that with my grain can I had enslaved him, conditioned him to captivity. Like a reservation Indian, he could never more be truly free. I had taken a wild, free spirit and turned him into a beggar who could not long survive off my welfare rolls. Migrate he might, but he would soon come panhandling in to some farmer's doorstep and end up in the pot. I was relieved when frost so painted my window panes that I could no longer look out upon my blunder, and I could once more return to Mike and the conditions that set up the end of his many years at Rock Creek.

According to Carrie Crockett, "In the spring of 1910, Mike and his family broke camp, packed up their baskets, grinding stones, digging sticks, bows, spears, and drums, as well as a large supply of staples such as dried camas, sego lily bulbs, wild onion, rose hips, dried fish and jerky, and headed out of the canyon on Indian Johnnie's trail leading west out of Rock Creek gorge and over the rounded timbered hills, driving a team of mustangs pulling a wagon Mike had purchased at the Jones Ranch not long before.

"I remember going by his camp above the stackyard," Carrie said, "but all that was left was a heap of fire rocks, a pot of black clay, and the willow bones of his hut. Since 1880 they had been part of the Crockett world; somehow not one of them ever came back to Rock Creek again."

Although the Crocketts, Larsens, and Hansens lost track of Mike completely that summer and the following winter, it was actually to be the most fully documented year of Mike's life.

At that very moment Mike, headed up over the western rim of the canyon and out of the gnats and mosquitoes for his summer range near Gollaher Mountain, was entering a more rapid phase of the story fate had written for him back in the 1870s. For those who were to play a part in the drama, however fast or slow the story sometimes moved, like those who fell with the collapse of the suspension bridge of San Luis Rey, there was no escaping their eventual involvement.

The events of 1911, at Little High Rock Canyon, several hundred miles away in northwestern Nevada, were fated as early as the 1870s, when the same Judge Tranmer who married John Hansen and Anna Petersen dropped off a wagon train bound for Oregon and chose instead to settle in the Snake River Valley. Had he gone on, the dramatic saga of Mike's subsequent life would never have taken place.

Doubtless Mike knew Judge Tranmer from the days before John Hansen bought out the Tranmer and Robinson store, but though he saw the judge often about the country there was little chance Mike knew the judge in professional capacity, since Mike broke no laws.

Mike generally arrived at the store on horseback, although when his purchases were to be heavy before a journey, he sometimes brought a horse and travois. He took care of his business without fanfare, traded a few items to John Hansen to cover his purchases, nodded politely to any who happened to be in the store, and departed. He never quite seemed to hurry, but then he never seemed to loiter as did the Shoshone, who whiled away endless hours squatting against the wall of the store or sitting, legs straight out before them, as people are wont to sit who have never used chairs.

Mike never allowed his women and children to accompany him to the store, as though the sight of wonders on the shelves might arouse in their breasts hankerings for luxury that might make them quit the band.

If Judge Tranmer ever conversed with Mike, it was probably only to ask Mike if, during his wanderings in the hills, he had ever run into his sons, Frank and Gay.

Frank was about forty-eight and Gay younger, and both were of a different stamp than the old man. The sons of a minister or judge never have it easy, and Frank and Gay from the beginning seemed out to prove they weren't sissies. Their chief love was running wild horses, which they sold to ranchers far and wide. Now and again there were ugly rumors that the boys were up to things the old man would never have sanctioned.

Sometime in the spring of 1910, the Tranmer boys headed out of the Magic Valley, bound for Mike's summer range. With them were a couple of boys, one their nephew of fourteen, named Frank Dopp, and the other a gangly eighteen-year-old Twin Falls boy named Nimrod Urie, who worshipped the ground Frank Tranmer walked on. With them also was a white woman who belonged to Frank Tranmer.

No one will ever know what really transpired that spring in the mountains and deserts surrounding the Shoshone Basin and south to Gollaher Mountain across the Nevada line.

Both the Tranmer gang and Mike's family roamed that lonely land. Soon rumors became rampant that ranchers in the Shoshone Basin were losing cattle and horses to rustlers, and that the thefts were perpetrated by wandering bands of Shoshone Indians.

Those who knew Mike were certain of his innocence. According to the sheriff of Elko County who investigated, some eighty head of horses were stolen. Mike hunted horses mostly for his own needs; it would have been very difficult for him to sell eighty horses, especially branded ones, without arousing white suspicions.

Furthermore, Mike had spent over thirty years on this range and knew only too well that his license to live there depended upon his reputation for honesty. He had never been known to steal, and there was no reason why he should start in a year when food was plentiful and what little money he required could easily be obtained merely by selling rawhide and buckskin items to ranchers and cowboys or by trading goods at the Rock Creek and San Jacinto stores.

It was probably the Tranmers who were guilty. Since they were unable to survive on roots and wild foods, groceries were a necessity only obtainable by purchase. Thus money became vital for their survival, and the best way to get money without working was to steal. Like many a white rustler before them, they tried to place the blame on the Indians.

It is now the considered opinion of old-timers that, whatever the accusations in the press were about Indian Mike and his band altering brands,* the thefts in the area were actually the work of the Tranmer gang. It is conjectured by those loyal to Mike that the Indians ran across the Tranmers altering the brands on a bunch of horses they had corraled and that the white outlaws, knowing of Mike's connections with the Shoesole, were afraid Mike might turn them in. The white outlaws followed the Indians to their camp, intending to wipe them out.

As Mike's son, Jack, was bringing some horses in to camp, some ten miles from San Jacinto, the outlaws ambushed him, shattering his leg with a bullet to such extent that Jack soon bled to death. The enraged Indians, stunned by Jack's death, managed to elude the whites and cornered them in some rocks without water. When the outlaws sent Frankie Dopp to the nearest spring, the Indians shot the boy in revenge. While the Indians were occupied, the rest of the outlaws made their escape.

If we accept this version as being close to correct, then the outlaws' trouble had just begun, for they were in real danger of being hanged as horse thieves. There was not only the probability that Mike, who knew them all, would report to his son-in-law, Lige Harris, but that the outlaws now had the additional problem of hiding the stolen horses whose brands had been altered both by cutting out sections of hide and by using a running iron to change the existing brand to Tranmer's iron. If they roped the horses again, cut the brands from the hide, and then turned them loose, there was the certainty that the horses would head for the range where they had been

* *Twin Falls Times* of May 9, 1910.

born or would soon be standing at some rancher's gate. If they drove the horses off to some isolated canyon in back country, it would be a simple matter for an Indian such as Mike to track them down.

There was not much choice. The rustlers drove the horses off into the sage, dug some long parallel trenches, shot the horses, and covered the carcasses with dirt so the buzzards would not give them away. Perhaps they threw Frankie Dopp into the same hole. Then the gang pounded leather to nearby Contact, where they wasted no time concocting a story that would place the blame on Mike for stealing horses and killing Frankie Dopp.

It was the word of a white man against that of an Indian, and the fact that the white man happened to be the son of a prominent Idaho judge insured that there would be no contest.

Gay Tranmer's story attracted much excitement, and newspapers all over Nevada carried the story on page one. On May 11, 1910, the following article appeared in the Winnemucca *Humboldt Star:*

STORY OF MURDER BY ELKO INDIANS

The *Elko Independent* gives the following particulars of the killing of a boy by Indians in the northern part of Elko County on the 25th of April. When the man whose name is given as Gay Tenly [Gay Tranmer] first saw the Indians, they were branding horses in a corral at the foot of a high hill. He and two companions [perhaps Urie and Frank Tranmer] were on top of the hill and started down to where the Indians were when one of them told them not to come to the corrals but to go to the camp. They started for the camp but before reaching there, they were halted by another Indian with a pistol who said to Tenly, "I am going to kill you." Tenly asked him why he wanted to kill him as they had always been friends. The Indian replied that he had no friends and was like a wild horse. The Indian then fired in the direction of Tenly but did not hit him. Tenly and his companions then started back up the hill. As they were going along, one of them happened to turn around and saw one of the Indians a short distance behind them raise his gun and shoot. The white men lost no time getting behind a big rock. The Indians also got behind a rock and a regular battle ensued. None of the whites were wounded, but it is thought that the Indian who began the fight was killed or so badly wounded that he has since died. When the firing ceased, the white men escaped to their camp. The Indians then got their horses and rode to the top of the hill overlooking the camp and fired several shots into the camp but did not hurt anyone.

While the battle was going on, a white woman and a boy were in the camp. The boy told the woman that he would go after the horses belonging to the camp. He mounted his horse and rode away and that was the last seen of him alive. After he had been gone for some time, Indians were seen riding around on the top of the hill at the foot of which the lifeless body of the boy was found. The name of the dead boy could not be determined. Excitement was at a high pitch in Contact when the news reached there and eight men volunteered to go with Deputy Sheriff Grim in search of the Indians. Had they been found, it is not likely that the county could have been put to any expense trying them.

The story worked precisely as the Tranmers had expected. They had framed Mike, pure and simple, and placed the burden of their own guilt on the shoulders of a gentle old Indian.

How they must have laughed around the campfire. The admiration Nimrod Urie had for Frank Tranmer knew no bounds. But Tranmer could not have been comfortable. He must have glanced often into the flickering shadows of the campfire in real fear that Mike might pay them a visit to get revenge. It was time to vanish, to seek new victims in new lands.

According to L.P. Larsen, the Tranmer gang killed a bartender named Harris at Twin Springs, near what is now Jackpot, Nevada, but before they fled the country, they fed another story to the press, this time to their home-town paper. Frank Tranmer wanted only to disappear, to be thought dead, but the story they concocted caused an outburst of Indian hysteria and increased not only Mike's peril but that of all other Indians in the area.

The *Twin Falls Times* for Thursday, May 12, 1910, bore the headline "CATTLEMEN OUT FOR BAD INDIANS" and carried the following story:

Rock Creek Man Murdered By Marauders. Roaming Bands Of Shoshone Indians Rustling Cattle In Nevada Kill Frank Tranmer.

Confirmation was received here Monday of the report, first brought here Sunday, that young Frank Tranmer of Rock Creek had been killed by Indians just over the Nevada line. Tranmer's death is ascribable to efforts of himself and other cowboys to recover their horses, stolen by marauding bands of Shoshones who have been causing much trouble to the ranch men and cattle and sheep owners this spring in the southern part of Idaho, whose herds graze in northern Nevada. So serious did their depredations become a few weeks ago, that the Sheriff of Elko County received many appeals for aid. He investigated and found that the Indians had stolen some eighty head of horses and after collecting same in the Shoshone Basin, Twin Falls County, ran them over the line. He sent word to citizens to "kill all the Indians, and every Indian that may be found roaming the Idaho country."

Accordingly, a band of cowboys last Wednesday started in pursuit of the renegades, and the sanguinary combat wherein Tranmer lost his life ensued as soon as the pursuing party overtook the thieves. It was not learned if any of the Indians were killed. When the report came to Rock Creek that young Tranmer had lost his life, his friends gathered in large forces Friday. All the rifles that could be mustered were secured and some 60 ranch men and cowboys formed a posse that left Rock Creek early Saturday, bound for the more southern country. Statements of ranchers from that section who came in Monday are to the effect that the intentions of the posse from this state were to strictly obey the instructions of the Elko County officer. The presumption here is, by the retired cattlemen and sheepmen familiar with that country, that ere the posse comes home, quite a number of Indians will have been sent to their happy hunting grounds. Frank Tranmer, the deceased, belongs to one of the prominent families in southern Twin Falls and Cassia Counties, and was an uncle of Mrs. O.A. Stalker of this city.

Frank Tranmer vanished for the moment from history, though he was soon to reappear, very much alive.

In this day and age such comment as that from the Elko sheriff about killing Indians would arouse a storm of protest from decent citizens, but when this article appeared in the *Times* back in 1910, not a single reader wrote in protest. Thirty-two years had passed since the Bannock War, yet even a false report of the murder of a ne'er-do-well such as Frank Tranmer by Indians could still set that lonely and vulnerable country ablaze with fear and leave it on the verge of hysteria.

At that moment in history, for Mike and his family, living their ancient existence in a land teeming with trigger-happy cowboys out to get-'em their Indian, any Indian, the chances for survival were exceedingly slim.

12

In spite of angry accusations against Rock Creek Mike, his friends refused to desert him. Those such as Sam Weighall, who knew him well, flatly refused to believe that Mike had as much as stolen a calf. Mike preferred wild meat to tame, had been a better neighbor than most white men, had an honest way of earning what limited money he could use, and risked being driven off his range if caught in any wrongdoing however small. It did not make sense to Sam that the grandfatherly old Indian would suddenly turn sour.

Mrs. Weighall was so beside herself with worry that one night she had a terrible dream that armed riders shot down Mike and all his band in their camp, and tumbled the corpses like so many dead dogs into a hole blasted into frozen earth. Upset by her fantasy, she sent word to the Elko authorities that Mike was a good, gentle Indian who had been their friend and neighbor for years, and that she was afraid he would be unjustly harmed.

The sheriff assured her that when Mike was found, he would most certainly be given a fair trial. This, of course, was the same sheriff who advised the Twin Falls posses to "kill all the Indians and every Indian found roaming the Idaho country."

Sam Weighall knew better. He was almost certain the sight of an armed posse sweeping down on Mike would panic the Indians into fighting for their lives. Even a rabbit fights back when cornered, and Mike's earliest memories were of white injustice toward the Indian people.

Perhaps it was Sam who located Mike and warned him of the dangers he faced from the senseless Indian hysteria that now gripped his land. But most probably it was Mike's daughter, Lizard, who, as wife of Lige Harris and part of the Shoe-sole community, would have had early access to news. Slipping unseen across the lonely sagebrush badlands, doubling back often to make sure no one followed, she could easily have located her family's hidden camp and warned Mike of the magnitude of his peril. At any rate, Mike and his family disappeared from the scene, leaving behind their cherished wagon in the sagebrush near what is now called Indian Mike Spring.

Without the element of surprise or the advantage of winter snows for tracking, the posse faced an almost impossible task. For efficiency, they split into small armed groups, combing hundreds of square miles of rolling hills, rocky canyons, and timbered, brushy mountain tops, visiting all known camps where anyone remembered having seen Indian Mike. The ashes of his campfires were many but cold, with no trace of recent occupancy. Mike and his family had vanished, leaving not a whisper of a trail.

One by one, as days passed and riders grew saddle-sore and horses weary, the ranks thinned. Cowboy after cowboy found excuse to head for town. Gradually the ranchers who had moved their families to safety went back to the routine of ranch affairs. But even then they cast apprehensive glances at the hills about them, as though they half expected to see Indian warriors outlined against the sky.

As time passed the Weighalls must have chuckled at the way the savvy old Indian had eluded his enemies, but just the same they missed his visits. Sometimes Mrs. Weighall would turn in her kitchen, half expecting to see Mike laughing in her doorway as she had seen him first so many years before. Often, as Sam rode the ranges tending cattle, his glance would catch and hold a far-off movement in the sage, but always it was only a magpie flashing black and white as it flew its daily mischief, a jackrabbit scampering up a hillside, or desert dust-devils playing pranks on tumbleweed or sage. As weeks became months, it was evident that Mike had disappeared perhaps for all time.

It was then that a new, unsettling mystery came to plague them. Not far from where Mike and his band had fought the Tranmers, Shoesole riders discovered the trenches where the outlaws had buried the stolen horses. It was obviously not something an Indian would bother to do. Suddenly even among those who only months before had lusted for a shot at an Indian, dread suspicions arose that perhaps Mike had been innocent after all, that most likely the horses had been buried by white rustlers to conceal altered brands, and that perhaps beneath the rotting heaps of horse flesh lay the bones of Mike Daggett and his family, killed by the very men who had accused them of rustling and murder.

There was even the ugly rumor that the Tranmer boys had been rustling stock themselves, that they had killed Frankie Dopp, their own nephew, to keep him from spilling the facts to the authorities, and that Dopp's bones too had been consigned to the same grave as the horses.

In the fall of 1910, when for the first time in many years the Daggett family failed to return to their camp at Rock Creek, friends wrote the Office of Indian Affairs, indicating their concern over the whereabouts of Mike and his family. The Office of Indian Affairs in turn notified the Department of Justice, but the mystery defied solution. Mike and his family could not be located on any of the reservations. Frankie Dopp and Frank Tranmer were supposed dead, and the rest of the Tranmer gang were thought to be off in northern Nevada somewhere, running mustangs. When asked of her father's whereabouts, Lizard Harris only shrugged and was silent.

The incidents of 1910 had dealt a telling blow to non-reservation Indians still living in the area. Frightened by open white hostility, they abandoned their occasional hunts, but huddled in their hovels at the outskirts of towns such as Elko, in Nevada, or moved to reservations such as Fort Hall, Duck Valley, or Fort McDermitt. To live in a tipi in the wild, hunting in the old way, gathering food as nature was harsh or generous with her bounty, was to arouse all sorts of dark suspicions among the whites and to invite blame for every rustled calf, every strayed horse. Though Mike had been innocent of any wrongdoing, the other Indians hated him for destroying the status quo, bringing down white wrath upon their heads.

In the decade following the turn of the century, there had been a certain laxity that had allowed Indians to come and go from the reservations or from the Indian towns to supplement their diets with wild food, such as venison, salmon, or pine nuts. Cut off from their wanderings by fear of white reprisals, the Indians now had less food than ever. Soon more and more women were forced into prostitution or into becoming dishwashers in cafes to earn a few pennies for their families. More and more, once-proud warriors sought escape from their frustrations in alcohol or opium brought in by the Chinese.

No longer busy gathering food, or controlled by tribal and family discipline, children who had once played games along Salmon Falls Creek or Goose Creek during occasional hunts now moped at the peripheries of towns, just one jump ahead of the local police, full of deviltry as though intent on earning every insult the whites had in store for them. Sadly enough for Mike, for every man who believed in him in spite of the fact that he was Indian, there were a dozen who believed in the Tranmers, simply because they were white.

The Tranmer gang had escaped by the skin of their yellow teeth, and without a backward glance at the lives they had ruined, at the heartbreak they had left in their wake. For several months they disappeared from sight, and ranchers, busy with autumn chores of gathering cattle off the ranges, cutting out strays, and weaning calves, shrugged off their disappearance as good riddance of bad rubbish.

But however destiny moves, fast or slow, it never ceases. On January 6, 1911, at Imlay, Nevada, a railroad station thirty-four miles south and west of Winnemucca and two hundred miles from where Tranmer's gang had last been seen, all hell broke loose. Frank Tranmer, once supposedly murdered by Indians, broke into headlines:

The Humboldt Star, Winnemucca, Nevada. Jan. 9, 1911. ATROCIOUS DOUBLE MURDER AT IMLAY. Masked Bandits Hold Up Saloon And Shoot Proprietor And His Wife—Murderers Are Captured.

One of the most atrocious and brutal crimes ever committed in Humboldt County was perpetrated in Imlay about ten o'clock last Friday night when Jean Quillici was shot dead and his wife mortally wounded by masked bandits.

The assassins, with masks made of flour sacks covering their faces, entered Quillici's saloon, which is situated about a mile west of the railroad station at Imlay, while the owner was counting the money in the cash register and was preparing to close the place for the night. As near as can be ascertained, there were three of the bandits, one staying at one of the outer doors, while the other two shot the proprietor and his wife and looted the place.

Upon entering the saloon, the robbers commanded Quillici to throw up his hands and when he hesitated, one of the robbers aimed a rifle at him and fired, the bullet entering the left shoulder. Quillici then started for the door when a second shot was fired, killing him instantly . . .

In the moments that followed, the bandits wounded Mrs. Quillici, then shoved a pistol barrel in the ear of her brother and ordered him to locate some money for them. The brother was only eighteen years of age, and having only recently come from Italy, could speak no English. He began to cry and the robbers gave up on him and began to search the house.

In the bedroom the four-year-old son of the Quillicis was standing up in his bed and the little fellow said to the robbers, "You killed Poppa, don't kill Uncle."

The bandits had vanished on horseback into the darkness. The sheriff of Humboldt County, Ralph Lamb, a highly respected lawman, was soon on his way by the first available train to Imlay, taking with him the noted Paiute tracker Skinny Pascal. At Imlay, Lamb formed a posse, and having found where the robbers had tied their horses, took out at daylight on the trail of the bandits, which headed for the Humboldt River.

They had just discovered a mask made of a flour sack with eyeholes lined with cardboard dropped along the trail, when they observed a man coming toward the posse, evidently looking for something he had lost. Arrested by Lamb and handcuffed, he was taken along with the posse, which followed the trail straight to the Blakeslee Ranch on the river. The prisoner was ordered to call out his partner, and when a man appeared at the door, he was quickly arrested. Both prisoners were taken to Winnemucca by train and lodged in the county jail.

Mrs. Quillici, who had been rushed to the Winnemucca hospital, died on the day following the robbery.

The two men were well known, having been camped on the river at the Blakeslee Ranch for some months; they claimed to be running wild horses. One of the bandits gave the name of N.R. Urie. He was only twenty-three years old and was from Twin Falls, Idaho. He had been working in Winnemucca on the sewer, and was in Winnemucca the day before the crime was committed. The other bandit refused to give his name, but from papers found on him when searched he was identified as J.F. Tranmer, about forty-five years old, and also from Idaho.

The arrest of Tranmer and Urie for murder convinced a great many of the Twin Falls posse members that they had acted too hastily in blaming Indian Mike for rustling and murder. They attempted to atone for their rash actions by saying kind words about Mike and his family, but the old man had vanished and was presumed dead, so their apologies went unheard and were soon forgotten, though it was obvious to every man concerned that their rash actions had affected many lives and had driven Mike from a stable, peaceful existence on a range that had been his for over thirty years. It was further clear that, had the Indians been found by the posse, Mike and all his family would have been shot down without a hearing. Now, since Nimrod Urie and J. Frank Tranmer were white, they would face a jury of their peers.

Confronted, however, with the weapons, the stolen money recovered from beneath the floor of their cabin, the mask he dropped upon the trail, and other damning articles, Urie broke down and made a complete confession.

The confession was not unexpected, since Urie, ever since he had been arrested, had been in a nervous state bordering on collapse, and Sheriff Lamb had kept a close watch on the prisoner's actions.

"My name is Nimrod Urie," the young man testified, "and my home is Twin Falls, Idaho. I have known Diffendarfer for about fifteen years and have been with him most of the time for the past year. I got acquainted with Frank Tranmer last spring while running horses in Idaho. I next met Tranmer at Imlay and he came down to the ranch to help Diffendarfer and I run horses. I did not like the way Diffendarfer and Tranmer were acting and I left and went to Winnemucca and got work on the sewer. I went back to get my things and stayed a few days. Nick Carter came down and asked Diffendarfer to come up and help him do work on some claims at Dutch Flat, and Tranmer took Diffendarfer up. I stayed at the camp and when Tranmer came back I said I would go out and work, but he said 'There's no need to work; I can tell you how to make some easy money.' I said, 'How's that?' and he replied, 'We will hold up the Dago saloon.'

"I said no, but he said it would be easy and explained how. He said, 'Well, you have to do it or I will kill you; we'll do it anyhow.' "

Urie went on to explain the workings of the crime, then told of the getaway. "I made the young man go out into the front room and Tranmer and I went out the back door. When we got to where the horses were I threw a cartridge from the gun and Tranmer took the gun away from me. When we reached camp, Tranmer asked me where my mask was. I looked for it but had lost it and he swore at me for doing so. He took me in the house and locked the door and told me to give him the money. Then he went out and rode off and when he came back he said, 'Now, kid, you are in for it as bad as I am.' He then told me to go back into the house and act sick and if anyone came to tell him he had gone for medicine . . ."

Undoubtedly it was Frank Tranmer who was the main force behind the robbery, but it was Nimrod Urie who was sentenced to death, while Tranmer, who had received a change of venue, was found guilty but sentenced to life imprisonment. Public outrage, perhaps, pressured for the later trial in which

SHAUG

TO START WORK AT BARRETT SPRINGS

EASTERN CAPITALISTS TO DEVELOP PROMISING RAMOLA PROPERTY.

A strong syndicate of Eastern capitalists, headed by the well-known mining engineer, Geo. W. Hartley, who is vice president of the Charleston Hill Gold Mining company at National No. 1, claim, at Barrett Springs. This property confines the southern boundary of the Nineteen Ten Mining company's holdings and two of the best located claims in that camp.

Messrs. Hartley and associates have incorporated a company known as the Barefield El-Metallic Mining company and here filed their articles of incorporation with the County Clerk. The incorporators named are George W. Hartley, Edward C. Fisher and Frank W. Wiltse, with the capital stock placed on a million shares at the par value of $1 each.

Already the new company has arranged for aggressive development work on the property which is to be under the management of R. S. Harlow, who will send a magonload of supplies to the property tomorrow.

NATIONAL MINES CO. SHIPS SUPPLIES

Frank Frey's big team arrived in the forepart of the week with the teams loaded with concentrates from the mill owned by the National Mines company at National for shipment from this place to a smelter. It has not been given out what the concentrates will assay, but it is presumed that they are rich, as it is the residue after reducing the extremely rich gold ore that is daily put through the company's mill at the rate of about $150,000 each month.

D. R. G. AND WESTERN PACIFIC ISSUE NEW MAP

The Star is in receipt of a large map issued by the Denver & Rio Grande system and the Western Pacific railway of the northwestern and far western states, showing the lines of railway controlled by these systems. The map is very neatly gotten up and will be very useful as it gives all the towns and stations along the Western Pacific railway, a practically new territory opened through the state of Nevada.

RETURNS FROM TRIP TO LAND OF ORANGES

F. J. Sutton returned yesterday afternoon from Redlands, Cal., where he had been inspecting the orange grove owned by himself and J. Pascal of this place. He reports a large crop of oranges on the property. He left a branch containing five oranges on exhibition in The Star's large show window.

Supplies for New Station.

The Caywood big team left yesterday with a load of pipe and supplies for the new station being built by L. F. Petersen near Cane Springs, on the road to National.

Left out for Montana.

O. J. Larson, who represented R. H. Barden & Co., in the construction of the new Winnemucca sewer system, left yesterday for Butte, Montana.

LOCAL NOTES AND PERSONAL MENTION

A. O. Pierce is in town from National.

Miss Fanny Harp is reported on the sick list.

Mrs. S. G. Lamb is reported on the sick list.

Joe Thomas of Chafey was in town Monday.

Miss Clara Young of Newport, Ky., is a recent arrival.

T. F. Rexburg is a recent arrival from Rexburg, Idaho.

J. S. McLaughlin arrived in town yesterday from National.

George House arrived in town yesterday from Paradise valley.

Geo. W. McCosh Jr. is a recent arrival from Montpelier, Ohio.

Frank Randohr a local dealer, is unloading a car of coal today.

Frank Nelson left yesterday with a load of supplies for his ranch at Chafey.

Eugene Thacker is spending a few days in town from his ranch near Mill City.

There will be services in the Catholic church at 10:30 next Sunday, Jan. 15.

Cummins arrived from Missouri will leave in a few days for National.

Mr. and Mrs. Charles Jenkins and son, Joey, are in town from National for a few days.

The big team, owned by John Leu left yesterday loaded with freight for his store at McDermitt.

M. Coleman, Dominic Bengoa, Joal J. Ace, E. Simois and Martin Echave of McDermitt are in town.

J. L. Wheelman has returned from a trip to San Francisco and gone to his home at the camp of National.

F. H. Lonsabory, route agent of the Globe Express company, was here yesterday checking up the local office.

Mrs. Charles Headfort has gone to San Francisco to be with her mother, who is quite ill at her home in the city.

James Brenin and L. Brock are here from Los Angeles to look over the mineral resources of this section of the county.

Clyde Welshons is here from Sparks visiting with his brother, C. B. Welshons, manager of the Orlando Telephone and Power company.

Mrs. Carl R. Squires of National and her parents here, Mr. and Mrs. W. A. Fogg of Reno, and are visiting at the Lafayette hotel. Mr. Fogg is County Clerk of Washoe county.

WESTERN UNION OFFICE NOW IN DOWNTOWN DISTRICT

The Western Union telegraph office which was formerly at the Southern Pacific depot is now fully established in the new offices of the company in the Nixinger building. The new office is being furnished with car furniture and is a great credit to the town. J. J. Mercer, who has been in charge of the company's office here for some time, is the manager and J. Tucker is the assistant manager. Mr. Mercer states that it will be at least three weeks before the place is fully equipped, when the company will multiplex nine trunk lines through the office, three have thoroughly established the office will contain sets of quadruplex and two sets of duplex Wheat stone automatic instruments. The basement in connection with the office is an interesting place, for here alone the 160 cells of 200 volts which are used in connection with the dynamo system and have. Another set of cell cells are to be moved from the office near the Western Pacific depot. Besides the ones mentioned there will have additional wells, the wires for which are already on the premises and read ready to be put in place. A gasoline engine and emergency dynamo are also to be installed in the basement. This office is to be known as "the transcontinental repeating station."

Eagles Install Officers.

The local lodge of Eagles held an interesting meeting Monday evening and installed their officers for the ensuing year as follows: J. W. Fitzpatrick, president; C. V. Drake, vice-president; John Weiner, chaplain; C. B. Smith, secretary; J. W. Oswald, F. W. P.; Bert Ellis, inside guard; Vic Giraux, outside guard; M. B. Johnson and E. S. Balloa, trustees. After the installation the members sat down to a banquet and spent the balance of the evening having a jolly good time.

Going to the Coast.

P. F. Snapp and daughter, Miss Pearl Snapp, Mrs. Simpson and daughter and Mrs. Kate Patten arrived today from the northern part of the county in the McConnell's auto en route to San Francisco.

Attended Bank Meeting at Reno.

J. Sheehan, cashier of the First National Bank, has gone to Reno to attend

URIE MAKES COMPLETE CONFESSION OF THE FOUL MURDER OF THE QUILLICIS

Claims that Both Were Killed by Tramner, His Partner in Crime, and That the Latter Was the Ringleader and Originator of the Whole Plot

Confronted with the rifle and revolver, the stolen money, the hideous mask which he wore and dropped upon the trail and the other damning articles found in their camp, a few miles from the scene of the crime, Urie, the younger of the bandits today asked for the murder of Mr. and Mrs. Quillici, committed in the saloon near Imlay last Friday. "Well, you have got to do it or I will kill you, we'll do it anyhow." Jack was broke and explained how. He said, well, you have got to do it or I will kill you, we'll do it anyhow." Jack brought up the subject again and I objected, telling him it would get all of us in trouble. He said that there would be no one following of the murder and then made complete confession to the county jail yesterday in the presence of Sheriff Lamb, District Attorney Callahan and Constable Rich of Imlay.

The confession was not unexpected as Urie, ever since he was arrested, has been in a nervous state bordering upon collapse, and Sheriff Lamb, who has kept a close watch on the prisoner's actions, has been of the belief that he would finally break down and tell the entire story of the horrible double murder. And this Urie did, making a lengthy statement to the officers in which all the horrible details of the crime were given, the story being an effort to exculpate himself as far as possible and throw the burden of planning the robbery and the actual killing of the Quillicis upon Tramner, the other bandit and partner in the crime, who the two bandits say another man, named Diffendorfer, have been scheming in the vicinity of Imlay for several months.

District Attorney Callahan and Constable Rich arrived from Imlay on No. 5 yesterday afternoon. The inquest upon the body of the murdered man having been completed there after a three days session before Justice Normann. Yesterday evening Constable Rich, who had been working hard on the case ever since the night of the murder, made another visit to the cabin where the bandits had been camped for the purpose of making a further search for the revolver which it was the theory of the officers had been used in inflicting the death wound of Mrs. Quillici. Constable Rich's persistence was rewarded, as he found the revolver, a 41-caliber Colt's and another 38-caliber, the one the bandits used in killing Quillici, hidden away under the roof of the cabin at the bandits' camp. A bell filled with revolver cartridges was also found and it and the weapons were brought here and shown to Urie, together with the other incriminating articles, when he was brought from his cell into the Sheriff's office yesterday afternoon and told that the game was up. He then made a complete confession. The confession was entirely voluntary and Urie was not promised anything in the way of immunity or that he would receive lesser punishment. The confession was taken down by District Attorney Callahan and signed by Urie, who was then taken back to his cell.

Urie Testifies at Inquest.

This morning Urie applied his desire to repeat his story at the inquest in the case of the murdered woman, Mrs. Quillici, which was set to begin at 10 o'clock before Justice Dunn and a jury consisting of James Ritchie, J. O. Mosstrop, C. W. McDeld, J. P. Ose and W. R. Paul.

Urie was brought into the courtroom and after having been informed by Justice Dunn that he was not required to testify and that if he did so his statement could be used against him, he said:

"I wish to testify and tell the whole story, the same as I did to Mr. Lamb and Mr. Callahan last night," and went on to tell the story straight and everything I know. I am and then Urie, after being sworn, told his story of the horrible crime. Throughout he maintained considerable nervousness, shown mainly by the trembling of his fingers, which he evidently tried to control by keeping his hands clasped together during the entire story of the brutal crime. But he gave no sign of emotion at any time, though it was only he who fired the shot with a mask drawn up to his throat that his face appeared the position he was placed in by the confession, he evidently placing difficulties upon some allegation of guilt. He went so far as to take part in the murder by the threat that would have met his fate, though Tramner had forced him to take part in the awful deed by the threat that he would kill him if he refused. Urie's story is in substance as follows:

"My name is Mustrad Urie, and I am here from Twin Falls, Idaho. I know Diffendorfer for about fifteen years and have been with him most of the time for the past years. I got acquainted with Frank Tramner six years ago. I met Tramner at Imlay and he came down in the ranch to help Diffendorfer and I cut hooves. I did cut for Mrs. Diffendorfer a while and after I quit they gave me $10. After I went to work for Diffendorfer and Tramner were acting and I left and went to Winnemucca and got work on the

some claims at Dutch Flat and Tramner took Diffendorfer up. I stayed at the camp and when Tramner came back I said I should go out and now, but he said, There is no need to work. I can tell you how to make some easy money."

I said, "How's that," and he replied, "We will hold up the dope saloon." I said no, but he said it would be easy and explained how. He said, "Well, you have got to do it or I will kill you, we'll do it anyhow." Then day he brought up the subject again and I objected, telling him it would get all of us in trouble. He said that there would be no one following of the murder and that if I tried to run off he would kill me if he had to follow me for ten years. Next day I came to Winnemucca and when I returned to Imlay Thursday night he was in Slaughter's saloon. We rode down to the ranch and he asked me again about holding up the saloon. I refused again and he said, "You've got to do it." Next day he said nothing about it until night, when he went out and got the horses and told me to get ready. After supper he fixed up the masks and we got on the horses and started to town. I took the guns. We tied the horses about 200 yards from the saloon and he told me to get out of sight and then cover the masks and things down by a brush. Tramner then took a rope and tied my hands to the saddle horn and he would tell worse." Then he said I would feel better." Then he handed me the rifle and handed it to me and instructed me to throw it down on Quillici when we got inside, the saloon. He made up go ahead and broke down the door and I said, "Let's not do it." But he shoved his gun against my head and said, "No, we will go in and I threw my gun down on Quillici and Frank said, "Throw up your hands." But Quillici didn't and grabbed the rifle and started to run me back and Frank said, "Frank then took the rifle from me and shot Quillici again. The woman started to run and he shot her. Then he told me to get the money out of the cash register and then go into the rooms and see what I could find. I saw the two boys in a room and went back and told Frank and he told me to go back and make them throw up their hands and tell where the money was. I made the young lads go out into the front room and I turned and I could not find out where that money was. When I came out the horses were I threw a cartridge from the gun and Tramner took the gun away from me. When we reached our camp Tramner told me to change clothes and said he where my mask was. I looked for it, but had lost it, and he swore at me for doing so. He took me to the house and locked the door and told me to give him the money. Then he went out and rode off and when he came back he said, "Now, kid, you are in for it as bad as I am." He then told me to get back into the house and set and wait for Tramner to come again. He did so and later on Tramner came and told him to get back and told him and Tramner grabbed the rifle and was going to shoot him and I ran from me and forced me up against the bar and then Tramner also him. Quillici then started to run toward the back door and Tramner grabbed the rifle from me and shot him again and shot Quillici's shoulder. Then Tramner handed the rifle back to me and pulled his revolver down. The cathedral and fired at Mrs. Quillici, who was passing me she ran for the back door. Then Tramner commanded me to lay my gun on the bar and go through the till, which I did. The money I took from the till appeared to be all small change, quarters, dimes and nickels.

"At this point Urie identified the revolvers which was taken from the till at Quillici's saloon.

"After taking the money from the till," continued Urie, "I went into the back rooms and made a hasty search. One of the rooms I entered and I could not get into it. I did so and my enemy in one of the other rooms. When I went into the room which I could not open I made the larger two boys open up their hands and I searched the room. Then I made the larger boy go into the back room of the house where his mother, who was in bed with him, and I then Tramner and I left the place. We threw the gun probably two or three bundles. There was an axe with us so we left the saloon and while we were riding away I lost my mask. If there is a revolver was taken the saloon I have three rows running in the saloon or so opening the trays to he mines...

Other Witnesses Testify.

At the official evidence of Urie at the inquest the evidence of Dr. H. Moran and Henry Robinson was given, the witnesses testifying to the wounds on the slain man and the slain woman, which the murders were committed with one shot in the head or neck. After ...

SHAUG

he was convicted of the death of Mrs. Quillici, and this time he did get the death penalty, and was later executed.

In the early days of World War I, however, at the request of Urie's mother, Nimrod was pardoned by the governor on condition that he would enlist in the Canadian army. Charlotte Crockett remembers playing as a little girl at the Uries', the day Uncle Nim came home from prison. He spent his days after the war as a sheepherder in the Twin Falls area.

But whatever the final designation of Tranmer and Urie, they are important to this account only as they served to alter Rock Creek Mike's life, and the story of their misdeeds is brought in only that we may more accurately weigh the accusations that were made against Mike. Sadly enough, even with their conviction, which forever tainted their reputations as honest witnesses, there was no returning to the conditions that existed when their lives first touched Mike's. The white hysteria against Indians touched off by the Tranmer gang's false accusations linking Mike with murder and rustling in northern Nevada would be years in the dying, with more tragedy yet to come.

13

The reason that posses scouring the vast lonely reaches of northern Nevada found no fresh traces of Mike in any of his favorite haunts, was, of course, that the old Indian, fore-warned of disaster either by his friends, the Weighalls, or by his daughter, Lizard, had ordered the hides stripped from the willow ribs of his hut and had headed south toward lands unknown.

Riding eastward from San Jacinto, a posse pushed across the wide sagebrush flats and over rolling treeless hills, forded Cedar Creek and Horse Creek, and passed into that drainage now known as Indian Mike Creek, which flows from the north shoulder of Gollaher Mountain northward into Hot Creek, and thence into Shoshone Creek. Here, where twin springs of sweet water flowed from the bottom of an otherwise dry wash, Mike had often camped.

Early that spring of 1910, Mike had stopped by the Jones Ranch west of Rock Creek and paid Harry Jones cash for a battered old wooden-wheeled wagon. Now when the posse discovered a wagon abandoned near the twin springs, they sent for Jones, who identified the wagon as the one he had sold Indian Mike.

But, although the posse found obsidian chips from arrowhead makers along the spring, as well as Mike's one major possession, the wagon, and the refuse of recent Indian habitation, the ashes were cold in Mike's campfire. They knew that buried somewhere in the neighboring rims were at least two of Mike's children and even imagined Mike watching them from distant rimrocks, but every day that the posse milled and circled in the area found Mike and his family farther and farther away.

It must have been hard to explain to the children why suddenly the family was on the run. No longer were there songs and laughter beside evening campfires; at night a guard mounted the rimrocks above the camp and watched for some danger the children could not fathom. In their father's eyes, where the happy twinkles had danced like spring breezes, now they read only a haunting sadness and confusion, and sometimes anger.

Often now, when the yellow moon smiled on the land, the band moved quickly across valleys and into the bordering hills. Sometimes in the distance they saw the twinkling of lights of ranch-house windows, and as the cool night air settled in the hollows, they saw the lights go out one by one as the white settlers put out their kerosene or carbide lamps and went to sleep. They kept their horses unshod so that their tracks—wandering, crisscross lines through the sage—would appear to the inexpert eye to be only those of wandering mustangs seeking a better range. They waited below the brows of hills or ridges until scouts had gone ahead and pronounced the landscape empty and safe. When dawn came they bedded down, making sunshades of the sage, while some man or woman watched from a high point and another herded the horses, letting them graze and rest.

According to subsequent testimony by his daughter, Heney, Mike's band drifted south to Tecoma, a rail head on the main line near the Nevada-Utah border. Today, little trace remains of Tecoma. In those days it was an important shipping point on the railroad, used not only by the Shoesole but other cattle and sheep operations from as far away as Idaho.

Mike had good reason to head for Tecoma, for here Jennie's sister lived, and Mike could readily slip in under cover of darkness to obtain food, money, and that which was most important to a hunted man, information as to the progress of pursuing posses.

The news from Jennie's sister must have added to Mike's anger and bewilderment. For many years he had lived in peace with the white man, and his only sins had been to reject reservation life and to refuse to give up his children to government boarding schools. He had taken pains to resist stealing the white man's beef even when he was hungry or to rustle new horses when his own had died on the trail, his moccasins were shaved paper-thin by rocks, and his feet were raw from stone bruises.

Now, unfairly, he stood accused of rustling, and the murder of Frank Tranmer, a man Mike knew from long association to be a thief. According to Heney's testimony, her brothers had killed Frankie Dopp, but only after their brother Jack had been brutally ambushed and mortally wounded in the leg. They had bound his leg tightly with a tourniquet of rawhide, and from a buckskin sack Mike had taken a handful of the dried leaves of Solomon's seal, rubbed it into powder, and applied it to the wound as a coagulator, but the medicine was too weak to staunch the flow, and soon Jack's eyes grew dim and the light of the hunt went out of them even as they watched.

Jack's loss filled Mike with a quiet rage, since he had been especially close to his boys, and had taught them hunting, fishing, riding, and the traditions handed down to him by his father before him. The squaws had set up a caterwauling of grief, but Mike was quiet and stared for a long time into the campfire. In Mike's veins burned the hot blood of a Bannock chief. Somehow he would lead his band to safety without further bloodshed, but let those be cautious who now got in his way or threatened the safety of his family.

Perhaps through his head came flooding now the counsel of other Bannock chiefs with whom he had sat around the council fires. What right, they had asked, had the white man's government to usurp the Indian's land without just compensation, while the Indian was left to starve amidst a feast of promises? What right to break its word, manipulate its treaties, find hidden loopholes, to cheat and lie, yet demand honesty of the Indian? What treaty ratified or unratified gave the white stockman right to graze the ranges into dust, the miner right to foul the streams so the fish floated belly up like so many white canoes on their way to the sea? What right had the whites to dam the streams and block the fish runs, the loggers to gut the forests and cut down the pinion pine orchards, the hunters to shoot buffalo for their tongues, and to run the elk and other plains animals to final last refuges high in the mountains? What treaty gave the white man right of dominion, the right to punish the Indian for acts the white man did with impunity, to rip family and tribal bonds asunder and shove down the Indian gullet a language foreign to his own, to offer a religion the white man preached but only pretended to honor?

For over thirty years, through Indian uprisings, white injustices, and outrages, Mike had kept his angers to his belly, but now his gorge rose. Fate in the form of Judge Tranmer's son had altered all the rules.

The disintegration of Mike's life pattern came swiftly, and at a time when food was not readily available for a long journey. The caches of food were empty from the demands of the previous winter and had not yet been replenished.

In the arid hills, antelope herds that once might have been corraled in canyons, shot from stone blinds along their trails to water, or lured close by waving flags above the sage to play on their curiosity were dispersed to bear their kids and the bucks scattered and hard to locate. Deer were trailing the melting snows into the high country, and the mountain sheep watchful from exposed rocky escarpments. Sage hens had ceased their blind strutting and booming and were nesting, dispersed and secretive. Much of the rodent population, including rabbits and rock chucks, were hidden in nests and burrows tending their young. What few seeds had survived last year's overgrazing had weathered and fallen to prairie horned larks, vesper sparrows, kangaroo rats, or insects. What tubers, bulbs, and roots not rooted out by hogs or destroyed by the farmer's plow had sent their strength upward into new growth would not store well until the flowers had faded.

For the unharried Indian, free to wander at will, gathering food was at best a slow, labored process. Now, for Indians on the run, who dared not show themselves, there was little time for gathering. Not only was Mike charged with providing food for a dozen Indians, many of them hungry children, and finding grazing for their horses, but he had to keep them all from blundering into the hands of the enemy.

In no way could Mike count on other Indians for help. Not only was he south of the Bannock range, into the land of the Shoshone, but any Indian who knew Mike's story would be resentful that Mike had, however innocently, unleashed white anger against all Indians in that territory. Where once the Indians might have respected his ability to exist in the old way, now they seized every opportunity to disclaim him. "Mike, bad Indian!" was the gist of what they told the whites, as though hoping to impress the authorities that they, on the other hand, were good Indians. Perhaps they sensed, too, that they were telling the whites precisely what they hoped to hear.

Once Mike had slipped south around the east shoulder of Gollaher Mountain, leaving behind his old hunting and fishing grounds at Goose Creek, Shoshone Creek, and Salmon River, he was out of context with the land, forced from a scene where he had been trusted and accepted; he now had to wander a land where every man he met was a stranger capable of evil and could only regard a family of Indians wandering as nomads across mountain and desert with suspicion and hostility.

On a point of land overlooking a panorama of sage traversed with game trails and shaded by three gnarled old juniper trees, one of the women left her pestle and mortar beside a massive, weathered trunk. She had no way of knowing that she would never pass that way again or that the utensils would be covered through the years with dust from restless desert winds and with falling refuse from the sheltering juniper until found by a road builder named Oran Jones, son of the man who had sold Mike his wagon, sixty-one years before.

Mike's horses were mustangs, hard-hoofed, small, compact descendants of Spanish stock. Raised on rocky plains, rimrocks, and mountains, they were used to arid diets and could thrive on fare that would have starved a barn-raised animal. The Indians broke their horses too young and used them too hard, with the results that their mounts were stunted, long-headed, and plain-looking. Whatever the Indian affinity for the horse and their dependence upon them, they took poor care of them, although, unlike the whites, they would never have dreamed of using them for food even if starving.

As Mike and his family moved slowly southward, they tried to keep ridges between them and ranch houses, mines, or settlements. Sometimes they watched bands of sheep drifting across the sage, then trailed ahead across the line of drift in order that the sheep might soon obscure their trail from any who might choose to follow. But they kept out of sight of the herders, for even at a distance the mustangs would be known as such, and even those who watched from afar would recognize them as Indians. Day by day, Mike's little band became more and more hungry, and Mike's resentment of what the whites had done to the land must have grown in him like coals spreading through the charcoal of a wind-harried fire.

He had been innocent, yet the whites had accused him of being a thief, driven him from his range where he had bothered no one and had raised his family with what the wilderness provided. Now, then, rather than letting his children starve on the wasteland the whites had made of the land, he would steal, if it took stealing to live.

In those days, theft for an Indian, however petty, was a dangerous game. According to a later account by Mike's daughter, Heney, given to the authorities at Carson City, Nevada (as translated by Captain Dave, Chief of the Paiutes), Mike's family was involved with a skirmish with the whites near Mt. Marie (now called Mt. Moriah) near the Utah line. She reported that the Indians were shot up with shotguns and an Indian named Gully was killed. Just who Gully was, or how he happened to be involved with Mike's band at that particular moment in history is not known, but he may have been a visitor to camp, a Ute related to Jennie, or even a swain of one of Mike's daughters. He was not, however, one of Mike's own family, and could not have been with the group for very long.

Heney also admitted that a Chinese prospector had been killed in another skirmish in this area, but the killing went unnoticed by local authorities.

While many of the killings ascribed to Mike's band were done by others, they were probably not entirely innocent.

Starvation develops its own morals and expediencies. Driven by hunger, they were forced to prey on any vulnerable mark. The Indian was only getting back what had been stolen from his people, and if it brought discovery and death, what did it matter? Really, death did not count for much when Mike could see the hollows and shadows of hunger in the faces of his children.

In general, Nevada's eroded mountain ranges extend north and south like giant wrinkles on rolling, sagebrushed plains, and the best food supply was concentrated on river and creek bottoms between the ranges. Here to tempt Mike down from the scab rock hillsides were nests of duck, magpie, and crow, as well as the emergent heads of cattails, tule roots, and willow shoots for their huts or for weaving into baskets for burden or winnowing seed. Here too were rank marsh grasses for seed, which by their very lack of palatability had resisted overgrazing.

The white man had fenced in many of these bottoms. Mike cut the wires by putting the strands against the blade of an axe and striking the wire with a stone; then he led his horses in the darkness down to water. In the daylight it was too risky, since the bottoms were often filled with cattle that would spook and run at the sight of riders. Such motion in an otherwise peaceful herd would attract the attention of anyone watching from afar.

Daytimes Mike's band slept or kept to the safety of the hills where within moments they could disappear into the canyons or place the screen of a hill between them and approaching danger. Here their principal food was rattlesnake, which they skinned and cut up into chunks for the pot. They also caught the rapid little rock lizards called swifts, either by stunning them with blunt arrows or by biting off their heads and eating them roasted or raw. Rabbits were scarce, and there was little time to hunt the watchful marmots in the rims. Whites with rifles had made the marmots wary; fat and lazy, with plenty of time on their hands, they spied the Indians from afar and backed into their holes to dream awhile until danger had passed. Already the sun had baked the shallow, rocky clay soils hard, but the Indians dug bulbs where they could find them, ate them raw, or roasted them in pits beneath a fire. They gathered ants from large anthills while the insects were still numb from the early morning cold, scorched their pincers off in the open flames, then mashed them into a thick paste. No one ate them because he liked them, only because it beat a hollow belly.

When they found a colony of ground squirrels, watching their approach by standing upright at their burrows like so many picket pins, two Indians went out and set feathers in the dirt around a hole. Around this they set a slip loop on a cord, so that when the cord was jerked, it would close on the circle of feathers and be thrown into the air. One Indian would depart while the other Indian would hide in the brush. Since the squirrels couldn't count, they would see the man on his way and stand to watch him leave, while the other jerked the loop and caught the rodent by the middle. One squirrel, however, divided among twelve people does not amount to much food, yet there was often little time to trap more.

There was a listlessness to the group as they wandered on like a bunch of mustangs drifting south in search of new pastures, grazing here, drinking there, wherever they were lucky enough to find a new waterhole. In truth the Indians were searching for a new range, where they could live the old life in peace.

But as they traveled south, the weather grew hotter, the land more desolate, and the water mineralized or alkaline, unfit to drink. Children bore the ordeal without a whimper but no longer chased and played; they limped silently along, remaining in the elusive shadows of their mothers. Constantly, scouts ranged out ahead, looking for cattle or game trails that might lead to water. The water in their buckskin sacks grew hot and fetid. How they must have yearned for the cool streams of the north, the shady aspen groves where breezes stirred the air with myriad tiny fans, the hunting, swimming, fishing paradise that was Gollaher Mountain.

During the heat of the day, exhausted by travel, they sought out some lonely fortress among the rocks, posted a lookout high on a bed of sagebrush bark, and built their cooking fires where they would be obscured from passers-by; the smoke, trailing upward in a blue haze, would be lost among natural chimneys in the rocky precipices.

The girls ground a few apronsful of seed gathered along the trail by rolling it on flat rocks, then tossed it expertly in shallow winnowing baskets, letting the breeze float away the hulls and dirt. If they killed a few rabbits along the way with their bows, they stripped the hides and hung the naked bodies from the saddles to dry. Within hours in the dry desert air they were hard enough to drive spikes in a brick wall. When mashed repeatedly with heavy stones, they broke up into fine powder that the women put into the soup, along with ground seeds, dried bulbs, and anything on the desert that even wiggled.

Mike must have wondered frequently how long he could keep his family together under such conditions. Eat-em-up Jake and Catchum Charlie could have hired out to any of the cow outfits they passed as cowboys; the women could have washed clothes at the ranches or even begged through the town and fared better than now. Traveling as a band they were far more vulnerable than if they simply dispersed like quail.

Perhaps it was the bonds of family that kept them together and the realization that if they broke up, they would never see one another again; perhaps they respected the old man's dream of keeping them as free as the wild-running mustangs;

perhaps it was fear of what the white man would do if he finally caught them and held them accountable for the crimes of which Tranmer had accused them.

But the dream of finding a new land was unreal. They climbed each ridge with new hope, only to have it dashed when they looked over the brow to see worthless desolation or a valley the white man had claimed before them. When they were too exhausted to travel farther, Mike took out his drum, and on the dry, taut rawhide chanted and thumped, trying to find a rhythm that would drive out their despair.

The increasing desolation of the new land made the land they had fled seem like a paradise. The heat waves shimmered; sweat soaked their headbands. As the promised land kept eluding them to the south, the boys grumbled more and more, and Mike, giving in at last to building tensions, turned westward again, passing just north of Ely, Nevada, then past Hamilton, across Little Smokey Valley, over the Diamond Mountains, and slipped past the town of Austin as it slept without even a dog barking at their passing.

Depending upon the food supply and the character of the terrain, they sometimes made five miles a day, sometimes if they felt insecure, thirty. During the rest stops, the gaunt-ribbed horses stood around for a few hours nibbling at the brush, then drowsed heads down, in each other's shade, against the oppressive heat, content to rest against another weary journey.

Day after day, week after week they journeyed on. From Austin, they crossed the Clan Alpine Mountains, camped and hunted for a few restful days hidden in the Stillwater Marshes east of Fallon, while the men hunted deer in the Silver Range. But fearful that they would leave too many tracks in the area and alert the ranchers to their presence, they headed for Wadsworth, soon turned north again up the east side of Pyramid Lake, past Martingale (Nightingale) and Lake Winnemucca, past Limbo, then headed off across the vast alkaline flatness of the Black Rock desert.

The heat seemed enough to fry a man's brains. Ahead of them the shimmering blue of mirages gave promise of lakes ahead, aroused their hopes for water, then vanished as they approached. During the days, they crouched in the bottom of washes, hugging the shade, waiting for darkness when traveling was cooler. Often they could see nothing in the darkness, but on the flat immensity of that dried-up lake bed there was nothing on which to stumble.

One horse died and then another, as though the second horse simply wished to sleep beside his pal. Within minutes the carcasses were black with buzzards, which came from miles around as if by signal, though it was their sharp eyes that had sighted the dying horses from afar. Without complaint the Indians took the burdens of the horses upon themselves. On and on they plodded, knowing that there could be only so many footsteps to a lifetime, only so many steps to the hills they could see ahead on the far side of the plain.

From those hills on, however, there were more hills and more wastelands. Their moccasins had worn through, and most of the band limped painfully. Mike gave his last pair of moccasins to Jennie and hobbled on painfully with his feet wrapped in burlap.

They were trudging up the floor of a hot dry canyon looking for water up ahead, when suddenly Mike stopped them and pointed high on the canyon walls. It must have seemed like a miracle, for here were the same towering rocks, the cathedral rims crusted with the same orange, olive, gray, and chartreuse lichens they had known in Rock Creek Canyon.

High above the canyon floor, amidst a fortress of towering cliffs and palisades, a tiny seep spring of sweet water made a generous pool, shaded from sun by the cliffs that gave it birth.

Great piles of fractured rock, weathered by time, had plunged from the rocky rims above to make a natural pocket. Here in this rocky bowl, a thousand feet above the floor of the canyon, the Indians made their camp.

It was well chosen, this fortress. The rider traversing the floor of the canyon on his way to Cedarville, California, to the west, or Winnemucca to the east could have stared hard at that city of rocks above and found no evidence of human habitation. Riders approaching from the sheer cliffs overhead would have plummeted headlong hundreds of feet before they could have leaned out far enough to spy the camp below beneath the overhang. Near the camp rose a pillar of rock, easily climbed even by squaws, where an Indian sentinel could scout dangers in all directions and warn the band with a low whistle.

If attacked, they had a dozen avenues of escape, up the small canyon to the west, through fissures in the rock if danger came from below, or along the narrow plateau to the east. One man could hold off an army while the rest could escape unseen. And what was most important, construction of a few short yards of rock fence strategically placed held their horses confined to a rock-rimmed pasture, where they could graze the bunch grass unseen and unattended, yet could readily be caught up for quick retreat.

The canyon itself looked as though the great eroded mountain had split asunder in one mammoth crack, exposing the rocky, petrified intestines of the planet Earth. They had no way of knowing that it was called Little High Rock Canyon or what a part it was to play in their future many months later.

14

The camp at Little High Rock could not have been discovered at a better time. Here Mike and his band rested, taking short expeditions to Summit Lake to catch giant cutthroat trout and to Virgin Valley to hunt antelope from rock blinds built a short bowshot from game trails leading to and from water by Indians centuries before. Along the willowed bottoms were large flocks of noisy valley quail, which the children caught with horsehair snares; along the rims were mountain sheep that came in almost to their camp to water at their spring rather than descend to the valley floor.

For the first time since they left Gollaher Mountain, they had food to spare, but they kept on hunting and gathering, storing their extra food in caves against some unforetold emergency. A little canyon wren sang around the camp as he crept in and out of the jumbles of fallen shale. Mike must have felt that this little brown bird was his own personal sign, for, since childhood, he had shared many a rock pile with that busy little loner, as though the soul of the Indian and the canyon wren had similar needs. In all of Mike's favored camps, the wren was a happy denizen, and from some hidden roost came its reassuring piping even in the silence of winter nights.

In late June, for reasons unknown, Mike and his family left their fortress in Little High Rock Canyon and journeyed westward. It may have been that the hills were not so lonely as the Indians first imagined, that there were too many nomadic bands of sheep, too many wandering cowboys poking about the range as they watched their summering cattle.

About that time, a man named Jerry Marsh left Cedarville for Winnemucca. His horse had a fancy saddle and his route would have taken him past the canyon. Marsh was never seen alive afterwards, though some years later a rider found a boot protruding from a rockpile and the bones of a horse and rider thought to be Marsh; yet, the murder was never solved. It could have been done by Mike's band, though they would have avoided taking Marsh's easily identifiable equipment. More likely, it was done by the notorious Pat Russel gang, who were then marauding and rustling along the Oregon border, or by any of a number of roughnecks envious of Marsh's fancy rigging. In coming years, however, it seemed easiest for people to put the blame on Mike.

Perhaps Mike moved on because he met cowboys who had known him in his Rock Creek days and had heard about the Dopp affair. And there are some local men today who claim that Mike was angered because lusty young Basque herders were molesting his daughters as they dug for roots in the hills, and that the women had taken to carrying spears pointed with the blades of sheep shears to ward off the herders. Heney was a very pretty girl of eighteen, capable of luring some brave into Mike's band, if some herder didn't steal her. The thought must have angered Mike, since he hated the sheepmen for what they had done to his land. Fresh in his mind were the sheep wars of his home range, where his allegiance had been with the cattlemen.

One of the Basque herders camped that summer of 1910 near Little High Rock Canyon and, now a wealthy sheepman, told me that he had been losing groceries from his camp while off tending sheep; one morning, after the camp tender out of Eagleville had delivered a fresh supply, he had decided to play a trick on whomever was doing the stealing. Calling his dogs, he headed out of camp in the direction of his band. But after a few minutes, he turned back on his trail and had just started over a ridge looking down on his camp when he ran directly into an Indian who crouched in the brush, calmly pointing a shotgun at his head.

The Indian motioned him back to his sheep, and when the herder returned to camp that night, his flour, bacon, and canned milk were gone.

Whatever Mike's reasons for moving on, pack up he did, traveling westward again toward California. One old-timer told me that the Indians camped at Tuledad Springs, near Surprise Valley, and he remembered investigating as a boy their deserted camp and finding a shotgun shell loaded with rusty nails.

From Tuledad, Mike moved northward up Surprise Valley, keeping above the irrigated hayfields, hugging the sheltering forests of the towering Warner Range of mountains.

Haying was in progress and the floor of the valley for miles was dotted with hundreds of fresh green stacks of loose hay. From the floor of the valley drifted the shouts of stackers directing the derrick crews, and if any looked up from their work to notice the passing band of horsemen near the hills, they were too busy to investigate. Mike was more relaxed now and rode more in the open, for he had crossed the magic line into California, where he knew the Nevada posses who had wanted him had no authority.

As Mike came to the town of Cedarville, he rode boldly into town with all his band, complete with horses, braves, squaws, children, and loaded travois; he left them in a vacant lot while he himself strolled across the street to the T.H. Johnson store.

Ernest Groves is now an elderly man, but he remembers that occasion well, for he was a boy working in the Johnson store when Mike's band pulled into town. He describes them as a wild-looking lot, dressed in blankets and moccasins, unlike the local Indians who had opted for the white man's cast-off clothing.

While the group waited silently in the lot, Groves watched the old man come toward him, his eyes seeming to miss nothing, ever watchful for danger. His hands especially stood out, big, short-fingered, and powerful, as though used to working rawhide. Mike was old, but still active, with the suppleness and easy grace of a mountain lion. He seemed to have plenty of money and bought staples like salt, coffee, and ammunition, but no frills. Moments later the band was gone and left only a trail of dust as it headed up the wagon road leading westward up Cedar Pass toward what, for the Indians, had to be the complete unknown.

The road over Cedar Pass was a narrow, twisting teamster's nightmare. Going up the pass empty was bad enough, but coming down with a loaded wagon threatening to overrun the slipping, sliding horses or mules was a major ordeal. Freighters would hitch onto heavy logs at the top of the pass to act as brakes on the way down, and these logs were welcomed by valley ranchers who eventually claimed them and sawed them into boards for their houses.

As it happened that day, while Mike and his band were going up the narrow road, they ran into a freight team coming down. The teamster was trying to negotiate his jerk-line team past a frightful hairpin curve at the edge of a precipice.

"Git out of the road!" the teamster roared at the Indians.

Calmly the old man, in the lead, whipped up a rusty shotgun, held the sweating teamster at gunpoint until the family had squeezed past and on up the hill, then, with a faint grin, he motioned the white man on. Once Mike and his family had crested the mountains and had begun their descent toward Alturas, the magnificent rockbound Warners screened out all sight of Surprise Valley and the Nevada hills to the east.

For a few weeks they camped in the lower hills, hunting deer and rabbits, roasting fat rock chucks over fires of mountain mahogany, digging camas bulbs in the meadows along Pit River and ipos or trail potatoes on the rocky flats. It was good land and a good time of year. The flapper ducks were growing fast but were still flightless along the river, and the grass was lush and strong for horses used to Nevada ranges.

At night, they camped out of sight in rocky canyons where their drums and chants would be heard only by the gods. They prayed to the deer that they would not run from them on the morrow, to the sage grouse that they would come to water and give them sweet, tender meat without the strong taste of sage. White men passed them as they hunted, but they all seemed busy and took little notice.

At dawn, Mike sent the women out to gather food, but he ordered the young men to the hayfields along the Pit River Valley to earn a few dollars against leaner times. Little by little the children began to laugh and play again and the mustangs to put on fat. One of his daughters was heavy with child, and when her time approached, the other squaws built her a tipi of her own off in the junipers, and there she was delivered of a little girl. Once the baby had been born, Jennie and the other women took time off from their labors to weave a cradle board of willow shoots bound with buckskin thong, which was then filled with dried algae or sagebrush bark rubbed soft.

Mike liked the area well enough, but there were too many whites around. Alone, he roamed the back country, looking always beyond the hills for lands the white men had not yet discovered, but to no avail. July drifted into August and still the family had not found a real home.

Some nervous energy or demon seemed to push Mike relentlessly onward, as though toward his inevitable doom. That they had no intention of wintering here was evident in that what they harvested they consumed as though there were no tomorrow. There were caves in the rimrocks around the camp, but these remained empty of more than a few days' stores.

As the August sun burned hayfield stubbles from green to brown, the ranchers finished haying, then turned their Indian crews, along with mower, rake, and derrick teams, out to forage on the range until the next season, so as to be spared the expense of feeding them. Mike's band headed south, skirting with wonder and awe the volcanic smokes of Mt. Lassen.

Sometimes, where food was in good supply, the bulbs lush and the digging easy, or where tracks of wild game indicated that animals were plentiful, they would camp a few days, so that horse and Indian could keep strong, but as it had been in many another camp, one morning they would be gone and the ashes cold in their campfire.

Days passed into weeks. According to Heney's testimony, the family journeyed until they came to a large body of water, across which they could see mountains. Most likely this was the Sacramento River, perhaps even where it empties into San Francisco Bay.

For some time, the Indians worked the fruit harvest, then in full swing, helping themselves to a staggering abundance of fruit. But again, in Mike's eyes, the country suffered from an epidemic of whites. "This no place for Indian," he observed, and once again the little band moved on, this time eastward from Oroville, California, pushing ever upward toward the moody and dangerous Sierras.

By now it was late autumn, and as they moved back into the

143

mountains, they met other travelers hurrying out. There were miners pushing mules and burros; cowboys with trail herds, their cows and calves sleek and fat from a summer in the high-country pastures; and Basques and Irishmen drifting their bands of ewes and fat lambs down toward some fall rendezvous with the owners. They stared in surprise at the Indians and shook their heads as Mike and his family persisted in their climb, which seemed to be taking them upward into the gun-metal-gray clouds.

The children grew silent with fatigue but did not complain. The baby's mother had lost her milk supply through fever, and the baby was kept alive by pine nuts ground into a paste; the infant ate this by sucking a finger dipped in the rich protein. Night storms dumped their burdens of snow upon the Indians' beds, leaving them wet and miserable but strangely resigned to their lot. Day after day, storm after storm laid its blanket upon the frozen land.

A white man would have followed the railroad, through Portola, but Mike was afraid his horses would be trapped on the track and be unable to mount the banks thrown up by the train's plows, and so he cut overland, picking his way through the more open hills, rather than the brushy wooded valleys.

Sometimes, when the sun broke through, the forests turned into a wondrous land of sparkling diamonds but made the eyes burn, the vision swim, and the stomach grow nauseated with snow blindness, as though in penalty for looking. The Indians painted their faces with charcoal, tied rags over their eyes, and peered through narrow slits, until the sun had mercifully been vanquished by another cloud laden with snow.

Overhead the Sierra strained to snatch every bit of moisture from ocean-laden clouds scurrying eastward toward Nevada on prevailing winds, as though intent that the deserts remain deserts. Silently, the Indians progressed, however slowly, with Eat-em-up Jake, Catchum Charlie, or Jim breaking trail, squaws and children following, and Jennie shuffling patiently along behind. In the rear, like a wild stallion herding his mares, was Mike, watching for stragglers or any precious scraps lost from the packs. Time and again they fought their way up one long ridge only to find more ridges and canyons on beyond.

Game had long since been driven to lower elevations for the winter. There were only a few pine seeds to eat, and these, falling downward on whirling wings to the snowy tablecloth, were preempted by flocks of fluttering finches and sororities of siskins. Sometimes the Indians robbed a squirrel's cache in rotting logs and, with frost-numbed fingers, tossed the pine seed in their winnowing baskets, but all too often the relentless winds, as though to conquer them, whipped both chaff and seed away. Sometimes, from exposed chambers in the shattered, rotting logs, great yellow winter-stupid grubs blinked out at them, but to rip the rotten logs apart took more energy than it brought back in food.

A few scant miles to the south, years before, the Donner party had failed the same crossing and had perished. It seemed now that Mike's little band might share their fate. One by one their mustangs broke their hearts in trying and simply died, soon becoming only shallow mounds in the persistent snow. At night, one Indian huddled close to another for warmth. Mike chanted with half-frozen lips, but the drumheads were wet and frozen and made little sound. Icy fogs hung heavy in the valleys, and often when, at last, they thought themselves headed downhill toward Nevada, the clouds would shift, cruelly exposing another towering range guarding the horizon.

Sometimes when Jennie faltered in the trail and seemed unable to rise, Mike would help her to her feet, but no look of tenderness passed between them as payment for the years, nor was one needed. In a leather pouch, Mike carried a few dollars left from summer work, but there were no stores in which to buy.

Pushing slowly onward, almost in a trance, the Indians must have thought of olden times at Rock Creek, fishing in the stream where it purled and bent its way through the Crockett Ranch, digging the great fat camas bulbs in wet meadows blue as a mirage with camas and pentstemon, beating the sticky cones from pinion pines with long sticks, roasting the cones over fires that sent the resinous fragrance even into the meat of the nuts, bringing a wagonload of deer off Gollaher Mountain for drying into jerky or sharing with a friend. Perhaps they remembered some lonely cave where they'd left some jerky against a future need. There was no going to it now.

But fate smiled at last when one day the storm clouds lifted and before them far below they saw not more white mountains but the gray-green of the Nevada sage. They had but three horses left, including a suckling colt who had, a few miles back, sucked the last bit of strength from his mother and left her dying by the side of the trail. But suddenly the family was happy again, as though the ordeal had never been. Mike took his drum and beat out a prayer, asking the mountain—to whom belonged the rabbit, antelope, and the deer—to give his family food. The band ate slowly at first, for their stomachs were shrunken, boiling the first jackrabbit into a soup for all and gathering some pine seed to make a gruel for the baby. Soon Mike shot a deer, gambling one of his precious shells, and it must have given the old man a feeling of pride that he was still a mighty hunter, could still carry a deer in on his shoulders, that his medicine was still strong. Behind them towered the great snowy fortress of the Sierra. A white man would have looked back in awe, but the Indians moved patiently on, their only concern their lingering weakness and the holes in their moccasins. The mountain was yesterday.

Along the shores of Pyramid Lake, they passed encampments of Washoe Indians, but the Washoes recognized them as strays, Idaho Indians far from their range, and refused them help. That night, Mike's boys raided the sleeping Indians, stole food and fresh horses, and by morning were heading north around the end of Pyramid Lake. Soon they had picked up their trail of the previous summer, leaving the angry Washoes buzzing like winter-stupid bees whose honey is being robbed but are helpless to fly and sting.

The Indians must have looked longingly eastward in the direction of Rock Creek and Gollaher Mountain, but there was no going home for them. Instead, they headed once more across the Black Rock desert toward the fastness of Little High Rock Canyon. The weanling colt they left in a rancher's field so that his constant nickering for his mother would not arouse the countryside. The little mustang was adopted by the rancher who found the unexpected bonus in his field, and for years the mustang was his favorite cow pony.

The land around Little High Rock was far more lonely than it had been in summer, although there still were cattle wandering loose on the range and some scattered bands of sheep being wintered near the Black Rock desert and Soldier's Meadows. What settlers there were, such as Will Denio and his wife, who lived about five miles west of the mouth of the canyon, stayed close to their fires during winter and could be counted on not to bother Indians if left alone.

Most of the sheep had been moved off the ranges for rendezvous with the owners and the weaning of lambs, while most cattle were in on hay at the Bare Ranch or other Surprise Valley establishments. Northern Nevada was cold, barren, and the grass was bleached and lacking protein. Along the rimrocks golden eagles patrolled for jackrabbits or carrion, or played the winter thermals. Over the sageland flapped long-tailed black and white magpies, winged jackals of the deserts, or ferruginous hawks hunting kangaroo rats. Among the rock

147

jumbles, the canyon wren braved the frosts, creeping deep into holes and jumbled rocky crevasses searching out hidden insects snugly dormant. How Mike must have grinned to hear its welcome call from the rims ringing the camp. It was good medicine and he felt at home.

The camp high in the rimrocks was as they had left it. Their horses were too weak to climb the steep slope, so Mike and his crew pushed them up bodily one by one to the rimrock pasture where the bunch grass had not seen a hoof since they had camped there months before.

Left to themselves, the younger members of the band might have rested from their journey, but at dawn, as the sun hit his bed, Mike was up pushing the rest into action. After a few cupfuls of rabbit stew and a handful of pine nuts, man, woman, and child began the task of preparing for winter. The men hunted, killing a mountain sheep, while the women descended the shale slopes to the canyon floor and cut long willow poles for a hut. These they carried back up to the rim, sharpened one end, stuck them upright in a circle, bound them with ribs secured with rawhide strips, then bent in the tips to form a dome-shaped hut. This they covered with hides and brush, leaving a smoke hole on top, should they need to build a fire inside. In front of the hut, they built a fireplace of stones and laid in a supply of the only fuel available, which was sagebrush. The floor of the hut they covered with several inches of soft bark stripped from the sage, as well as apronsful of leaves stripped from the leaders, which gave the hut an aroma that would have overpowered most whites.

Across the dangerous shale hillside leading from the camp the women engineered a path by fitting the fractured rock together in a careful mosaic, then lined the rock with bark and leaves so that even the clumsiest horse could traverse the slide without causing an avalanche into the canyon below.

On a pinnacle beside the camp, they made a soft bed of

sagebrush so that a lookout could lie hidden but comfortable to spy the slightest movement on the encircling hills or up and down the canyon thoroughfare.

While mountain sheep had once been numerous and a part of Indian diets, in northwest Nevada only a handful remained, and these clung to existence along those very rims where Mike camped. They were considered a nuisance by sheepmen, for often the rams would make off with bunches of domestic ewes, and the herders shot them and let them lie whenever they came within rifle range.

It did not occur to the Indian to save the species. He considered them a gift from the mountain, and by lying in wait along the water holes or attracting them by thumping logs together to sound like two rams fighting, they soon wiped them out, save for one old ram who fled the canyon under pressure and ranged the rims that year eweless and alone, until cut down by a rancher the following autumn. Thus did the mountain sheep pass from the scene until their reintroduction over half a century later.

For the Indian, the camp at Little High Rock was unique in its perfection, and Mike must have looked around him with both relief and satisfaction. Plenty of sagebrush for fires, water only thirty yards away, caves handy for storage of food, shelter from winter winds, security from attack, naturally enclosed pasture for their few remaining horses, wild game in fair abundance, and scattered cattle to kill if the meat supply gave out. Moreover, the first rays of the morning sun caught the Indians in their beds, filling the whole camp with a pleasing, rosy glow. Here they could rest and fill their bellies. Perhaps by the time spring came, the law would have forgotten them and they could return to their old haunts at Rock Creek and Gollaher Mountain.

Cut off as he was from contact with other Indians or sources of gossip, Mike could not have known that time had run out

149

for Tranmer and Urie, who had caused his exile. It was on January 9, as Mike and his family were setting up camp, that Tranmer and Urie robbed the Quillici store at Imlay, eighty miles south of Little High Rock Canyon.

Ironically, once Tranmer and Urie had been caught and Urie had confessed to their crime, their reputation as witnesses would have been shattered, with the result that Mike and his family, after routine questioning, would have been free to head home to Rock Creek to the bend above the Crockett house.

He would perhaps have been astonished at the eagerness with which the Crocketts and the Weighalls would have jumped to defend him. Mike had merely to tell his story, that the Tranmer gang, caught rustling, had ambushed and killed his son Jack, and, in the ensuing fracas, Frankie Dopp was killed. The posses had hunted him for killing J. Frank Tranmer, who, with the murder of the Quillicis, had proved himself still alive. By now it was general knowledge, though never admitted by the gang, that they had been responsible for the rustling in the Shoshone basin. Curiously, even to this day, no one has ever proved that Mike killed anyone. Under Indian law, braves act as individuals, and the tribe is not held responsible.

But Mike did not know his freedom, and even his daughter would never have been able to guess his whereabouts to tell him. At both Rock Creek and San Jacinto, it was thought that Mike and his family had been wiped out by the Tranmer gang.

In judging Mike, we can neither be harsh nor lenient. The good qualities that had so impressed the settlers at Rock Creek and the Shoshone basin went only so deep. But then, perhaps there is murder hidden away in many of us, lying dormant, awaiting circumstance.

It was not long before the presence of a band of Indians in Little High Rock Canyon was known to others. People even identified the band as that of Rock Creek Mike, and it was rumored that they had killed a white boy over by the Utah line. Sometimes cowboys would trail the Indians for short distances to see what they were about, but they soon grew interested in their own business when Mike took to leaving cairns of rock marked with Indian signs warning people that anyone following them could expect death. The Indians, frightened of more trouble, wanted merely to be left alone to live out their winter in peace.

At night, they sat around a hidden fire in the stone fireplace, snug in their bowl high among the rims; they sat in the orange light of a sage fire, watching the familiar pale dancing ghost of smoke, and drummed and chanted. They celebrated the killing of the first mountain sheep, chanted for the mountain to give them many rabbits in tomorrow's drive, chanted to thank the deer for possessing such delicious meat, to ask the rock chuck to bring up many delicious babies from his burrow in the spring, and even to thank the sun for warming their winter-morning beds. For the first time in months they could laugh, sing, and enjoy themselves around the fire, though such belly-slapping jesting and revelry they limited to darkness when travelers were asleep across that icebound land.

There were signs easily read by Indians that indicated to old Mike that a major storm was on its way. Perhaps it was by reading the restlessness of the little canyon wren, or by noting the feverish activity of the long-tailed kangaroo rats in the brush, or merely by feeling pains in his old bones. But Mike knew, and sent the Indians into a flurry of activity to ready themselves for blizzard conditions. Since the few remaining mountain sheep had been killed, and there was no time to mend their nets for a rabbit drive, the Indians turned to slaughtering some beef, driving the animals toward camp and butchering them where they would be most accessible. Most often they roped the animals by the head and heels and cut

151

their throats, or shot them with arrows, so that the sound of guns did not attract travelers to the scene. Soon two beeves were killed, cut into strips, and stored in caves. On January 15, 1911, just as they finished cutting up the last of the beeves, there began the worst storm since the winter of 1889–90. Soon the canyon was knee-deep in snow.

Perhaps it was the wildness of the storm that made the Indians careless. From the rims they saw three cows drifting down the canyon for shelter from the winds and butchered them where they fell. They had almost finished skinning them when the sentry barked like a coyote to warn them of trouble. The Indians had time only to fade into the rocks on the hillside, leaving the beef exposed. Snow soon filled their footprints and for a time they saw only the black and white flashings of bold, hungry magpies braving the fury of the blizzard for tallow. Then, suddenly, they heard the bell of a shod hoof scraping on rock, and, head bent against the flung snow, a Basque sheep herder came riding slowly up the canyon into the face of the storm. He would have passed the carcasses without seeing them, had not his dog scented blood and started to bark.

For a few moments, the herder huddled on his horse at the scene of carnage, squinting around him as he felt the full force of hostile eyes upon him. Then, quickly, he reined his snow-encrusted horse around and vanished into the snow, heading toward the Denio place.

The Indians let him go. Pursuit in the storm on the four worn-out horses left them would have been next to useless. Short of fleeing, there was only once choice open to the Indians and that was to gamble that the herder would be so busy worrying about his sheep that he would forget to notify the cattle owners about the rustling.

There could have been little rejoicing in the Indian camp that night. High in the stormy darkness, the lookout, his face grotesquely masked with snow, crouched on his bed, watched, and waited for any lights in the hills. As the fire gasped its last under the assault of the storm, and the big, wet flakes hissed on the last hot coals, the storm seemed to abate, and, as the firelight died, more and more of the surrounding hills took shape. Perhaps the old man himself came out from the hut and stood for a moment looking up at the skies and the empty white hills, spoke a word of encouragement to the sentry huddled in his blanket, then went back to Jennie's side. They had to fear even night attack, but thought probably no one would come until after the storm had broken. When they came—if they came—Mike would have to make the most desperate decision of his life.

15

Will Denio's young, dark-haired wife Mattie charged out of their tiny shack, hurling a white-enameled chamber pot at the flop-eared, winter-starved jackrabbits that seemed to have flocked from a hundred bleak empty miles around just to feast on her sparse postage stamp of a lawn. Tears of discouragement must have welled to her dark eyes as she saw how the frozen stems, so carefully nursed through summer, had been eaten into the ground. And if it wasn't the rabbits it was Will's horses or Harry Cambron's stupid cows!

How easy to picture her, as that pretty woman, posed there all unknowing upon the threshold of history, stood more than sixty years ago with sharp cold wind pressing across the northern Nevada desolation and whipping her long, black, wool skirt around her slender legs. As she lifted her tired face toward the bald hills encroaching on the meadow that was home, her heart must have leaped when she saw riders etched against the leaden, ominous skyline and then sank as she saw

Camp Denio fifty years after the massacre.

them to be Indians. There was something sinister about the way they kept to the back ridges, instead of the more sheltered valleys, and she must have shivered and been glad that this was January, 1911, when Indian massacres were a thing of the past.

Once, on one of my many trips back into Mike's past, I stood at the Denio place and let myself drift back into that era, while the wind drummed around the eaves and the deserted house seemed filled then with the murmurings of times long ago. The winds seemed to talk in voices that were gone, and I seemed to hear Will Denio as he was then, young and full of hope, asking his young wife to share a life with him that was bound to be difficult, happy to have her there to share his lonely homestead but a little embarrassed too at how coarse and hard the life suddenly appeared now that she was actually there. His calloused hands must have stolen around her shoulders as though ever ready to retreat, and when he hugged her to him it was as though begging her to share his dreams.

By then the Denios were long gone, but the old buildings had stood the relentless buffetings of a million winds and were much as they had been left. Scattered around the area was a convention of farm machinery—some museum pieces, some more modern, but all worn out and rusting. Surely the old wooden wagon wheels were rolling in Mike's time. Through the windows, etched by blown sand, I could glimpse the furniture, utilitarian, starkly Pilgrim, and practical. A pack-rat palace: even the souvenir hunters of this day and age had left it alone.

I could think of Mattie Denio only as delicate, unsuited for her life, but then maybe it was she who had the stuff for the life of a pioneer. That night I lay outside in my bedroll among the rusting wagons, and some time during the night I awoke with the wind howling around the eaves like a cat trying to catch its tail, and I got to thinking about other pioneer women, such as old lady Bare, down in Surprise Valley.

One time when the Winnemucca Indians, a poor, starving lot, went on the war path in frustration, they caught the old lady alone at home with the menfolk all gone. The hungry Indians went howling around and around the stockade fence. Peering through cracks in the logs, Mrs. Bare watched them trotting around as though trying to get courage to storm the wall. She felt so sorry for them, all hungry and naked like that in the cold, she went inside and cooked up lots and lots of nice hotcakes, and every time an Indian passed her station on the way around, she just put a hotcake on a stick and passed it out to the astonished brave. This went on until the braves were full and the howling had all died down to a mere belly rumble. By then the braves couldn't remember why they wanted to attack that nice old lady anyhow. Or so the story was told to me one night in the Eagleville bar.

In those years, northern Nevada was far more heavily populated than it is today. The homesteaders came, tried to tough it out, but finally gave in to the reality of kids needing schooling and the wives wanting it for them. Homesteads and one-room schools somehow went together hand in hand, as did wives and the need for refinement. Usually the kids moved in to town to visit Uncle Fred for a week for the Fourth of July rodeo maybe. Next time it was two weeks, and pretty soon the old man was out there putting up hay with just his wife driving the team, and soon after that they were both living in town, visiting the kids. They soon forgot the hardships and the loneliness. Their talk was ever of the good old days.

If there were times when Mrs. Denio longed for town, this was one of them. It was seventy miles to Eagleville and to her sister, Laura Murphy. Not far, perhaps, for a saddle tramp of a cowboy on a good mustang, but a long bumpy wagon road for a woman driving a team. She must have missed Laura desperately, for Laura was engaged to marry Harry Cambron on the following Saturday, and there could have been much girl-to-girl talk planning the coming event.

Of course Mattie kept abreast of the news, since Harry Cambron was overseer of the Humphry-Moffat cattle that ranged in the Little High Rock country, and he could always be relied upon to fetch and carry the latest word, though it wasn't half so much fun as lying snugly abed with Laura in the old high-ceilinged family home, giggling over secret things.

Seldom did a letter arrive without a coating of dust and more fingerprints on it than stamps, but generally the mail did get through. Sometimes she prevailed upon camp tenders coming out from Cedarville with supplies for the sheepherders; sometimes a rider came by heading for Winnemucca or Gerlach with letters in his saddle bags, knowing that a handful of letters would buy him welcome in any house. Sometimes letters went by way of a vaquero, heading into town for a good time after months out on the wagon, and lay forgotten for days in some ramshackle brothel until mailed by the madam.

Winter was a slow time after the calves had been weaned and driven west to Cedarville, and the cows turned out to fend for themselves on winter-leached bunch grass, white sage, and Indian tea—after the herders had left with their bands for autumn rendezvous with the owners in Surprise Valley and were taking their own good time grazing back over the California-Nevada border, scattering far and wide over the vast Nevada ranges.

If the herders passed through at all, they always left their bands on the hill and trotted down to camp for a cup of coffee. Not speaking much English, most of them merely sat and grinned at her as they drank or ate a piece of cake. It was all a real treat for lonely men used to campfires, drinking wine from leather *bottas* and sleeping under canvas and stars. Now they were here, now gone, to remain away for months, sometimes years. Some made their stakes and went back to Spain or France, others took their pay in ewes and became big sheepmen in their own right.

Late in the afternoon of January 17, 1911, as Mrs. Denio, huddling in her husband's greatcoat against the raging blizzard, went out to pump her evening bucket of water and do her chores, she saw a horseman fighting his way through the storm. He was coming from the east, against the wind, as though he had just come from the mouth of Little High Rock Canyon, about four miles away.

The man's horse gasped for breath; his sides heaved; the melting snow made dirty rivulets down his flanks. But Mattie caught the flash of a grin beneath the ice-encrusted moustache and she recognized Bert Indiano, who herded sheep for Peter Erramouspe and John Laxague. She invited him to put his horse in the shed, throw him some rye hay and grain, and come to the house.

Indiano was only the first of her visitors, for soon from the west came Indiano's bosses, Erramouspe and Laxague, along with the bridegroom-to-be, Harry Cambron.

Always full of fun, Cambron livened up the supper conversation and continued to joke even when Indiano related that he had found three freshly butchered cows on the floor of Little High Rock Canyon.

Worried about the condition of their sheep in the raging blizzards, the two sheepmen were on their way to Soldier's Meadows, about nine miles away, while Cambron was on his way to Winnemucca and Gerlach to buy grain. Since the scene of the rustling was not far out of their way, the three decided to investigate. By morning the snow had abated, and they asked Indiano to accompany them to show them the exact spot. At first, the Basque refused to come.

The herder tried his best to beg off. He was weary of snow; he had just come from there and lost nothing on the way, and besides the bottom was drifted with snow and was as cold as a well-digger's wallet. In reality he had felt hostile eyes upon him and was still spooked by the experience.

It may be that Indiano had other reasons for not wanting to go back. It was known that Mike was in the area and was angered at the treatment his daughters had received from the herders. At last Indiano's bosses prevailed. Cambron had his pistol and it must have seemed highly unlikely that a band of rustlers, unless caught in the act, would elect to fight, when it was easier by far to run. They had no way of knowing Mike's desperation and that, due to the condition of the band, flight was impossible. On the morning of the eighteenth, the four men left Denio camp in the direction of the canyon.

Instead of fighting the deep snows of the bottom and the cold winter gloom, the men rode up over the windswept north rim, where the snow had all but blown off the rolling hills with the violence of the winds. The men knew the country well, and it is thought that they descended into the main canyon by a narrow rocky gorge that hits the main canyon bottom not far from where the cattle were butchered. In descending, they must have passed only a hundred yards from where the Indians were camped, but the camp was conveniently screened with rocks, and the men were probably so preoccupied with picking their way down the snow-encrusted rock falls that they had little time for sightseeing.

Through the years, I have gone often to that spot in Little High Rock Canyon, armed with a skeleton of facts, and have huddled there in the snow, trying to piece together the events of January, 1911. Forever in my mind will be the winter day in 1956 when I first climbed to that rocky bastion. I had determined its probable location from photographs taken in 1911 by a Cedarville photographer named Mathews. As I climbed the steep canyon, pausing often for breath in that high mountain air, I followed the trail the squaws had paved with stone across the treacherous rocky slides. I would have settled merely for the chance to stand where Mike had stood, but, as I moved on up over the pile of rubble that had fallen through the centuries from the overhanging brow, there before my eyes stood the skeleton of Mike's hut, its poles broken and lying in shambles from wind and weather, but there. The poles had been cut from the willow thickets on the floor of the canyon. Some had been sharpened with an axe, others hewn square.

On the rocks close by lay the remains of Mike's travois poles of aspen wood, the ends scrubbed smooth from miles of dragging over rocky ground. Still visible was his fireplace of rocks, charcoal from his fires, a rusty milk can stolen from a sheep camp, stabbed not daintily in white man's way, but slashed across the top as with a rough stone knife. In the neighboring caves were bones of mountain sheep and a full curl of a ram's horns.

That night I camped among the remains of Mike's tipi, built my fire of sage, and cooked a piece of antelope meat. For a time I watched the brush burn, the weak limbs flame and vanish while the strong held on stubbornly, saw the rabbit-brush twigs curl with the heat like the toes of a dead chicken's foot when the tendon is pulled.

The brush burned quickly with sweet, heavy smoke, but left a bed of hot, red coals. I sat for a time watching the drip of grease from the meat, then as the firelight died, the rimrocks around me became visible, as did those across the canyon. Somewhere a canyon wren piped, and there were far-off sounds of rattling stones tumbling to the canyon floor, dislodged by some midnight hunter.

By now I had been in so many of Mike's camps that I felt at home with him, and suddenly, vivid as though real, his family drifted over the rocks into camp and sat silently watching the fire. Jennie was there, her brown faced wrinkled by close to six decades out-of-doors, Hattie clutching a doll made of sagebrush, little Cleve, fat-faced with a tiny bow pulled close to him as though I would steal it from him, Heney, pretty and shy, not above casting a flirting glance, Eat-em-up Jake, Catchum Charlie, Jim bare-chested, blankets draped loosely upon their shoulders. There was Heney's older sister, Snake, too, carrying her baby in a blanket on her back. Only Mike was missing, and by chance, as I stood back against the cliff, I raised my hand and suddenly, as the flickering firelight cast my shadow against the wall, visible to anyone passing up or down the canyon, I was suddenly a giant Mike with a shadow thirty feet tall.

As the firelight glowed and the circle of light intensified the outer darkness, the images would fade, only to return again when the light grew dim. There was a shyness about them, and they kept their eyes averted from me toward the fire. In my vision there was an extra man whom history has not recorded and whom I shall mention later. Years later, when I at last found pictures of the children, there with astonishing clarity were some of the faces I had seen, that night so long ago, sitting alone along the rims of Little High Rock Canyon beside Mike's fireplace.

Not long ago, I crouched on a bed of sagebrush on the lookout tower at Mike's camp and imagined the drama that took place the morning of January 18, 1911. The canyon has not changed much in sixty-one years. The snow was there, the rocky cliffs, covered with lichens, the canyon wren, the sage, the loneliness, beauty though desolate, mystery, grandeur even. How helpless the feeling, sitting in Mike's bastion, looking down with Mike's eyes, with the eyes of God, all-knowing yet mortal too, and helpless to avert history, watching as four men leaning back in their saddles go slipping and sliding down the canyon.

I can see the shadows of Indians lurking in the rocks, the sky lowering, and the snow coming down on me as it came down then, perhaps, quietly at first, a few hard round bullets, caroming against the lichened overhang of the wall, ticking against the bleached, frozen bunch grass and wild rye; then suddenly the clouds seem to lean upon the land. A chill wind sweeps the canyon, rushing headlong a thousand different ways. Then, suddenly, the flakes come big and wet, slanting in with the gale so that the beetling overhang no longer shelters me.

To the Indians it must have seemed that the law they had so long feared had finally caught up with them. Visions of the white man's prison in Carson, which had haunted them for so long, must have thrown them into a blind panic. Now they had been caught rustling beef, and with horses too weak to travel in the storm they had no choice other than to make a stand.

The riders are ghosts. They drift slowly toward the floor of the canyon. I call out, trying with my shout to change the past. While the men are still off balance on the steep, before they can gain their footing at the canyon bottom, a rifle cracks. Harry Cambron jerks in the saddle, falls, his pistol sending a burst of useless, unaimed shots ricocheting across rocks now thundering with gunfire, while his white horse shies at his tumbling body and with a sunfishing kick plunges away. The other men fall almost in unison. One horse gains the floor of the canyon, saddle empty, reins trailing, and stampedes around the first bend, but the others mill in confusion. Unarmed, an angry Erramouspe stands shouting Basque curses, searching for a way to fight back, upright, blood filling his boot, helpless and vulnerable but defiant. The next volley cuts him down as if he were a rag doll falling off a clothesline.

The snow comes fast and heavy now. Heney claimed that she was in camp and could not see the fight, but she had only to look down the slope. The bucks seize the remaining horses, shouting to the women to hurry down. Methodically, they strip the bodies of all clothes not stained with blood, for they are desperate in their needs. Mike takes Cambron's thirty-eight automatic and what ammunition he can glean from the pockets, and hands it to his son, Jim. Cambron's watch and checkbook he keeps. Then the bodies are dragged down into the wash on the canyon bottom so that next spring's freshets can cover them with sand. They are stacked head to toe, like cordwood, and mercifully the drifting snow covers their nudity against the bitter cold of the Nevada winter. I shiver with cold, and my face is wet with the cold tears of snow, coming down now as a final curtain over all I have envisioned.

One of the horses belonging to the murdered men escaped and was never found again. It may have been wounded in the battle and may have died somewhere along the rims or, in trying to return to its home range, stood in a fence corner, anchored by the bridle reins, and starved in the snow.

Mike and his family packed the other three horses with all the meat they could carry, tore the lodge covers from the pillow poles of the hut, then headed across the canyon and up over the southeastern rim. They left a frozen bucket of water, piles of jerky, a graveyard of cattle and mountain-sheep bones, scraps of buckskin, a pair of old moccasins, two clay dolls, aspen travois poles, the ribs of the tipi, and the combings of a woman's hair.

According to Heney, they did not hurry. The wind hurtled the snow in constant mist across the flats, filling in their tracks, blotting out all traces of the tragedy. The immensity of the storm had tied up the West, and the Indians knew it would be weeks before anyone had time to search for the missing men. The party moved slowly east, camping frequently, sometimes making no more than five or six miles a day in the heavy snows. As Mike struggled on and on through the drifts, he must have felt his age, and his thoughts must have been often on Rock Creek and the summer ranges at Gollaher Mountain. It was time to visit his daughter, Lizard, at San Jacinto and to see his friend Hansen at the Rock Creek store, time to grow old among the rimrocks where wandered the spirits of his family.

On the desert a record forty-eight inches of snow had fallen, and temperatures following the storm plunged below zero. Mustang Smith was working out of Gerlach when the storm hit, and had headed down to Smoke Creek to celebrate. It took him thirteen hours to go eighteen miles. At times his horse was breast-deep in snow and the visibility was almost zero. Lost and desperate, he finally heard a dog barking in the storm and, at last, the bawling of hungry cattle in the distance. Soon he was holed up before the stove in a warm, snug homesteader's cabin.

In the Sierras, snow fell to a depth of ten to twelve feet, and savage winds hurled the snow into monster drifts thirty to forty feet deep. Westbound trains, stalled at Gerlach, Nevada, were forced to backtrack to Salt Lake City, Utah, while the eastbound trains were snowed in at Portola, California, as all available rotary plows tried to clear the drifts. A train running between Lakeview, Oregon, and Reno, Nevada, was stuck in drifts eighteen feet deep on the Madeleine Plains, and food had to be carried in to the passengers by men on snowshoes. In northern Nevada, sheep clustered in the canyons and died when the relentless winds piled the canyons rimrock deep in suffocating snow. Stockmen let their horses out of their corrals so that they might move about and not freeze in the lethal icy blasts.

Mike's family huddled where they could, piling hides across narrow washes, covering the shelter with brush and snow. With fingers benumbed with cold, the squaws altered the clothes taken from the murdered men into warm garments for the patient but suffering children. The horses were weak from fighting the drifts and carrying their diminishing supply of food, so even the children had to walk or be carried through the banks. Their tiny feet, wrapped with sagebrush bark and strips of burlap to keep them from freezing, left the tracks of monsters in the snow.

Skirting Mud Meadows and Soldier's Meadows, they fought their way around the northern end of the Black Rock desert, perhaps the largest barren expanse in all of North America. Near Paiute Meadows, they killed a thin, half-starved cow for food. The horses plodded on, heads hanging, as though hoping to catch a wisp of rye grass sticking above the crust, or nibbling hungrily at the tail of the horse ahead on the trail.

At Quinn River, the Indians crossed on the ice of the frozen stream. Ahead of them, Mike could see mountain ranges white with snow, and so he turned south toward Winnemucca, into more open country, though there would be little shelter from the driving desert wind.

16

My visits to Little High Rock Canyon could tell me only so much about those tragic events so long ago. Somehow I had to find someone who had been in on the making of that history. Many of those who subsequently became involved were afterwards inclined to embellish on their adventures with each telling. Already many of the original participants had died, taking their stories with them for heavenly campfires. Others had lost the events through a hole in the pocket of their memory.

In 1958, I interviewed a dignified old cowboy named O.D. Van Norman. In semi-retirement, Van Norman was then batching it at a line camp on Lost Creek, southeast of the Bare ranch in Surprise Valley, living alone miles from a neighbor and awaiting death calmly in that same desert landscape he had known as a boy.

As I approached the camp, Van Norman threw a gray-enameled dishpan full of soapy water out over the thirsting earth and stood for a moment watching the iridescent bubbles burst as the dusty ground stole their moisture. Only when the last globules had burst and released his stare did he glance at me. His face showed neither hostility nor welcome, only the slight suspicion a lonely, unarmed man always has for an approaching stranger.

But when I introduced myself and mentioned mutual friends, he invited me into the line camp, which, though furnished by necessity with furniture no one would bother stealing, was clean and neatly cared for.

Van Norman was slender enough, only slightly stooped with the years, quiet, unassuming, and intelligent. His face was cherry-red with a recent scrubbing in the wash basin now poised like Don Quixote's helmet on the crude drain board. His moustache was large but neatly trimmed.

As I settled at the board table, listening to the wind in the cottonwoods and the plaintive, lonely nickerings of his horse down at the corral, Van Norman fried me a buckeroo meal of beans and beef on the glowing wood stove; then, when the dishes were done and stacked to dry, we sat over steaming mugs of coffee, and I heard out his story.

Van Norman and I got along well, and our talk when not of Mike was of many things—of cowboys we'd both known, young men to him, old men to me. Of line camps in the desert, chuckwagons, roundups, runaway teams, mustang runners, and mustangs. In my youth I had listened to a hundred like him grow expansive before a bunkhouse fire.

That evening I helped him with his chores and, when all was done, I sat in the shadows listening to the soft roll of his reminiscence, interrupting now and then with a tale of my own if only to put him at ease, to prove that even though I admitted to being "one of them writers," I savvied the lingo and could only be a man of ranch tradition.

When his bedtime came he signaled its arrival with a sudden

yawn, stripped down to his long-handles, padded out into the darkness, his bowed legs keeping only slight control of his carpet slippers, stood for a long moment looking, I suppose, at the stars, then returned to the house. In a few moments only a few gray hairs showed from the cocoon of his bedroll.

I blew out the kerosene lamp and lay on my blankets, not yet ready for sleep, seeking to digest what I had heard and to put it into context with what I already knew, listening to the restrained voices of a fire damped down for the night, musing at the ticking of expanding and contracting metal, the patter of kangaroo rats in the corners, the inconsiderate monotony of a pack rat rolling a treasure stone back and forth in some playground in the eaves, and the creakings of frozen cotton-woods in the night winds off the sage.

When in the chill half light of dawn I awoke, the firelight danced again on the wall of the shack through chinks in the battered stove. The old man was already feeding his livestock. Unaware that I stood watching from the house, he stood for a moment at his horse's muzzle, cupped his hand, and gently rubbed the animal's eyelids. Soon thick slices of side pork crackled in the frying pan, and a mountain of steaming sour-dough biscuits turned golden in the crude oven. In mid-sentence he took up the story of the Indians where the yawn had interrupted the night before. Time had not mellowed his resentments, any more than it had been able in fifty years to alter the face of that arid, immutable land.

"A bunch of animals," Van Norman growled, putting me in my place for hinting some sympathy for Mike. In Van Norman's account, the Indians were only elusive shadows from a far-off land, and their importance seemed only that they had been the quarry, and without them there would have been no chase.

"Like I said," Van Norman put in, "I'd seen those Injuns off in the distance sometimes near my claim in the Little High

Rock country, and didn't give them a second glance. You didn't in those days. There was a bunch of Injuns up at Summit Lake who were always off hunting and they never bothered anyone. After all, that was 1910. Custer was killed way back in '76, thirty-four years before. We'd heard about Indian fights from our folks, but that was all. Now and then you saw family groups of Injuns roaming the deserts, but winter sent them high-tailing it to some reservation or another where the white man would give them handouts.

"There were lots of Injuns hanging around ranches in those days, too. Every ranch of any size had its own Indian camp not far away. The Indian men weren't much for work, but occasionally they hired out for haying, gathering, or breaking horses. If the bucks hired their women out to do laundry at the ranch house, they sat outside and waited. If you gave the woman lunch she had to go outside to feed her man first, and, of course, he was right there at quitting time to collect her pay."

The hours spent with Van Norman were all too short. The old man told me all he remembered, and I left him then, thinking I would come back another time, but little by little the epicenter of my search for Mike became Rock Creek or Gollaher Mountain. Periodically, however, I would return to Little High Rock Canyon to sit atop the rims and muse, trying to capture the flavor of that awesome land, trying to move back into time, back to 1911, so that I could better understand my story.

When Harry Cambron parted from his sweetheart, Laura, in Eagleville, he promised to be back in two weeks for the wedding. The fact that Harry was heading out alone into one of the most desolate and ruggedly immense wildernesses left in North America, a frozen, wintry desert, where even a broken leg could be fatal, did not worry Laura especially, for Harry was used to roughing it and could survive and flourish

170

where the city-bred would have perished. At best, communications in that part of Nevada were poor, and the only sure way to let the home folks know you arrived safely was to turn around and take the message back yourself. Men went often alone into that bitter land and sometimes were not heard from for months on end. There was a curious resignation about the breed. They either made it back or they didn't. It was quietly accepted that to find an injured man in that great, rugged country would be nearly impossible.

Herders and buckaroos lived often in isolation, their only company their animals and their only contact with the outside world camptenders or owners who came sometimes with stock salt or fresh supplies, or to see how the livestock were faring. Often when they stayed in the line camps, the cowboys marked each passing day, so that when the owners came and they were off on a circle, a mere glance at the unchecked dates on the calendar showed how long the man had been gone.

Years back I borrowed a saddle horse from Butch and Jack Powers in Cedarville and rode into one of the Little High Rock line camps to stay with one of the Powers' vaqueros. But the rider was off making a tour of the ranges, and, by calendar, hadn't been back in thirty-nine days.

But the fact that Harry Cambron failed to show for his wedding worried people in Surprise Valley. Laura persuaded a young cowboy named Warren Fruits to ride the fifty odd miles to the Denio place to find out any information he could about where Harry had last been seen. Erramouspe and Laxague were both married men and the fathers of children, and, in due time, their families began to be concerned.

Several theories were advanced as to the whereabouts of the men. Some said, hopefully, that the sheepmen had gone on to check their bands at Quinn River, others that the severity of the weather had required the owners to stay with their bands until the animals were out of danger. The pessimists had them dying of eating tainted canned meat or being killed by either a gang of train robbers said to be headed that way or by the Pat Russel gang from across the Oregon border. Some less imaginative thought they had just plain perished in the storms.

The last theory was discounted, since the men were warmly dressed, well mounted, experienced, and there were plenty of caves in that rocky country in which to take refuge from a storm.

Will Denio knew the dangers of the country well, but had not given the absence of the four men much thought, since he had respect for their prowess on the trail. Indiano had left a herder in charge of the flocks, and now the herder began to wonder why neither Indiano nor the owners came to check the sheep and bring him more grub. And so he set out for the Denio place, where he learned that his bosses had gone to see him two weeks before.

On learning that the men had never arrived to check their flocks at Soldier's Meadows, only nine miles away, Will Denio became immediately concerned. He wrote to the families of the missing men, warning them that some tragedy might have befallen them. Fruits and the herder took the letters back to Eagleville.

Within hours of their arrival the little ranching community was abuzz with activity, as men wrangled horses in from frozen pastures, tacked on horse shoes, and packed their gear for a journey in the snow. There were many volunteers, but in the end, the search party came to consist of ten men, including Ben Cambron, Harry's brother, Dr. Milo Kennedy, Warren Fruits, Ed Hogle, Henry Hughes, George Holmes, Mort West, George Reeder, and O.D. Van Norman. Since Van Norman had a small land claim in the Little High Rock area he could be counted on to know the country. Such a body of men needed supplies and bedrolls, so a pack outfit, donated by a man named Bill Scott, a well-known freighter, trailed on after.

On Wednesday, February 8, the party set out in a blinding snowstorm and headed east, fighting their way through massive drifts clogging the East Warner Range to the Denios' meadow.

On February 10, 1911, *The Humboldt Star* of Winnemucca, Nevada, contained this lead story:

BELIEVE SHEEPMEN WERE MURDERED. Disappeared On January 17, And Have Not Been Seen Since. A dispatch from Eagleville, Cal., published in yesterday's *Reno Gazette* says that no word has been received from the searching squad of ten men that set out Wednesday morning to find the bodies, if possible, the living members, of the party of stockmen who went out into the blizzard of January 12, and never returned.

It was portentous that the ten men went forth heavily armed. The significance of their armament is realized today, when rumors are flying thick and fast that Cambron, Laxague, Indiano, and Erramuspe [Erramouspe], did not perish with the cold or other natural causes, but that they were foully murdered.

The persistent rumor is that a bunch of outlaws from across the border in Oregon attacked and killed them and made way with their horses and camp equipment.

The people here are wondering why the Nevada State Police have not been put on their trail, as the men were lost or killed in that state.

Ben Cambron, brother of H. Cambron, will arrive today from Constantia, and will follow the searching party. J.B. Laxague and Peter Erramouspe, two of the members of the lost party, are men of families. They own ranches in Surprise Valley. B. Indiano was unmarried . . .

If there was conjecture that the party had gone on to Quinn River, where they had another band of sheep, one by one possibilities such as this were checked out and eliminated. It was brought out, too, that recently a party of nine hostile Indians who were said to have murdered a white boy some time before were seen in the area. The Indians had been piling up stones and placing signs as warning of death to any who might follow them, and there was the possibility that the renegades might have trapped the stockmen and killed them. Even across the vast deserts that separated one corner of the state from the other, Mike's tarnished reputation had preceded him.

On February 11, 1911, the search party left the Denio place at dawn and decided to fan out over the Little High Rock Canyon area and work it systematically for evidence. They agreed that any of the party making a major find should fire two shots into the air as a signal.

Soon after, Warren Fruits was wading through the snow along the creek that meanders the floor of the canyon, leading his horse through a scrubby patch of red willow, when he tripped and fell over something buried in the snow. It was a gloved, human hand frozen upright, as though purposely to seize anyone who wandered by.

Hardly more than a boy, poor Fruits was so shaken he forgot the signal agreed upon and emptied the magazine of his rifle in a wild fusillade of shots, which echoed and re-echoed about the rimrocks. The scattering party of searchers, thinking someone was being attacked by outlaws, converged at a run and came flooding down over the cliffs to his aid. When they got to Fruits, he was in a state of shock, muttering and cursing until someone gave him a long slow drag on a whiskey bottle to bring him to his senses.

Scraping the snow off the bodies, they found that the men had been neatly placed face down in a row, the head of one body at the feet of the other. Missing were gold teeth, genitalia, and the spectacularly moustached lip of Erramouspe.

174

Such murder and dismemberment threw the white men into a rage against all Indians. No one seemed to remember for the moment the outrageous Walker Lake massacre in Nevada, where white soldiers slaughtered an encampment of peaceful Indians, including women and children, cut out the genitalia of the women, and wore them as hatbands. Obviously, Mike and his band had reverted to a state of total savagery, though many now believe that he was only getting even with the Basques for past offenses to his women.

Once the parties had gathered about the bodies, Warren Fruits and Mort West were dispatched back to Eagleville with the news that the lost men had been found and that help was needed. It was not long before the rest of the search party, with time on their hands, had climbed up the steep slopes into Mike's stronghold and found the remains of his camp—the litter of bones, human feces, stacks of abandoned jerky, clay dolls and horse figures left by the children, and rock and willow barricades fencing in the natural pasture where the Indians had kept their mustangs.

Since the murder seemed now definitely the work of Indians, a wire was sent to the Secretary of War, requesting that troops be sent to Nevada, but Washington must have taken the request for what it was, an act of hysteria, and no troops were ever sent.

As was required by law, messages were sent out to officials of Modoc County, California, at Alturas, and to the coroner, county physician, and police of Washoe County, Nevada, at Reno. In order to get the Washoe County officials out to the scene of the crime, a special train was chartered on the N.C.O., which ran from Reno to Lakeview, Oregon. Coroner Lee J. Davis, and County Physician S.K. Morrison, along with other officers of Washoe County, went by train to Alturas, at a cost of $300.00, then took saddle horses over the same pass

175

Mike and his band had once traveled when leaving Cedarville for the Sacramento Valley.

In Eagleville, the Washoe County men were joined by Sheriff L.C. Smith of Modoc County. The inquest in Little High Rock Canyon was held in the dead of night by lantern light with a temperature of twelve below zero. The inquest was made more difficult by the fact that the bodies were frozen together solid and that the fingers, noses, and wounds had been gnawed by mice.

According to Dr. Morrison's report, all the shots were fired by thirty-thirty high-powered rifles, except two, which were from a thirty-eight pistol. The thirty-eight used may have been the pistol captured from Cambron, but Mike's arsenal was old and primitive, consisting mainly of black powder pieces. Either Morrison erred in his report, or Mike did not keep the thirty-thirties long.

In the camp, searchers found six head of beef that had been butchered and the tracks of seven Indians, including those of a squaw and her papoose heading in the direction of the Black Rock desert and Winnemucca. They also found the remains of the Indian horses, which had died of starvation. These horses had been rebranded B. In those days, while many Indians branded their animals, it was seldom that they bothered to record the brand legally with the state, so the brands would not have been too valuable in identifying which Indians had been on the scene.

Possession of property stolen from the murdered men, however, would have been irrefutable evidence as to their guilt, so the state police published a description of the articles stolen from the four stockmen:

One bay horse, white stripe on face, white foot, weight 1100, 5 years old and branded H.P. on left shoulder, J.A. on left side.

Sorrel horse. Light mane and tail, white face, weight 1100, L.T. right thigh. Mule shoes.

Black Oregon horse, 7 or 8 years old. No brand known.

One gold, open face watch, number 13,997, 831.

One silver hunting case watch; C.H. Cambron on back.

Once the coroner's inquest had been held, the party faced the difficult task of getting the bodies through the deep snows of the canyon. It was impossible to get wagons down Little High Rock, so the frozen remains were lashed to crude stretchers made of saddle blankets and poles, and carried up the canyon to where a flimsy sleigh drawn by a team awaited them. Holding the frozen bodies on the sleigh over the rough ground proved an almost impossible task, so the cowboys walked alongside, helping the sleigh stay upright in washes and rough hillsides never meant for such means of transportation, pushing the bodies back on whenever they began to slide. Once the canyon widened, the bodies were transferred to teams and wagons for the long journey over the California border to Eagleville.

Hundreds of people lined the streets as the party came to town. Each wagon creaked and rumbled a funeral dirge of its own as the procession, followed by a large, sorrowful contingent of horsemen, passed along the streets to the church.

The stockmen were taken into the little white church and laid out on the floor to thaw out sufficiently so that the mortician could place their bodies in caskets. As the bodies thawed, blood dripped onto the wooden floor, making grisly stains that would still be visible half a century later, along with those of a beehive between the walls that melted in the heat. On February 14, 1911, the four men were buried in the Eagleville cemetery.

Once the victims had been brought in from the hills, a posse was organized to head out on the trail of the Indians. From the surrounding ranches came volunteers, warmly dressed and mounted on good, if winter-thin, horses and armed to the teeth with high-powered repeating rifles, pistols, and enough ammunition to fight a war. There were those who were friends of the dead men and were eager to avenge their senseless deaths, but there were more who sensed that this was the last great Indian chase of history and who would not have stayed home on a bet—men whose sole purpose in going was to get themselves a legal Indian.

Uppermost in the minds of several were the lucrative rewards offered for catching the culprits. The state of Nevada offered $5000, Mrs. Erramouspe $2500, Mrs. Laxague $2500, the citizens of Surprise Valley $2,000, the Humphrey-Cambron Cattle Company $2000, and the state of California $1000—a grand total of $15,000. The sheriff wanted to deputize the men, but, knowing that if they were deputized they would not be eligible for the reward, they refused.

The higher the reward money became, the more pressure developed within the posse to cut down on the number of men with whom they would have to share. Eventually, the great hue and cry of volunteer Indian fighters was lessened by the realities of a lack of conditioned horse flesh and a raging snowstorm that swept down from the Warner Mountains. At last the posse was reduced to about twenty-two men.

From the Nevada state police, only recently formed, came Captain J.P. Donnely, Sergeant Buck, and Privates Stone and Newgard; from Modoc County, California, came Sheriff L.C. Smith, and from Washoe County, Nevada, Sheriff Ferrel. In addition, there were Henry Hughes, William Parsons, Ed Hogle, George Holmes, Joseph Reeder, Jack Ferguson, Ben Cambron, Warren Fruits, Mort West, Frank Perry, O.D. Van Norman, Charley Demick, Sid Street, Fred Hill, Gilbert Jackson, and Jim Baty.

On February 15, 1911, the posse left Eagleville for the Denio place. If Mrs. Denio had ever been lonely out on those Nevada barrens, it now seemed as though civilization had moved in with her. Behind the shouting, noisy posse came a pack train pushed by thirty riders. Supplies for the fifty men had to be carried by mule, since the next source of supply was Winnemucca, Nevada, over two hundred miles away. Not only was a large remuda of fresh horses needed for the posse, but hay, grain, bedding, cooking gear, ammunition, and supplies of food.

The Denios had only a couple of extra shacks to spare, so that night men took turns crowding in to get warm. Men outside waited their turn patiently, then resignedly lay down to sleep in the snow, as the floors of the shacks became covered rib to rib with snoring men. True to the hospitality of the West, the Denios made everyone as welcome as possible and would take nothing in the way of pay for the great inconvenience caused them by the posse.

That night, the horses were night-herded in a fence corner and fed from a wagon load of hay brought in from a neighboring ranch.

On the morning of February 16, nearly a month after the massacre, the posse left Little High Rock Canyon on the trail of Mike and his family.

The search party that found the bodies of Harry Cambron and his companions had brought along a photographer. The following plates and their "explanations" appeared in The Humboldt Star.

179

PLATE NO. 1, This view is of the deserted tepee, and the location is marked "Camp" in plate No. 2. About 25 or 30 feet to the left of the tepee was a couple of large rocks which were used as a lookout, and from which point they could guard the canyon in all directions. Leading from the tepee to this lookout was a trail covered with sagebrush bark and behind the rocks forming the lookout was also a bed of sagebrush bark, on which one could lie concealed and guard the canyon from all directions. This camp was located in a depression and could not be seen for only a short distance. The deserted camp, together with finding the combings of an Indian woman's hair, Indian arrow heads snow shoes and other Indian curios, was considered conclusive evidence that the four stockmen had been murdered by Indians.

→

PLATE No. 2, Is a general view of the canyon, looking in an easterly direction. The four men came off the upper rim-rock to the left of the camp, and through a narrow break in the lower rim-rock and over the slide, as shown in the left of the picture, to where the beef was found by Indiano, which was near where the three horses are standing in the center of the picture.

From the confession of the young squaw that was captured, it was learned that the four men were seen by the Indians from their lookout near camp some time before coming over the upper rim-rock and some of the Indian bucks secreted themselves in the willows near where the bodies were found, and shot the four men when they came to examine the beef the Indians had killed. A cap and other remnants of clothing were found near this point, which led to the finding of the bodies thrown in a narrow creek-bed surrounded by willows at the "X" in the picture. In the front of the picture may be seen two men with one of the bodies on a stretcher, starting up the canyon to where the sleigh was in waiting, one and a half miles distant. (See Plate 3)

CAMP.

HIGH ROCK CANYON, NEV.

BODIES FOUND.

X

LATE NO.

PLATE NO. 3,

CAMERON

INDIANA

ERRAMOUSPE

FROM STRETCHERS TO SLED LITTLE HIGH ROCK CANYON, NEV.

COPYRIGHT 1911 BY G. L. MATTHEWS CEDARVILLE, CAL.

PLATE 3. This plate shows the bodies after they had been carried on stretchers up the canyon, through brush and over rocks for 1 1/2 miles; this being the nearest available point to which the 4-horse team and sleigh could be brought. From here the bodies were taken to Denio's, where the inquest was held by the aid of a light from a sagebrush fire and a lantern, with the mercury several degrees below zero.

BODIES AS FOUND. COPYRIGHT 1911, BY G.L. MATTHEWS CEDARVILLE, CA.

PLATE No. 5. This picture shows a general view of Camp Denio, five miles west of where the murder was committed. In the foreground can be seen the corral, with some 50 head of horses. To feed those horses it was necessary to haul hay some 10 miles, and owing to bad roads 500 pounds was a sufficient load for four horses. The first building back of the corral is a small bunk house, probably 10 feet square. The other building in the distance is Mr. Denio's house, about 12x16. In this building was cooked and served excellent meals for at least 50 persons, and for which Mr. and Mrs. Denio refused to accept pay. Much credit is due them for their generous hospitality.

NIO. 5 MILES FROM SCENE OF MURDE

PLATE 4. This plate shows the bodies as they were found in the creek-bed, as they had been placed there and left by the Indians. The bodies were in a good state of preservation, having been frozen solid shortly after being placed there and owing to severe cold weather had remained frozen, and it was with some difficulty the bodies were pried apart. The place where they were found was surrounded by brush and the bodies could not have been seen unless one had gotten within 15 or 20 feet of them.

PLATE No. 6 shows the posse with animals packed as they left Denios' ranch to take up the trail of the murderers on February 16, 1911.

The posse was composed of the following persons: Sheriff Ferrill, Capt. Donnelly and Messrs. Newgard, Stone and Buck, of the Nevada State Police, Sheriff Smith, of Modoc, with Henry Hughes. Wm. Parsons, Ed Hogle, Geo. Holmes, Joe Reeder, Jack Ferguson, B. F. Cambron, Warren Fruits, Mart West, Frank Perry, O. D. Van Norman, Chas. Demick, Sid Street, Fred Hill, Gilbert Jackson and Jas. Baty, of Surprise Valley.

The forming of the posse in a severe snow storm at Eagleville, Cal., Feb. 13, 1911, is shown in Plate No. 7.

Wounds on the Murdered Men.

Harry Cambron was shot four times—in right breast, through left hip, in the head behind the right ear and through the left elbow.

Peter Erramouspe was shot four times—in the head, through the left breast, in the left thigh and in the right thigh. His mustache and upper lip were entirely removed.

J. B. Laxague was shot twice—in the right breast and the top of the head.

B. Indiano was shot four times—twice in the head (left eye displaced from the socket) through the shoulder and in the upper part of the chest.

17

It is the very nature of deserts that time seems stuck at high noon. Of all the land mass, they are the area most resistant to change. What does it matter, really, whether Mike's saga happened today, yesterday, sixty-one years ago, or, for that matter, a thousand? While seasonal changes are often spectacular, only the skilled observer can spot changes that are often so subtle as to be only long-range trends.

In the northern Nevada of today, the desert soils still wander willy-nilly with the winds, jackrabbits lope and play, nibble without care or conscience, and solve an immediate problem merely by loping over the next available dune. Gravity and spring team up to send snow water ever downward to form vast sinks or playas of muddy, silted water on impermeable bottoms. The golden eagles still circle, when we let them alone, nesting along the decaying rims. Magpies chatter, and the sage thrasher, canyon wren, and vesper sparrow still sing atop the highest perch of rock or sage. The horned lark tinkles with too thin and silvery a voice to be lauded by our local poets, though our dogs can hear. The Indian, too, could hear. Coyotes still hunt and howl, happily unperturbed that sheepmen hate them so. The tumbleweed steals a free ride on the wind, with one throng, all unknowing, helping its later comrades over fences.

We men believe in dominion of man over nature; but in reality we do what nature intends. In time. We too are of the scheme. The antelope runs and is a bit silly and curious. If he were not so fast to compensate for his faults, there would be no antelope. The mountain sheep lies about a good deal of the time being conspicuous, but also out of reach, and alert. The slow hawks, broad-winged Buteos, are the most patient, as if knowing their dinner will eventually appear. Each in his place serves, unthinking, to avert natural disaster, the hawk serving partly as a genetic tool, or all ground squirrels would become idiots.

Creating God in his own image, man considers himself above change, believing that natural laws are fine for the ground squirrel, but not him. He cannot accept the fact that all species are on their way somewhere and in transition into other forms, even he. He sits complacently, thinking that somehow God will overcome natural laws to provide for his most errant species.

There is no other way to look at Mike's saga, at the great chase across that timeless desert and its ultimate dramatic end, except for what it was, the simple pursuit of one predator after another. One heartless, savage, and unreasoning predator preying upon a weaker subspecies to usurp his territory. The "reds" were merely first. In time, inevitably, blacks, whites, and yellows will, in turn, flourish and fail.

The whites could achieve only a temporary victory in destroying Mike's little band, then they too had to yield. Each species, man included, is vulnerable; nothing nature has yet

192

designed is perfect. The seed rots, grows, or is eaten. In human nature are the seeds of man's destruction; he is but part of the system, and not the system itself, weak as all in nature are weak, imperfect as all are imperfect, enslaved by greed and lust, hampered by lack of foresight, and in his own way as silly as the antelope.

Since the first mountain was created as a thrusting of crust in the smooth plain, there has been a counter force of change. Wind and rain were forces, the buffalo was a force, the salmon fertilizing the food chains of the upper watersheds with its death was a force. And man was a force. Change, though inevitable, is not necessarily a stampede toward cataclysmic annihilation, but the slow doom of one gene rotting, one lesser seed failing.

We have failed to grasp the concept of time. What is a million years to us, really? What is reality to us now is too often only the moment we are in the process and ecstasy of orgasm. The saga of Rock Creek Mike was the story of change. Mike could no more have understood the real significance of why he was being pursued than the white cowboys could have understood where it all fit and why they were pursuing.

The first campsite found by the posse, after leaving Little High Rock Canyon, was not far from High Rock Lake. Here they found an incriminating piece of evidence, a scrap of leather bearing Harry Cambron's name, which the Indians, as a precaution, had cut from his saddle. From that camp, the Indians had crossed the ice on the lake and headed eastward. A heavy snow had fallen since the Indians had traveled here, but in places it had blown away so that the route of travel could be established by Jim Teham and Henry Barr, Indian trackers brought in for the job. In some places the snow had been scoured clean by the winds; in others it was belly-deep to a horse, or piled in huge spoil banks fifty feet deep along the rims. Often for long stretches the trail vanished, and the trackers swung wide on each flank until the tracks showed again.

The Indians, all wearing moccasins, some riding, some walking, did not seem hurried, nor did they seem to fear pursuit, for in each camp the posse found eloquent evidence as to their guilt, such as scraps of cloth discarded as the Indian women fashioned stolen clothing into warm clothes for the children. Once they found Harry Cambron's checkbook, which the Indians finally fathomed was a risky bit of evidence, best hurled off into the sage. The trail led on through the Calico Mountains. The whites had originally assumed that the band was heading for a no-man's-land of broken lava, where they could have holed up for some time, but instead, the Indians had passed it by.

Since the Indians had nearly a month's head start, it was necessary for the posse to cover as many of Mike's camps as they could in a day. Time was of the essence, for if Mike was able to reach the brakes of the Owyhee, he would be safe forever in that tortured jumble of inaccessible canyons.

The trail led northeast past Soldier's Meadows, where the posse, numbed to the bone by subzero temperatures and long cramped hours in the saddle, spent the night sheltered by the old stone buildings of historic Fort McQuarry. From Soldier's Meadows, the trail led past Mud Meadows, skirting the foot of the Summit Lake range of mountains, crossing the desert to Paiute Meadows, a Miller and Lux ranch on the east side of the Black Rock desert. Here the Indians had rested for two days, killed a beef, and lost a draw knife used for scraping hides. They were traveling in fresh powder snow under even worse weather conditions than the posse, and from the way the Indian mustangs avoided the bare patches of sharp rocks, the Indian trailers knew they were tired and sore of foot.

At that point, most of the posse headed for Quinn River Crossing, but six men, including Jim Teham, headed southeast toward Albert Lay's ranch, twenty-five miles east and north of

Sulphur, and some fifty miles south of the crossing. Here the Indians had crossed on the ice, but recent thaws had made a strip of open water down the center of Quinn River, which was still ice-encrusted, swollen, and ugly from record autumn rains.

First Newgard, the big, stoop-shouldered policeman, tried crossing the stream, but when the water got over his waist he hollered quits, and the others pulled him back on the end of a rope. When Jim Teham, the Warm Springs Indian, gave it a try, he too was forced back to shore by the swirling torrent. It was Frank Perry, who, angered by the failure of the others, dashed in ahorseback, breaking ice with the butt of his rifle, and finally made his way across, to emerge dripping and half frozen on the opposite shore. Soon, the whole party had crossed, with the exception of Henry Hughes, who volunteered the long ride north to Quinn River to tell the others that the Indians had headed across the river on the ice and moved toward the fastness of the Jackson Mountains. Soaking wet, the rest of the men rode off in a blinding snowstorm to try to find the Lay ranch. United with the rest of the posse the following day, they crossed the north end of the Jacksons to the edge of the Willow Creek desert.

It was then that Sheriff Lamb, of Humboldt County, entered the chase. Ralph Lamb was a famous law man, generally loved and respected throughout his territory as a brave man and one eminently fair. To the criminals who drifted into Humboldt County, Sheriff Lamb, his brother, Kise, and a famous Indian tracker, a Paiute named Skinny Pascal, must have seemed an unbeatable team. Lamb solved so many crimes in the area, and with Pascal's unerring eye tracked down so many criminals, that his exploits became legendary, and seldom did a bar-room conversation go a whole evening without someone mentioning an adventure of Sheriff Lamb's.

It was Lamb and Skinny Pascal, for instance, who tracked

·down Tranmer and Urie after the Quillici murder at Imlay, and, within hours, had criminals and suspects locked up in the nearest jail.

As Mike and his family moved into Humboldt County and Sheriff Lamb's personal fiefdom, it is perhaps understandable that the Eagleville posse began to get nervous about possible loss of the reward money for which they had worked so hard. Then, too, the Nevada state police had only recently been formed, and there was a lack of cordiality between the police and the sheriff's office, since Lamb got the lion's share of the glory and the operational budget.

No one today really knows who sent the message designed to throw Sheriff Lamb off the trail. The message was sent by messenger from the Miller and Lux ranch to the telephone at Amos, forty miles east, then telephoned in to the sheriff. It was purported to have come straight from Captain Donnely and indicated that the Indians were hiding in the lower end of the Jackson Mountains. In reality, by this time Mike was at least a hundred miles east of the Jacksons and closer to safety every day.

On February 20, *The Humboldt Star* reported the following:

INDIAN MURDERERS ARE HIDING IN FASTNESS OF JACK-
SON MOUNTAIN
Sheriff Lamb Will Leave Tonight With Posse And Join Pursuit At Sulphur.
News of the capture of the Indian murderers of the four French sheepmen may be expected at any time.
The first definite news from the pursuing posse was received this afternoon from Superintendent Donnely of the State Police in a message telephoned in from Amos. The message was dated this morning at Quinn River Crossing, Miller and Lux's home ranch, situated at the head of the Black Rock Desert, forty miles west of

Amos, the dispatch having been sent by messenger from the ranch to Amos. The message is as follows:

"Quinn River Crossing, Feb. 20. The party of Indians that killed four men crossed the Black Rock Desert fifty miles below here. Some of our boys crossed their trail. The rest of us are crossing here and getting fresh horses, and are going out this morning. The Indians we believe are in the lower end of Jackson Mountain.

J.P. DONNELY"

Sheriff Lamb immediately forwarded the message to Governor Oddie, who had asked to be kept fully informed of the pursuit of the murderers. Sheriff Lamb also telegraphed to Superintendent Ogilvie of the Western Pacific at Elko to have a special car on tonight's Train No. 1. This car will be loaded with horses, and Sheriff Lamb, his brother "Kise" Lamb, with Indian trailers and a local posse will leave over the Western Pacific tonight for Sulphur which is the nearest railroad point to the place where the murderers are supposed to be located. Sulphur is only about thirty miles distant from the southern end of Jackson Mountain, and Sheriff Lamb and the posse will take up the pursuit bright and early in the morning. From Superintendent Donnely's dispatch it seems that his posse is divided and that the party which is on the trail of the Indians is likely to be somewhere in the neighborhood of Sulphur. A junction between the other two posses and Sheriff Lamb's will likely be effected some time tomorrow. Sheriff Lamb and his brother know every foot of the section of the country in which the Indians are supposed to be and it seems impossible that the murderers can evade capture longer than a day or two, unless it happens that the State Police posse has been following a cold trail, in which event the Indians may be far away from the Jackson Mountain country by this time.

As of course they were. Donnely's posse, in fact, did not head for Sulphur at all, but having taken care of any competition from Sheriff Lamb for a while, headed southeast on Mike's actual trail.

Sheriff Lamb ran into immediate difficulties in preparation

for his journey when he found that Superintendent Ogilvie of the Western Pacific was absent from Elko, and there was difficulty in getting someone to authorize a special train. In addition, when volunteers for his posse discovered that they would have to pay their own expenses, their desire to do community service quickly left them, with the result that when the special train pulled out of Winnemucca at 2:35 the next morning bound for Sulphur Siding, Sheriff Lamb, Kise, and Skinny Pascal were the only ones aboard.

Understaffed as he was, when Sheriff Lamb unloaded the horses at Sulphur Siding and prepared to ride for Jackson Mountain, he did not hope to engage the Indians himself, only locate them and put Donnely's party on the trail.

It was Lamb's opinion that Mike's band had passed Sulphur some ten days before and would probably by now be south, along the shores of Pyramid Lake, with a host of other Indians waiting to catch the huge, black-spotted native cutthroat trout as they ventured out of the saline depths of Pyramid to spawn. While Lamb thought it might be several days before the Indians were located, he did not anticipate any trouble in their capture.

Virtually all the old-time Indian fighters were following the chase and had varying opinions as to who the Indians would turn out to be and where they were hiding. Some were sure that the Indians were Jim Winnemucca's band. Jim was a nephew of old Chief Winnemucca, for whom the town was named, and had a very bad reputation, to the point where some people even suggested that if Jim wouldn't change his name the town should change its. Another of Winnemucca's nephews, Jerry Winnemucca, had a good reputation, except that in war time he was apt to forsake his peaceful ways and fight until the war was over. The reputations of many a peaceful Indian suffered from conjecture merely because lately they hadn't been seen about town.

To the old-timers living out their days in old folks' homes, poor houses, and family attics, the massacre at Little High Rock was the most exciting event to come their way in years, and it gave them a glorious excuse to gather together in clumps of twos and threes, on porches or park benches, and, brandishing their canes, relive the glories of the past.

On the chance that Sheriff Lamb might be right about the Indian murderers heading for Pyramid Lake to fish, nervous citizens besieged Governor Oddie's office until a posse led by Inspector Cablan left Carson City for the lake.

In fairness to Sheriff Lamb, who knew the habits of wandering Indians as well as any man, assuming that the Indians had headed south as Captain Donnely's message indicated, his guess that the Indians had gone south to Pyramid Lake was based on sound knowlege that Indians for hundreds of miles around did indeed converge on Pyramid and the other remnant lakes from ancient Lake Lahontan, at precisely this time of year to gather huge tonnages of fish. At this point in their journey, the renegades had to be hungry, and the old Indian might well head for the fishery, where he would have no trouble feeding a dozen hungry mouths.

It did not take Sheriff Lamb long to determine that Donnely's lead was wrong, and the Indians were neither hiding in the fastness of Jackson Mountain nor had ever passed that way. Quickly, Lamb spurred on north and caught up with the posse east of the Jacksons, at Willow Creek.

Those knowledgeable about Indians did not think that once the Indians were discovered they would make a stand. An article in *The Humboldt Star* of February 22, 1911, stated:

The average Nevada Indian has no scruples about committing murder, but he has an overpowering dislike of losing his own life. And they have no particular fear of being compelled to suffer the death penalty as punishment for the commission of murder. They have been taught this by the action of the Nevada Board of Pardons, which in years past has commuted the sentence of nearly every Indian who has been condemned to death. There have been plenty of murders committed by Indians, but very few Indians have been hanged in the history of the state. All of which is undeniable reason why the murderers of the French sheepmen, in case they are Indians, are very likely to surrender when they are run down and find escape impossible, rather than make a fight and be shot to pieces by the posse. They would rather take the chance of being hanged than to stop any of the posse's rifle bullets.

At the time of his death, Harry Cambron was riding a fine white horse. This horse, although for some reason it was not among those listed in the police reports as stolen, was taken by the Indians. But now, since Mike was entering a land more thickly populated than the desolations through which he had been traveling, perhaps he felt the animal was too conspicuous. The horse may have escaped the Indians, but it is more probable that they turned the animal loose to return to his native range. At any rate, Cambron's white horse was now found wandering alone, complete with saddle and bridle, by a sheepherder who tried in vain to catch him up.

In modern times, of course, planes would have circled the desert and Mike's story would soon have been over. But though airplanes existed in 1911, the state of the art was such that any attempt to use them to locate Indians might have resulted in more deaths than had already been caused by Mike's band.

In San Francisco, a daring pilot had taken off from the heights above the city to attempt the first airplane landing on a ship, and the only casualty was one of the onlookers on the hill, who was running alongside the plane as it took off and in his excitement ran right off the precipice.

It was in September of 1911 that a man named Fowler,

preceded by an agent collecting subscriptions of money along the route of the flight through Nevada, attempted a transcontinental journey. Fowler was delayed by an accident at Alta, California, which was a great disappointment to local Winnemucca people who had been waiting patiently by the baseball field down by the stockyards for his arrival.

Perhaps the state of transportation in that era is best indicated by a notice in the *Silver State* of February 23, 1911:

BUY NEW STOCK FOR THEIR FREIGHTING BUSINESS A.S.F. Rankin, of Gorham and Rankin, arrived in town Monday evening, trailing in six head of fine large four-year-old geldings of the Double Square brand which Summerfield and Pearce had bought to put into their freighting outfits.

While automobiles had begun to demoralize the horse market, they would have been of little use in pursuing an elusive band of Indians through the mountains.

On the same day, the *Silver State* announced:

TRAIL OF MURDERERS LEADS THROUGH HUMBOLDT COUNTY. Indians, Said To Be Shoshones, Evidently Headed For Owyhee Country . . . Posse Will Camp At Tollhouse Tonight . . . Sheriff Ferrel Goes To Elko By Rail.
Sheriff Ferrel of Washo County and Frank Buck, a member of the state police, arrived in Winnemucca via the Western Pacific at about three o'clock this afternoon, coming from Jungo by freight train. When seen by a representative of the SILVER STATE this afternoon, and asked the latest news regarding the hunt for the murderers of the four sheepmen, Sheriff Ferrel replied,
"The murder was committed by a band of Shoshone Indians, composed of one old man, three young braves, two old squaws, one young one, 17 years of age, and three children. That these Indians committed the murder there is not the slightest doubt, for at several of the camps we found remnants of the clothing taken from the

murdered men, which the squaws were undoubtedly changing to fit the men in their party. On the twenty-fifth of November, they stole a quantity of cartridges from a man named Van Norman, who has a small ranch near Little High Rock Canyon. He is a member of our posse and is able to give a minute description of all of them. Sheriff Lamb with his brother and 'Skinny' Pascal, the Indian trailer, joined our posse at Lay's Ranch yesterday morning, and are included in the 14 men who are on the trail today. Last night the posse camped at Lay's Willow Creek Ranch, and tonight will reach the Tollhouse.

"The Indians are headed for the Owyhee country, but are making slow progress. From their camps we have ascertained that they have not made any more than twelve miles in any one day, and indications are that their stock is almost worn out. Although the posse this morning was twelve days behind, there is no doubt but what they will be overtaken and captured."

Sheriff Ferrel is of the opinion that this same band of Indians murdered a boy in northern Elko County some months ago, and for the purpose of confirming this theory, visited Tranmer and Urie at the county jail to talk over details of that crime.

Sheriff Ferrel and State Policeman Buck left for Elko on No. 10, this afternoon. While for reasons of public policy, the Sheriff did not care to discuss his future movements, it is the reasonable assumption that he hopes to form a new posse in Elko County and head the Indians off before they reach their destination in the Owyhee Country.

Through notoriety gained in the fight with Tranmer's gang, Mike was now a marked man, known across northern Nevada and southern Idaho. Had the family split up at this point and scattered like quail into the anonymity of either the rough country or resident Indian populations, they would have had an excellent chance of escaping detection. Mike must have known how vulnerable and conspicuous his band was as they traveled in a bunch. But they all realized that, like the mustangs, once they were separated there was no coming together again as a band to wander wild and free as their ancestors before them. Desperate in their need of each other, they clung together, ready to accept whatever fate had decreed.

18

Once Mike and his family had crossed Quinn River on the ice, some fifty miles upstream from Quinn River Crossing, they were faced with a sudden change of weather, a warm chinook wind that turned the snow to slush and made muddy playas of the bottoms. Ducks fed happily and Canada geese set up territories on shallow lakes that would be gone by mid-summer.

The Jackson Mountains lay directly ahead, and, instead of detouring around them north or south, the Daggetts pushed up over Rattlesnake Pass, fighting the heavy waist-deep snows rather than leaving lasting dinosaur tracks in the sticky gumbo of the plains.

There was little food, and the once lusty cry of the baby was now only a plaintive, fretful whine that must have cut Mike to the quick. He sat more and more at his drum, chanting to the mountain to give them of its food, but Mike's medicine was weak. To the north, Mike could see the Lay ranch, where he had traded some harness the summer before, but he could not go there without being recognized. He preferred to drift through the territory unnoticed in case any should take up his trail.

Crossing the Jacksons, one of the dogs died, but the dog had been sick and, even in their hunger, the Indians were afraid to eat it. This was a dangerous area for Indians and Mike paused often to reason his course. Just across the Slumbering Hills lay Winnemucca. And north of Winnemucca, all along the valley of the Little Humboldt, lay a string of ranches scattered clear to Paradise. It would be difficult, if not impossible, to cross this valley without being seen, yet there was no way past without cutting through the heavy snows and high elevations of the Santa Rosas, to the north.

Mike moved cautiously, sending scouts on ahead to examine each new valley for sign of danger. Making good use of each ridge or gully, they passed a scant eight miles north of Winnemucca, trailing through the sand dunes and heading on between Barrett Springs and the Bloody Run Range of mountains.

However close the sand dunes were to Winnemucca, they were a good place to hide and rest. There was no snow on the south hillsides, and with every afternoon wind the sands began their travels, screening out tracks, moving on their slow interminable way across the deserts, forming brand new dunes out of the old. Few whites came here, except sometimes a few children rode out from town to slide down the slopes or write their names on the smooth, immaculate, cherubic cheeks of white sand.

Here the Indians succeeded in catching a few rabbits for the pot and in raiding the anthills for good quantities of red ants. The Little Humboldt was swollen from melting snows, but still the women were able to wade out deep under cover of darkness and dig out a few tule roots with their bare toes. In the distance they saw the lights of the town, and they must have thought of the white people there with plenty to eat and the great piles of food on the shelves of the stores. But there were no complaints to Mike about their condition. They accepted their lot with stoicism; they had elected to be free of the white man's yoke and this was the price they must pay.

The long run across the valley of the Little Humboldt was made at night. Even the children stripped naked and, holding their clothes above their heads, clutching firmly to the backs of the adults, made it across the churning, swirling undertows of the stream. One of the horses, pitifully weakened by months on the trail, became mired in the ooze along the Little Humboldt and soon was lost to sight, while another, numbed and exhausted by immersion in the cold, icy water, went down the next morning near the camp they made in the rocks at Long Canyon, and they slit his throat to end his suffering.

In desperation, Mike sent Jim and Jake to the store at Paradise. The storekeeper looked them over carefully enough, but served them and took their money eagerly. They went off with all the food they could carry, but in their weakened condition it was hard to pack enough food for a dozen starving people.

Mike was against staying long in the area, but he had little choice. The mustangs' feet were worn to the quick, and left bloody, scarlet tracks in the snow. Even though no one, even of the children, complained, he knew that they were almost at the end of their strength. They were free to leave, to scatter like tumbleweeds across the sagelands to safety, but somehow the old chief must have known how deeply family ties bound them all together. Whatever there was to face, they would face together.

Mike rested, but not well. He knew that it would be only a matter of time before they would be sighted by some miner seeking gold or some rancher tending his stock. Scattered through the Osgood Mountains were mining claims owned by corporations whose guards might mistake them for prospectors pilfering ore.

Once he had passed over the Osgoods, however, he had only to cross Clover Valley and ease past the Kelley Creek ranch, to enter one of the loneliest desolations in North America, a land that had sheltered many an outlaw, white and Indian alike. No white man would dare pursue him into those rocky badlands. Here his ponies could graze out this last month of winter, and his family could rest and find sustenance to build their strength against one final journey back to their old range at Gollaher Mountain.

He had sent the boys on ahead to scout snow conditions in the mountains to the northeast, when, suddenly, he ordered the rest to break camp. Perhaps he sensed that he had been sighted by the lone prospector, a gray-beard who had been hammering among the rocks of a neighboring canyon. Summoning all their strength, they heaped dirt upon the embers of their fire and moved on.

They plodded slowly, silently, along the western foothills of the Osgoods, then, pausing frequently to rest, began the long ascent of Soldier's Pass. That night in the distance they could see the gay sparkling lights of Winnemucca at one end of the valley, and at the other the lights of Paradise, with a generous sprinkling of ranch-house lights in between.

They did not stop to camp. As they ascended eastward in the dawning and gained the summit, they could see great snowy mountains to the north, Clover Valley stretching south. Far ahead they could see the small patch of cleared land, the buildings and trees of the Kelley Creek ranch, and the great rocks where Kelley Creek rushed from the hills. Mike must have pointed with triumph toward the horizon. One day's hard journey away they would be safely into the hills.

As the old Indian stood looking eastward, memorizing the

lay of the land, he must have noticed how lonely and vulnerable the ranch at Kelley Creek appeared. One strike there and they could have fresh horses, and then within hours they could vanish into the rugged hills.

The snow lay knee-deep; their feet, bound with burlap and sagebrush bark for warmth, were chafed and blistered. Soon they had trailed down off the Osgoods, keeping to the gullies and washes deep enough to obscure their horses from hostile eyes. The hills were gently rounded with only an occasional outcropping of rock. On the lower elevations the snow was only three or four inches deep and on southern exposures had melted entirely, while the sage was low and crisscrossed with rabbit tracks. Atop the long low ridge that forms one shoulder of Rabbit Creek wash ran a wagon road, but the band kept the ridge on their left and traveled down the wash, moving as far eastward as they dared. Ahead of them the ridge seemed to end abruptly, and a few more minutes would have brought them out to a point where they would be exposed upon the plain. There was little else to do now but sleep until darkness came and then make a run for it across the valley to the beckoning hills.

Just off the main wash they found a short, eroded gully, which they covered with hides, weighted down against the wind with stones. They blocked one end of the wash with brush, making a simple but effective three-sided hut. There was no water, but the horses ate snow for moisture, then were herded up the shoulder of the ridge to graze on bleached bunch grass and sage.

The sum total of their rations now were a few scrawny jackrabbits and some ants worked from one of the few anthills to which sage grouse and flickers had not laid first claim. But now the hunger must have seemed easier to bear. Miraculously they had managed the long, hurried march past Winnemucca and Paradise, through the very heartland of the enemy. By the next dawning they should be safe in the lonely hills, where once more they could shoot their rifles at game without fear of attracting attention.

Always before, Mike had posted a guard, but now he failed to fortify the camp. Even with warning, there could be no escape in their condition. The fortress rocks across the valley were as out of reach as though they were the mountains on the moon. The sagebrush around them furnished scant cover, and only the zig-zag run of Rabbit Creek furnished any sort of battlement. Mike must have had qualms about their vulnerability, but to go back to the nearest rocks would have added miles to their coming journey across the darkened valley floor. In the tired silence of the children and the thin faces of the adults, as well as the gaunt ribs and lackluster eyes of the horses, he read signs of man and beast pushed to their limits. The old chief sent Heney up on the ridge to tend the horses and ordered the rest of the band to sleep the daylight away. Perhaps the scudding clouds would clear and the moon would shine its lantern to light their way.

19

Mike could not have known how tight the noose was drawing about his neck. To the north, along the southern border of the Duck Valley Reservation, straddling the Idaho-Nevada line, Indian police had set up patrols to prevent Mike from slipping onto the reservation, where presumably he might be sheltered by Indians sympathetic to his plight.

From Elko, Sheriff Ferrel and Private Buck had formed a posse to head northwest toward the old mining town of Tuscarora, and at Tuscarora itself, Constable Dean H. Young had formed a tough, hardened posse of miners and cowboys who knew every wrinkle in the land to move west to guard the mountain passes through which Mike would have to travel. In Carson City, Governor Oddie had authorized Nevada State Police Inspector A.W. Cablan to send police to Elko if requested. All local, county, state, and Indian officials had been alerted. From behind, nosing along Mike's trail in relentless pursuit, came the noted Paiute tracker Skinny Pascal with the posse of Surprise Valley boys led by Captain Donnely, all thirsting for sport, revenge, and prize money.

The *Sacramento Bee* had sent a reporter to Winnemucca, as had many other newspapers, and the men were now running over each other in an effort to uncover facts about the dramatic chase from a land reluctant to yield news. What little copy they were able to glean, however, made front pages far and wide.

Just before he left for Elko, Sheriff Ferrel interviewed Tranmer and Urie to obtain further information about the Indians, and the outlaws, of course, were more than willing to repeat their original testimony implicating Mike's family in rustling and murder. The number in the party and the composition tallied with the tracks the posse were following, so that they were positive now that, if they finally caught up with the Indians, they would turn out to be Mike and his band.

On February 23, *The Humboldt Star* reported:

The Indian murderers left the Duck Valley Reservation in Northern Elko, over a year ago [incorrect]. They have been rustling horses and cattle ever since, committing murder whenever their operations have been interfered with. After killing Frank Dopp, they disappeared from that section, and went westward, probably taking about the same route over which they are now being pursued on the back trail. Last July, the Indians stopped at Lay's ranch and traded for some old harness. Later they were seen in Limbo Canyon in the extreme western part of this county, where they were running off horses. An Indian who was hunting started to ride up to one of the young bucks when the outlaw pointed his rifle at the other and warned him to keep his distance. The Indian hunter did as he was told. . . . The feeling of the members of the posse from Eagleville is said to be so strong that they will stay with the hunt until the outlaws are finally captured, no matter how long that takes. . . . J.F. Tranmer stated to a representative of this newspaper that he is satisfied that he knows the Indians and that they made their home around Twin Falls, Idaho. They were the same band of Indians that were in the battle in which young Dopp was killed. Tranmer says that Dopp, who was only fourteen years old, was his step-son and was killed at Cow Creek, Elko County, last May. He has known the leader of the Indians who committed the murder for at least fifteen years. He is known in that country as Indian Mike and is an old man.

On the evening of the twenty-third, Sheriff Lamb returned to Winnemucca, accompanied by a number of the posse who came in to get supplies and to have their horses reshod. The remainder of the posse, including Captain Donnely, stopped at Tollhouse, twelve miles north of Winnemucca, and took up trail the next morning. They had followed the trail through the sandhills between Barrett Springs and the Bloody Run range of mountains, found where they had passed but eight miles north of town, and had even camped one night at the Miller and Lux well on the old Thacker Road, just beyond the sandhills in Bloody Run Valley.

Mike and his family pulled out of Long Canyon just in time. On a Friday night, a prospector named Schnitzius telephoned to Sheriff Lamb from Willow Point that a party of Indians answering the description of the fugitives was camping in the first canyon above Sardorus Canyon, known as Long Canyon, in the vicinity of Dutch Flat. On Saturday morning, Deputy Nofsinger was dispatched to Golconda by rail on No. 4, to convey the news to Captain Donnely. Nofsinger secured a team and wagon, and Donnely and his men were taken to Dutch Flat to investigate the story. There they met Charlie Byrnes, Constable of Paradise, and his deputy, Merril Prussia from the Cathcart Ranch, who had come in on Lamb's advice and found the deserted Indian camp, complete with dead mustang, live coals in the campfire, the sagebrush lookouts where sentinels had stood guard, and other evidence that Mike had camped there.

Even while Donnely was investigating the camp at Long

Canyon, Sheriff Lamb received another phone call, this time from a man named George J. Meyers, who had discovered the trail of the fugitive Indians at a spring, a short distance east of the Clover Valley ranch, where the Indians had watered their horses. Sheriff Lamb sent word to Captain Donnely, and Donnely in turn sent half his posse on ahead while the rest kept to the known trail.

By finding the trail in Clover Valley, authorities concluded that the Indians had crossed the Osgoods over Soldier's Pass, the same route traveled by Butch Cassidy's gang when they robbed the First National Bank of Winnemucca some years before.

By now, however, it was generally believed that the Indians were closer to the Idaho line than Winnemucca, and perhaps already safe in the Owyhee brakes. Actually, Mike and his band had spent nearly ten days under their noses in rugged Long Canyon, forced to lie close with hunger and fatigue. While it gave the posse a chance to catch up, it nearly cost the white men the trail, for, in their eagerness, they almost swept past, searching a vast, uninhabited land for tracks that did not exist.

Perhaps there was another reason besides the condition of his family that made Mike hole up in the canyon. He could ill afford a mistake, and was forced to hang tight while the boys went ahead to scout snow conditions to the northeast.

Some sources claim that Mike's whole band crossed Clover Valley and tried to head up Squaw Valley, but were turned back by snow. If this were true, the band would not have crossed back past the Kelley Creek ranch into an exposed position at Rabbit Creek, but would have skirted north of the ranch, keeping the ridges between them and the buildings, and disappeared into the upper reaches of Kelley Creek.

Most likely, it was Mike's boys who tried to push through the snows toward Squaw Valley and were forced to turn back.

Having been thus repulsed, the young men may well have tried a more southern route toward Tuscarora to the east.

On February 25, the *Silver State* reported that an Indian, supposed to be one of Mike's band, showed up at the I.L. Ranch, thirty-five miles from Tuscarora. Posses left Tuscarora immediately to investigate the rumor. Soon another report had it that all the Indians were at the I.L. Ranch and that their horses had sore backs. Sheriff Ferrel's forces were at that time camped at Winter Station, on their way to the Spanish Ranch. Hearsay had it that Constable Young's forces were within four miles of the Indians.

Mike's boys, however, perhaps realizing for the first time the danger of their predicament, beat it back toward Long Canyon, some fifty miles west, where they probably rejoined their family as they headed over the Osgoods under cover of darkness.

The situation was indeed desperate. The Tuscarora country was on full alert; Squaw Valley had too much snow; every pass was guarded by armed men; to the south lay settled ranch country. Only the northern route above Kelley Creek seemed open, into the mountains spawning the South Fork of the Little Humboldt. From the ridge above their camp at Rabbit Creek, they could see the friendly yawn of Kelley Creek's rocky canyon, splitting the domed hills as if by a giant axe.

Saturday night, February 25, 1911, Donnely's posse, made up of Sheriff Smith of Modoc County and the Surprise Valley men, camped at the Stewart Ranch near Willow Point, and early Sunday morning the posse gathered at the northeast corral gate. Fresh horses were in short supply, and although some of the posse had fresh mounts, others were riding jaded plugs that had difficulty keeping up. Nonetheless, they proceeded to the vicinity of Scott's Springs, about ten miles northeast of their starting point, where they picked up the trail of Mike's band, which led northeast toward the Bliss Kelley

Creek Ranch. The trail was followed until noon when the posse noticed smoke rising some distance ahead. It was Sunday, February 26, and sixteen days since the posse had begun the chase at Little High Rock Canyon, more than two hundred desolate, wintry miles away.

20

If there were twenty-one members of the posse who charged down the hill toward Mike's little family, there were nearly as many versions as to what happened during that dramatic afternoon at Rabbit Creek wash. Since the events occurred as late as 1911, the battle between wild Indians and whites was itself an anachronism, a holdover from times past. Each member of the posse had to be aware of his role in a happening unique for the time, maybe the last Indian skirmish in history. Each member had to be aware that if Mike surrendered peacefully, there could be no battle, no satisfaction of revenge for the murders at Little High Rock Canyon, no stories rivaling those of their fathers to tell around bunkhouse fires on winter eves.

We know from accounts that the braves fought back with guns; the women with bows, arrows, and spears; the children with rocks and gravel—all to the accompaniment of war whoops, drums, chants, and dances as the Indians tried to drive the terror from their own hearts into those of the enemy. What we will never know from the accounts of the avengers is whether the Indians were ever really given a chance to surrender.

The members of the posse went home heroes, wined and dined by all, chased by pretty girls previously unavailable, slated for fame and glory the rest of their days, with their names bywords in barrooms, whispered in reverence by history buffs. A century from now, the names of Cambron, Donnely, Fruits, Hogle, and Van Norman may still live, accumulating luster with each passing year for their part in a dramatic event that modern times could not duplicate. But there is just a chance that in a hundred years we will have acquired such maturity as a people that we will see these men not as heroes but only as actors in an unfortunate tragedy that destroyed the last of a people whose culture was old while ours had only begun.

When I stand at that lonely site—that forgotten battleground amidst the wild, unchanging sagebrush desert northeast of Winnemucca—armed with perspective, there are scenes that haunt me. I see the little family of Indians, the last holdouts of their culture, stumbling in near-exhaustion down the snowy wash. The hooves of their unshod horses are worn to the quick, bleeding crimson snowberries into the remnant snows. The feet of children and adults are wrapped with sagebrush bark and rags against the cold. The faces of all are haunted with sadness, their cheeks hollow and eyes dull with malnutrition. I see no hero makers here.

Their weapons are laughable. Only the thirty-eight Savage automatic taken from Cambron's body, and in Jim's possession, can be termed "modern," and there well may be only one cartridge left for it. Mike has a forty–fifty-two Henry black powder, while another of the boys has an ancient Colt cap and ball. The shotgun in their possession is a black powder blunderbuss that shoots a charge of small rocks or anything that will fit down the barrel.

These against a posse equipped with new, high-velocity repeating rifles and sidearms. There are only four able-bodied men—Jim, Eat-em-up Jake, Catchum Charlie, and Mike—fighting for their lives against twenty-one. But they are Bannocks, and ready to die like Bannocks. A cornered wolf does not surrender while there is breath in his body, nor does a corraled mustang stallion.

Most of the posse were superfluous. Three men armed with thirty-thirty rifles could have stood atop the bluff overlooking the camp and wiped out Indian Mike and his whole family without exposing themselves to danger. No need of heroes or heroics; three plain average, even cowardly, ranchhands—one up the dry wash, one down, and the other perched above, just over the bulwark of the hill—could have popped them off one by one, as if they were shooting long underwear hanging from a clothesline.

Of all Mike's camps I have visited, this alone was exposed and vulnerable to attack. He must have realized when he ventured as far out in the valley as cover permitted in order to shorten the next night's march that he was taking a calculated risk. He was protected from the north by the one low ridge, and behind him was a flat expanse of low sagebrush where even a running jackrabbit would have been visible and vulnerable for a mile. Only the wash itself provided some protection, yet it was impossible to crawl far up or down that winding arroyo without being exposed to enemies watching from the bluff overhead.

But the old chief had little choice. Across the valley, the fruits of freedom were dangling before him. Of all the possibilities, this route seemed least hazardous.

As the story was told to investigating authorities, the posse heard a dog bark, spotted smoke in the distance, and discovered the camp. Skinny Pascal then rode forward and called to Mike to surrender. According to the account of the posse, Mike fired back in answer and the battle was on.

Surely Mike was not such a fool. If he were indeed watching that long skirmish line of riders poised for attack, he had to know that there was no chance for escape. If he retreated down the canyon the wash soon terminated on the broad flat plain. He had simply to surrender to Skinny Pascal and take his chance in the white man's court.

Heney claimed, "White man shoot first. Indian had gun. Maybe one, two. Maybe not many powder."

What really happened is that when the posse was observed by Heney, she started to drive the hobbled horses down the hill toward camp. Immediately the posse broke down the wash in a wild, undisciplined charge, a mob of shooting, shouting, laughing, whooping cowboys, killing Heney's horses as they came, waking the Indians from sleep, and sending them scurrying for such cover as they could muster in such mass confusion that the Indians had little opportunity to grab the right cartridges for each caliber of gun. Whether or not, at that moment, the posse had actually fired on an Indian is beside the point. Hearing gunfire, seeing the posse and Heney running toward camp, the Indians had to assume that they were about to be massacred.

Twenty-five years after the event, one of the posse members, Mort West, wrote an account of the event for the *San Francisco Examiner*. Part of this account appears in Effie Mona Mack's book, *The Indian Massacre of 1911* (1968):

"At noon, we had covered 35 miles. Entering a deep, narrow canyon under a great cliff, I spoke to Captain Donnely of the N.S.P. saying 'We are apt to get shot up in there, Cap. You had better send in scouts. I volunteer to be one of them.'
" 'No need,' says he.

" 'Then let's string out so we will not all be in a bunch as a target.'

" 'No,' said Cap. 'We will keep together so we can help each other.'

" 'And get shot to hell!'

"Joe Reeder said: 'Oh, Hell! Let them have their way. The Injuns are just as apt to shoot a son of a b——— of a state policeman as one of us.'

"We had beds and grain with our packtrain so as to camp on the trail, but the State Police had insisted on staying on ranches ten and fifteen miles off the trail and at one place these hardy barracks fighters left a hay mattress to go three miles further to get feather beds. They had in general so delayed and disgusted us that the vaqueros had but one answer for them, 'Go to Hell!'

"Everyone including sheriffs, cowboys, and state police themselves, had gotten to relying on Cameron [Cambron] as leader!

"So we strung out as the vaqueros wanted to do. Jack Ferguson leading and I close behind while Captain Donnely and the Deputy from Paradise [Byrnes] went to the rear end of the line as we drove the pass. Then [at that time] we thought they were afraid but looking back across the years I realize the wise old captain knew we wanted to kill the murderers of the Surprise Valley men and probably stayed back on purpose so we could have our way and he could later say he was not there and could not prevent it.

"Watching the rocks above, every man with his rifle at the ready and expecting at any moment to feel a bullet, we rounded a great cliff, when Jack Ferguson said 'There they are!'

" 'Where?' someone said as we started around.

" 'Down there!' said Ferguson pointing to the rolling country beyond the pass.

" 'I don't see them but I see their hobbled horses.'

"Half a mile away, grazed eight hobbled horses which we had to watch closely to see that they were hobbled.

"I was following two faint draws through the snowy plain rod by rod with my eyes until I saw a faint bluish haze against the snow.

" 'Yes,' I said. 'It is their horses—there is their camp.'

" 'Where? Where?'

220

" 'There is their smoke in that draw.'

" 'Oh, you're crazy. I don't see any smoke.'

" 'No, he isn't,' said another.

" 'I see it myself now,' said a third.

"And so we gathered under the great butte where the Shoshones could have slaughtered us had they not thought all danger was past.

"We charged around the cliff, dropped into a hollow and across without being seen.

"A young squaw was guarding the horses and tried to drive them into camp. We shot three, one falling partly on her knocking her down before she gave up the attempt. On the far south end of the line Bill Parsons and Charlie Stone of the Nevada State Police were shooting horses.

" 'Watch me get that horse the squaw is chasing,' said Sergeant Stone.

"Charlie was a good shot and he took careful aim. As he shot, the squaw fell over a bush.

" 'You shot the squaw,' laughed Bill.

" 'Oh, God! Did I?' said Stone aghast.

"But just then the squaw got up and the horse fell knocking her down again.

"Bucks came yelling and war-whooping out of the draw and began shooting.

"Ben Cambron was just ahead of me laughing and shouting for these Indians had killed his brother.

"We had Skinny Pascal, Indian Trailer, tell the renegade Shoshone that if they gave up we wouldn't kill them. They listened a minute then went on yelling and shooting. We took to the bushes afoot like the Indians. Bullets went flying past our heads. Indians yelling, warwhooping, shouting. Vaqueros yelling, laughing, shooting, horses stampeding, and so began THE BATTLE OF KELLEY CREEK, NEVADA. And so began hell, many would say.

"No! Joy unbounding to us youngsters. That day and the summer that followed was the crest of our lives; and few of us will ever be happy again, for that year we were heroes entertained and sought after by all."

221

It is the habit of the white man to label as vicious any animal who fights to defend himself. If Mike fired the first shot aimed at a human being, he had no way of knowing that the hundreds of rounds that preceded his had been confined to shooting horses. The confused, frightened Indians did the only understandable thing. They fought back savagely to defend themselves.

Boldly, Mike ran out alone from the camp to try to decoy the attackers away from his children. He was thus the first to fall.

In later years, of course, many of the posse members claimed to have shot Mike. Most probably he was downed by Skinny Pascal, then wounded again by Captain Donnely. For some time the old Indian, refusing to die, propped himself on one elbow and encouraged his family to fight on, until eventually the tide of battle passed him by. Later, virtually every cowboy who came along emptied his gun at him until his body was half shot away.

The war whoops and wild drumbeats were all intended to frighten off the enemy, but drew only laughter from the posse, who knew themselves to be in command. In all the confusion, the cowboys were in far more danger of being hit by one of their own bullets than by the infrequent bullets or arrows of the Indians. In vain Jim, Eat-em-up Jake, and Catchum Charlie tried to hold off the onrushing posse so that women and children could retreat down the wash. But the women refused to flee. Instead, they rushed back and forth between the boys trying to straighten up the mixup of the ammunition, beat the drums, chanted, or fired arrows at the advancing party.

The whites made little attempt to distinguish between woman, child, or man, but instead fired upon anything that moved in the brush. One little boy of thirteen panicked under the assault, and was shot as he turned to run. As he fell, his brother, fourteen, jumped up crying, caught the boy in his arms, and was shot in turn. Later, when the frozen bodies were collected, the two boys, arms still locked about each other, could not be pried apart and were buried together. Mike's wife, Jennie, was shot as she tried in vain to crawl to Mike's side. As the Ute woman fell, Heney ran to her screaming, ignoring danger, and held the old woman's wrinkled brown face to her breast until her eyes dimmed forever.

Little by little the Indians gave way down the wash, as the cowboys whooped and hollered obscenities, mounted, galloped, dismounted, and fired at some new real or fancied target. Bullets struck the rocky soil and ricochetted off across the expanse, whining like a thousand angry bees. Horses reared, plunged, screamed like banshees in pain or terror, ran off dragging reins, and had to be gathered by other riders. Ben Cambron's horse was not recovered until the following day.

Heney left her mother's side and ran back into the melee, brandishing a short spear at any who tried to attack her. Crawling on her hands and knees, she found her brother, Jim, in a wash. Bullets were cutting switches off the sage over his head. Jim was unarmed except for one bullet left in the thirty-eight automatic pistol taken from Harry Cambron. Heney wormed her way to Jim. A young cowboy was advancing on Jim's hiding place, his gun cocked like that of a hunter expecting a covey of quail to burst from the grass. He was out in front of the others, but Jim could not risk his last shot at that range. Bravely, Heney stood up before her brother and faced the advancing Ed Hogle. She pulled up her skirts to expose her womanhood, smiled, and moved toward the astonished cowboy with a weaving, shuffling dance, holding her ragged clothing wide as she advanced. As Hogle stared in fascination, she suddenly dropped, exposing her brother Jim, who had been hiding behind her, and Jim fired the last shot in the automatic before being cut down by a snarl of bullets. Bewildered, Hogle staggered back, holding his arm tightly to his chest. "My

God, boys, I'm shot!'' The boys thought it was just his arm until he walked back some forty feet and fell dead.

Long after the Indian guns had ceased, the posse fired and fired, lacing the sage with bullets. Throughout the battle Indian dogs barked and ran searching for their masters. A tricolored collie, later adopted by the state police, bounded back and forth wild with excitement.

Henry Hughes scaled the ridge and lay watching as the squaws danced and chanted just below him. Suddenly they detected his presence and began lobbing arrows, trying to hit him.

According to Hughes, the arrows would go up into the air until they looked like knitting needles, then they would turn and fall to thump into the frozen ground beside him. As each one fell, he gathered it for a souvenir.

In the meantime, Heney's sister, Snake, with the baby strapped to her back, huddled in the wash. Snake was nineteen, round-faced, and jolly—a pet of the camp. She lacked Heney's serious nature, and though she worked hard, laughter was never long from her lips. Because of the baby she stayed out of the fray, but as the sound of rifle fire ceased for a moment, she raised her head, only to be caught in a sudden crossfire. She pitched backwards and lay still, the baby's head hanging in the snow and mud, its terrified, angry wails adding to the din of battle.

Eat-em-up Jake and Catchum Charlie were both wounded in a frenzied charge as the posse learned about Hogle's death and went berserk, forgetting their safety. In the rush one of the posse members was struck by an arrow, but it barely penetrated his clothing. Jake and Charlie were hit again and again, but somehow managed to crawl away to fire again from another point in the gully. Great crimson trails of bloody snow marked their crisscrossed paths until, their ammunition expended, both died in the bottom of the dry stream bed.

224

Even Hattie and Cleve took part in the battle. Picking up rocks and handfuls of gravel, they made a brave stand before the advancing party, flinging stones at them as they pushed forward, their dark eyes sparkling with hatred, which for the moment overpowered their terror.

Quietly, Heney slipped in and took them down the wash, then crawled off with them across the flat where the sagebrush afforded some cover. But it was not long before two of the cowboys found their tracks in the snow and followed them. Heney tried valiantly to defend the children with a short spear tipped with the blade of a sheep shear. For a time she held them off, then one slipped up behind her as she faced the other, threw his coat over her head, and wrestled her down. Hog-tied, she lay in the snow screaming invectives in a language known only to her.

Cleve scampered away from a cowboy who tried to outrun him on foot and left him as though standing still, but the man regained his horse and roped Cleve in the sage, then dragged him, terrified, into the saddle in front of him, where the poor frightened boy tried to beat his brains out on the saddle horn. Hattie huddled by the trussed-up body of her sister, too young really to comprehend the full magnitude of what had happened.

During the battle, the Indians had managed to retreat about a mile down the wash. Now, as the firing slackened, Van Norman galloped back up the wash to where Mike had fallen, catching up with Cambron, who had lost his horse, just as the burly, heavy-set cattleman reached the spot where Mike lay beside a light-green bush. As they approached, the old Indian tried in vain to reach his rifle. He was riddled with bullets and his stomach was shot away, but still he stared them down, his eyes sparkling with hatred. His once-proud head-dress, plumed with snowy eagle feathers, lay dirty and disheveled stained by blood and mire.

It was here that Van Norman told me Cambron cursed the old Indian and asked him, "What kind of damn Indian are you anyway?" And Mike replied, "Me Shoshone! Me Shoshone!"

Cambron then pried his mouth open with his rifle barrel to look at his teeth and would have finished him off had not Van Norman pulled him away. The old man returned their stares, still unconquered, until at last the eyes glazed and a faint trace of a smile announced his arrival in the happy hunting ground of his ancestors.

Over the battlefield the posse searched for surviving Indians, half expecting more shots to come from the brush, but there were none, and a curious silence hung over the sagelands. Once the battle was over, they sent a messenger on to the Bliss Kelley ranch on the floor of the valley perhaps six miles to the east to borrow a wagon for the captives and for the body of Ed Hogle, while another messenger was sent to North's ranch, thirteen miles away, to summon Coroner Buckley from Golconda.

The gathering cowboys seemed hushed, almost disappointed that the three-hour battle was over. That night the men gathered before the fireplace in the Kelley Creek ranch house to talk over the deeds of the day and to guard the prisoners who huddled together mourning their dead. The firelight died, but still Heney's banshee wails rent the night, and there were doubts in some minds as to whether she was more interested in giving her dead a good, mournful send-off on their journey or in seeking revenge upon their slayers by making sure they got not one moment's sleep. Muttered curses from the bedrolls sprawled about the room brought only fresh gushings of grief from the pretty Indian girl.

Now and then some cowboy, rising from his bed to put another log on the fire, found her still huddled with her arms about the children, sobbing as though her heart would break.

226

21

On Monday, the day after the battle, members of the posse flipped coins to determine who would have the dull chore of guarding the captives, and the winners trotted westward across the valley to scavenge for souvenirs and poke about the frozen corpses for anything that might be of interest to the folks back home. About noon, Sheriff Lamb arrived from Winnemucca to view the carnage. An eminently fair man, he was enraged at what he saw. "What the hell has been going on here?" he roared, looking at the dead mustangs and the bullet-ridden women and children. Through the years, there has been speculation that, had Lamb been along, the Indians would have been given a chance to surrender, and there would have been no battle.

It was not the sheriff's fault he had been absent. Once again the state police had tricked him to avoid sharing the glory. Lamb had been good enough to send them hot leads, which had been phoned in to him, enabling them to pick up Mike's trail beyond Long Canyon, and he expected to meet the Surprise Valley men at Willow Point and go on with them, but the state police phoned in the information that they had inspected the trail and it was stone cold. Every man in the posse who had seen the tracks of course knew differently, and so when the battle was fought, Sheriff Lamb was in Winnemucca attending to the routine business of his office.

Methodically, the cowboys fanned out through the sage, picking up spears, arrows, bows, drums, Mike's tattered headdress, a bundle of otter skins trapped in the Warner Mountains, and Mike's guns, as well as any evidence linking the Indians to the murder of the Surprise Valley men. There was a brief flurry of excitement when the state police discovered a twenty-one-year-old Golconda cowboy named Walter Polkinghorne riding through the hills; they arrested him, thinking he might be a renegade white attached to Mike's band. Walter and two other mustangers were camped in the hills some three miles away, and, striking the trail of the Indian mustangs, Walter followed them down the wash. Since Polkinghorne was of an old Nevada pioneer family and his father ran the store in Golconda, he was released after a few hours' custody to join the rest of the curious at the battlefield.

When I interviewed Walter in Winnemucca in 1971, a few months before his death, he told me that he had inspected the camp the Indians had made by covering a small wash off Rabbit Creek with hides and brush. He found that the Indians were near starvation, having only a small flour sack of dried ants and a couple of partly eaten rabbit carcasses.

As I sat in the Polkinghorne living room, surrounded by mementos of Nevada's past, I recorded his words on tape as he told me that, some days previous to the battle, he had been loping across the foothills of the Osgoods heading for camp when his horse stumbled in a badger hole and was so badly injured he had to be shot. As he headed across the hills afoot, he was taken into camp by some of Mike's boys, who later released him. This could not have been the main camp at Long Canyon, but had to be a scouting camp used by the boys alone.

Walter was not present at the battle, but heard many an excited firsthand account from members of the posse in dire need of an audience.

According to Polkinghorne, when Coroner Buckley finished his inquest on the scattered Indians, he ordered them buried on the scene. Using a case of dynamite brought by buckboard from Golconda for that purpose, the whites blasted a hole in the frozen ground, snaked in the Indians with horses and reatas, and dumped the bodies into the mass grave. Precisely as Mrs. Weighall had dreamed so many months before, the Indians more than filled the hole, and Polkinghorne claimed that one big Indian slid off the pile to one side and had to be covered separately.

The grave was marked with a pole but soon forgotten. In the 1930s, engineers from the Getchell Mine, which sprang up on a hillside overlooking the battlefield, searched the area for remnants but found only a few scattered bones dug up by animals. Later a cairn of rocks was stacked around the post and a sign was erected that read, "SHOSHONE MIKE AND HIS BAND OF MARAUDERS," but frost-heaved and neglected, the sign post soon succumbed to desert winds and was taken as a souvenir by a Winnemucca man. In recent years, a van load of university students paid a miner at Getchell Mine five dollars to show them the site, dug up the grave, and hauled off many of the bones. It is an atrocity hard to defend, since there was little to be gained scientifically from such desecration. Had the grave been that of a white man, it would have remained inviolate.

The bones the thirsty students missed were left scattered on the surface amidst a hoard of bottles, until I gathered the remnants where they lay scattered over the gravelly bottom and buried them on a lonely rimrock on Gollaher Mountain, near the grave of one of Mike's daughters.

When Skinny Pascal, the tall, handsome Paiute tracker, arrived back in Winnemucca with Sheriff Lamb, he received a hero's welcome, although folks in Humboldt County were understandably upset over the treatment their intrepid sheriff had received at the hands of the state police. To Skinny it had been a job, and a distasteful one at that. His tale was terse and to the point, and his tale confirmed that the battle had begun before he called to Mike to surrender.

"We took trail at 6 o'clock on Sunday morning. There were about nineteen men in the party. We followed the trail from place the Indians had left Saturday morning and went across the mountains to upper end of Clover Valley. Traveled about twenty miles. I saw smoke Indian's camp first in little canyon just edge valley. Donnely gave orders forward and Indians first saw us as we got top ridge. Indians started run down canyon main body posse after them.

"Mike separated and ran into brush. I started after him. He dropped behind brush. I shouted to him. He raised up and shot at me. I shot too and again into brush. Guess got him as trail of blood afterwards found where he crawled back nearly to camp where he found dead.

"As Mike lay dying, Donnely rode up and Mike took shot at him but missed. Maybe Donnely finished him. We caught up balance Indians about two miles down canyon and here they made last stand and had war dance. Posse surrounded them here and we finished them." (*The Humboldt Star,* March 1, 1911.)

Once they had combed the battlefield for souvenirs, the posse dutifully piled them in a stack that was quickly usurped as evidence by Policeman Newgard. Members of the posse immediately jumped in, upended the protesting Newgard, and helped themselves to reatas, rawhide reins, arrows, and such other souvenirs they felt belonged to them as victors' spoils. The otter skins they left for Captain Donnely, who said he wanted them.

It was a triumphant posse that rode down out of the hills escorting a buckboard containing the hog-tied bodies of the prisoners, followed by a spring wagon bearing the body of Ed Hogle. Still wearing chaps, Hogle's body was covered with a bed canvas and surrounded by trophies of the battle—the drums, Heney's spear with its decoration of feathers, and Mike's blood-bespattered war bonnet. The trip from Kelley Creek ranch to Golconda took most of the day, and while still miles from town the men were met by throngs of the curious in sleighs and buggies. Since the road paralleled the railroad track, one enterprising soul even pumped out from town on a handcar and cheered along with the rest of them.

Onlookers had come by the hundreds from Winnemucca and the surrounding country to see the historic spectacle. Women in long dresses and broad-brimmed hats braved the cold wind and crawled awkwardly out upstairs windows to sit on porch roofs and watch across the broad, rolling hills for the first glimpse of the caravan.

Though the party had started at dawn, it was three in the afternoon when it finally dragged into Golconda. The onlookers had expected to see the bodies of the wild Indians, and there were mutterings of anger when they learned that the Indians had been left piled on the desert awaiting burial. Cheated of one spectacle, they thronged around the living Indians.

Heney, Cleve, Hattie, and the baby were placed in the boxlike jail, where the girl covered her face with a blanket to avoid the stares of the curious. Indian women were permitted in the cell, and from these, Heney signaled for a pair of scissors so that she might cut her hair to mourn her dead properly. But the request was refused for fear she would kill herself and the children.

That the Indians had been guilty of murdering the four livestock men was easily proved by the fact that they were found to be still in possession of the sheepmen's horses. In addition, on Mike's dead body they found Cambron's watch. The watch was set on railroad time, which may have meant that, when the Indians passed Winnemucca, one of the bucks slipped in to town to get food and to learn the news.

At the inquest over the body of Ed Hogle, the jury decided that he had died of wounds suffered in the battle with the Indians and accused Heney of complicity in his death, but none of the testimony indicated that she had fired a gun or shot a bow and arrow, although she had defended herself often enough with her spear. Eventually, all charges against Heney were dropped, and she was sent to Reno in custody of Sheriff Ferrel and State Policeman Buck. For a time, Heney was terrified of the train, but soon she settled down, comforting the little ones, and took the trip in stride.

In Reno, huge throngs met the train, but had only a fleeting glimpse of the captives as they were whisked into a closed carriage and driven to the Reno jail. Cheated, the crowds had to settle for a look at the trophies gathered from the Indians.

One of the most interesting was an ingenious vise found by Sheriff Lamb, made from two large bull horns. The curved horns were bolted together at the tips, and the large ends with sawlike teeth formed the jaws of the vise, while the natural spring in the horns held the jaws tightly together. To use the vise, one had to pull apart the jaws of the vise and place the article to be held between them. None of the Nevada Indians had ever seen anything like it, and, along with other souvenirs, it was used to demonstrate the extremely primitive nature of Mike's existence.

The battle occurred on a Sunday, but it was Friday before members of the posse were excused from further testimony at the coroner's inquest. The men were naturally anxious to get back to their professions, and besides that, some stood in extreme danger of being caught up in matrimony by Golconda and Winnemucca girls.

Leaving Golconda, the posse staged a celebration in Winnemucca, where Sheriff Lamb quartered them in the Humboldt County Court House. The next day they were taken to talk to Tranmer and Urie in the Winnemucca jail about their fight with Mike's band.

When souvenir hunters began to deplete their stock of relics, the men left Winnemucca for Gerlach on the Western Pacific, taking their horses and rigging with them in a box car ahead of the caboose. Still heady from their experiences, the men swaggered onto the train, playing the role of Indian fighters to the hilt. The trainmen protested their taking loaded guns aboard, but fell silent under their withering gaze. Once under way, the men amused themselves by shooting at wild horses and antelope as they passed over the alkaline flats and sagebrushed plains.

More than a few of them fancied a pot of gold waiting for them upon their arrival home as their share in the rewards. Day and night they talked of little else than how they would spend the booty. Unloading at Gerlach, they immediately began the long ride home.

The first night they camped at Clear Creek ranch, then, traveling along the Granite Range of mountains, they crossed the pass in a heavy snowstorm and spent the last night on the trail at Lost Creek, a Gerlach Cattle Company ranch, and the very ranch where, years later, I was to interview O. D. Van Norman.

On March 8, one month to the day after the posse left on the great Indian chase, they rode into Eagleville, California,

233

and the wildest homecoming celebration in that town's history.

The men, who had held little place in Surprise Valley society, now found themselves feted all around, giggled at by coy matrons, and boldly eyed by the daughters. A reception was held in the church, where services, partly Catholic, partly Protestant had been held for the murdered men; people flocked in from the length of the valley, Fort Bidwell to the Bare ranch, filled the church, and overflowed into the street. The main speaker for the evening was state senator-to-be, Frank (Butch) Powers, who later became lieutenant governor of California.

In the words of Mort West, "Delia McClintock recited a poem she had written in our honor. Ethel and Floy Patterson, and Zella MacCormic played and sang. Ben Cambron and Elzie Smith, Modoc County Sheriff, made talks, while even Henry Hughes and I had to face that crowd and tell the story of the trail. Henry stammered, cleared his throat, and nearly swallowed his tongue before he finally got going. Hughes said afterward, 'I would a damn sight rather face any Injun than that crowd.'" (Mack, *The Indian Massacre of 1911.*)

There was first one banquet and another, then even another to eat the leftovers from the first. The boys who had stayed at home were given short shrift by the girls, who seemed to think that the sun rose and set just to shine on the members of the posse.

For a few weeks, peace and quiet reigned over northern Nevada, but among those lonely, vulnerable families who lived their solitary lives miles from towns or neighbors, an after-shock soon followed, and rumors of coming Indian reprisals sparked a rebirth of the Indian hysteria that had long plagued the red men. Sales of ammunition jumped, lonely cabins became arsenals, and ranchers kept close watch on the surrounding hills, while their wives left them to cook for themselves while they headed for civilization to visit relatives.

Those Indians given to hunting found it safer to travel in larger parties, since the solitary Indian stood a good chance of being shot first and questioned later. Although the size of the parties gave them some measure of safety, the sight of them crossing the deserts only fanned the rumors beginning to run rife that Indians were now on the warpath to avenge Mike's death.

Alarmed by white attitudes, Chief Harry Preacher, head of the Shoshone in Elko, requested an interview with the Wells, Nevada, *Herald*. An article published March 22, 1911, read:

Harry Preacher, chief and leader of the Shoshone Indians of Elko, called at the Wells *Herald* office a few days ago and stated that it had been reported to him that some of the white people, especially those living in the northern part of Elko county, were afraid that the Indians might go on the warpath to avenge the death of Indian Mike and gang who were killed by the State Police and posse in the battle of a few weeks ago.

Harry stated that he does not believe that there is any danger of any of the Shoshones making trouble for the whites. He says that Indian Mike and his band were Bannocks and that the Shoshones have no particular love for them. In fact he rather intimated that the Shoshones were pleased to know that Mike was out of the way, as they believe that they murdered a couple of their tribesmen some time ago.

The Shoshone Chief wishes to impress upon the Shoshones the necessity of being friendly with the whites. He wishes to advise them to be careful that they do no act which will offend the whites as they are certain to be sufferers in the end, and no good could come of incurring the enmity of the white people. He also wants them to be friendly with each other and not get into trouble among themselves.

He states that if the Indians would only leave whiskey alone that they would be far more prosperous and happy.

Despite Harry Preacher's statement to the press, rumors persisted that Indians resented Mike's death and were thirsting for revenge. Near panic resulted when the newspapers announced that eighteen Shoshone Indian bucks, wearing warpaint, had escaped the Duck Valley Reservation and were on the warpath near Little High Rock Canyon to avenge the killings in the battle at Rabbit Creek wash.

The *Silver State* reported:

The Indians are heavily armed, unimpeded by squaws or superfluous baggage, possess a large extra supply of horses and have donned the war-paint in token that before long some unprotected white man or woman will pay the blood toll for the killing of Indian Mike's band.

Law men made every effort to warn the lonely inhabitants of the area to stay clear of the path of the hostiles if they valued their lives. Forewarned, miners and sheepmen headed for town, taking the story with them and spreading distorted facts like wildfire through the whole of northern Nevada.

Skinny Pascal caused further uproar when he told a former state policeman that Mike's eldest son had not been killed in the massacre but had escaped the fighting, since he was off on advance patrol, and on hearing shots watched the demise of his family from a distance, then fled for the Duck Valley Reservation, where even now he was in charge of the party of youths. According to Pascal, however, the Indians were camped at Soldier's Meadows on a hunting trip rather than seeking trouble.

But the youths were armed and Pascal's report did little to soothe frayed nerves. When the report reached Washington, authorities there ordered the Indian agent at Owyhee, George R. Daggett, to investigate the matter. Since the battle at Rabbit Creek, the Indian office had been keeping the situation in northern Nevada under close scrutiny. Daggett ordered every Indian on the reservation to report for roll call and soon determined that, save for a few Indians working on adjoining ranches, none were unaccounted for. The identity of the eighteen bucks remained a mystery, and they soon vanished without ever acting on their supposed desire for vengeance.

The next reported uprising came on July 31, 1911, when Sheriff Lamb received a letter from John B. Hoover, superintendent of the Indian school at McDermitt. Mr. Hoover wrote that the Indians who lived in the McDermitt section had reported to him that they had seen a brother of Mike with a band of four braves and three squaws, and that they were traveling westward toward Little High Rock. The Indians told Hoover that they spotted the party a few days before and that they were on the warpath to avenge the slaying of Rock Creek Mike and his band.

This is the first and only reference I have found to Mike's brother. Most likely confusion arose from similarity of names. Many assumed that the Indian sometimes called Salmon River Jim, Rock Creek Jim, or Indian Jim was a brother to Salmon River Mike, sometimes called Rock Creek Mike or Indian Mike.

In a letter to the Wells *Herald,* concerning the rumors putting Salmon River Jim on the warpath, a well-known rancher named James O'Neill wrote that Jim was a gentle old Shoshone while Mike was a Bannock, and that far from being on the warpath Jim at that very moment was out working in the O'Neill ranch hayfields.

Undoubtedly Jim's reputation suffered from the similarity of names. In *The Indian Massacre of 1911,* Effie Mack states:

No one wanted Heney and/or the children; and they had no known relatives. Someone suggested they could be turned over to Salmon River Jim in southern Idaho, himself a known outlaw.

Even poor Jim, the gentlest of the Rock Creek Indians, thus patiently acquired a burden of blame simply because he was an Indian.

It was not until the coming of World War I that the Indian scares died out in northern Nevada. Though the land remained much the same, the Indians were simply forgotten by government and news media alike, as the nation became preoccupied with problems abroad.

After the Indian captives were transferred to Reno, Sheriff Ferrel took a special interest in their comfort and even became quite attached to them. On the first day of May, 1911, Heney, Hattie, Cleve, and the baby were transferred to the Carson Indian School, and the sheriff personally took them out on the Virginia and Truckee local to Carson City.

The Reno *Gazette* commented:

The squaw was resplendent in a late model black hat with cream puffs and red ribbons galore. They were the best clothes they ever had for before the outfit started on its murderous career it was satisfied to simply keep reasonably warm, but the good women of Reno opened their hearts and surrounded the group with choice garments, neatly tailored, and excellent material.

The children by now were learning to play with dolls and toys, which were a far cry from those made of sagebrush or clay, though they would have welcomed a sagebrush doll as a friend out of their past and played with it readily. As she said good-bye to her friend the sheriff, Heney wiped her nose on a hem-stitched handkerchief just as the photographer recording the transfer had her in the center of the field, and the picture proved no better than those taken of her by previous cameramen.

At Carson, once Heney got over her fear that she would be punished for her past, she became a model inmate. She was greatly attached to the three younger children, but in time she began to trust them for increasing periods to the care of others as she began to associate with other Indians in the school.

Assigned at first to household duties, she was slow to catch on, due to her wilderness upbringing, but she was a good pupil and gave no more trouble than any others in the school. They were really not under commitment at the school, but had been taken in as a humanitarian gesture by Superintendent Ashbury.

On September 13, Heney again made headlines. With her best friend and confidant, Ida Best, a Shoshone girl from the Silver Peak country, Heney vanished without a trace. Ida Best was a chronic truant and invariably returned after a short time. It may be that the girls missed the smell of sagebrush and the taste of wild foods cooked over a willow fire, and could not resist a journey back into history. But Heney's attachment to her family proved strong, and she slipped back one day, quietly and without fanfare, and took up life at the school as though completely unaware that she had been away.

Since Mike's family had not been enrolled on any of the reservations, there was a problem as to what to do with the survivors of his band. Perhaps because they feared trouble with the whites, her two relatives, Lizard at the Shoesole and the aunt at Tecoma, had no desire to assume their care.

Mack claimed that the baby was adopted by Harry Eastep, at Chimawa, Oregon, where there was an Indian school similar to the one at Carson; Heney remained at Carson, and the other two children, Hattie and Cleve, were sent to the Shoshone Reservation in Elko County.

But according to an article in the Carson *News,* Heney and

CAPTAIN J. P. DONN

Some members of Captain Donnely's posse in Golconda after the massacre. Standing, from the left: Charles Byrnes, Charles Stone, Peter Itziana (not a member of the posse), George Holmes, Joe Reeder, Skinny Pascal, Frank Perry,

POSSE

Captain J. P. Donnely, and P. M. Newgard. Seated, from the left: William Parsons, Warren Fruits, Merril Prussia, Henry Hughes, Mort West, Sheriff L. C. Smith, and Ben Cambron. *(Nevada Historical Society.)*

OFFICIAL PAPER OF HUMBOLDT COUNTY

THE SILVER STATE

PIONEER MINING JOURNAL OF NORTHERN NEVADA---ESTABLISHED 1869

WINNEMUCCA, NEVADA, TUESDAY, FEBRUARY 28, 1911.   VOLUME 43, NO. 106.

SEASON TOMORROW

FORMER RESIDENT TELLS OF OLD DAYS

BAND OF MURDEROUS SHO-SHONES WIPED OUT BY POSSE

Information Furnished Sheriff Lamb by Prospector Schnitzius Enables Captain Donnelly and Posse to Trail Fugitives to Point Near Bliss' Kelly Creek Ranch, When Desperate Battle Ensues

NEWS NOTES OF NATION'S CAPITAL

(From F. J. DYER.)

FEB. 22 OBSERV-ED AT M'DERMITT

Kelley Creek Ranch, where Heney and the children were taken the night after the massacre.

Some of the Eagleville boys at Golconda after the battle. Left to right: Warren Fruits, O. D. Van Norman, Skinny Pascal, Joe Reeder, George Holmes, Bill Parsons, Frank Perry, and Peter Itziana. *(Nevada Historical Society.)*

The bodies were piled into a grave blasted out of the frozen ground. This is the only known picture of Mike. *(Nevada Historical Society.)*

The open, desolate land of Rabbit Creek Wash provided no cover for the band: defense was impossible.

The citizens of Golconda lined the streets and sat on their roofs to get a glimpse of the posse and prisoners after the fight at Rabbit Creek Wash. *(Nevada Historical Society.)*

Skinny Pascal, the famous Paiute tracker who led the posse to Mike's camp, carries Hattie to the jail. Heney and Cleve are hiding behind Pascal. *(Nevada Historical Society.)*

Heney and the children leave the jail in Golconda. Cleve is hidden behind Heney's skirts. *(Nevada Historical Society.)*

Sheriff Ferrel and the captives at the Washoe County Courthouse. *(Nevada Historical Society.)*

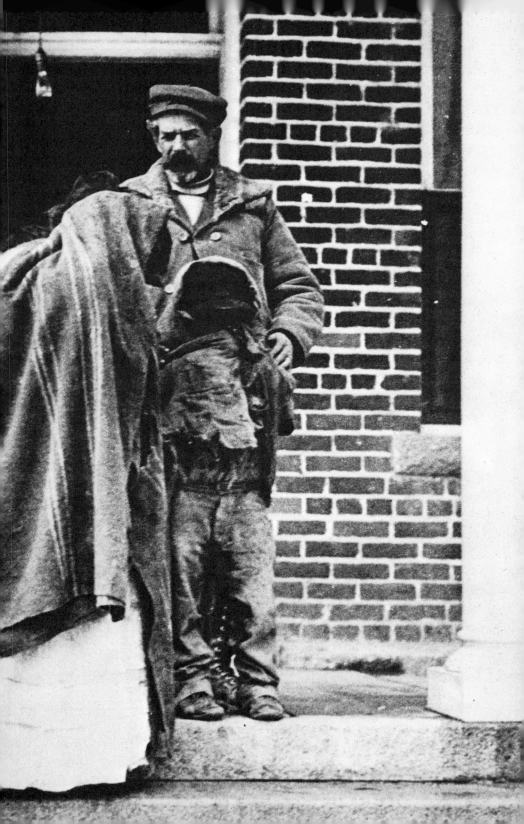

SHOSHONE MIKE
BAND OF MARAUDERS

the children were taken to Fort Hall, since that reservation had more of their tribe of Indians than any other reservation, and it was thought that they would feel more at home than at Carson. Carrying specific authority from the Indian department, the Superintendent of the Fort Hall Indian Reservation himself traveled south to make the transfer.

Here at Fort Hall, the trail of the Indian children vanishes. There is even a possibility that some of them might be alive today. Heney would be eighty, Cleve about sixty-eight, and Hattie sixty-six. Most likely they were rapidly absorbed into Indian life at Fort Hall, and soon forgot the past hardships and the old free life at Rock Creek and Gollaher Mountain. If ever they came back to Rock Creek to view the old wintering ground, they did so quietly and without contacting the whites who had played with them so happily among the hills.

22

If the Surprise Valley posse had heady dreams of dividing the promised $15,000 reward money among themselves, they were jolted to reality when the funds proved as elusive as the desert winds. Not only was the sum less than originally reported, but also it was tied up for some months in litigation. In the end the men received not the $700 or more they thought they deserved, but the paltry sum of $126, and this for a hard month's work. The men from Humboldt County were given $50 each as their share.

It was late summer before their trophies, held as conclusive evidence of Mike's guilt, were released by the authorities and distributed among the men. Sheriff Smith was awarded Mike's head-dress, Captain Donnely took the otter skins Mike's band had trapped on their way over the Warner Mountains, Sheriff Lamb ended up with at least one of the guns, while the rest of the trophies, such as bows, arrows, spears, drums, reatas, and other rawhide creations, were passed out as fairly as possible. The fifty dollars cash found on the bodies of the dead Indians was used to help defray the expense of the inquest.

For a few years, collections of the trophies were welcomed as displays in various hotels, drug stores, and annual fairs, but as memories failed and a younger generation grew up the artifacts began to attract more dust than attention and soon were scattered or even discarded by the children of deceased posse members settling their estates. One of Mike's arrows, steel-tipped and beautifully bound with sinew, still rests on display in the Elko, Nevada, museum.

In Rock Creek Canyon, above the Crockett place, in Mike's absence his campground soon grew up in willow and river birch, garlanded with wild clematis. Of the Bannocks and Shoshone who had hunted the canyon for centuries, there remained only Indian Jim, last of Chief Tuanna's Shoshone.

In 1924, when a neighbor found old Jim dying, he rushed him to the hospital in Twin Falls. According to Charles Walgamott, in *Reminiscences of Early Days* (1926),

Some of the old timers tried to contribute some comfort to his last days and when they called he was indeed glad to meet his old friends, but it soon developed that he still doubted the white man, when he told one of the old timers, "White man he take 'em all land, all water, all game he no more. Now white man he take 'em all my cattle, my horse, you get 'em my moccasin, I go."

When told he could not get his moccasin, and if he should go out in the cold he would die, he says "mebbe so die, mebbe so no die." And when told if he would take care of himself he would get well and strong and be able to catch more buck skin, he says "Mebbe so no more buck skin."

When Indian Jim died on September 20, 1924, old-timers gave him a Christian burial and a headstone in the cemetery with this inscription:

ROCK CREEK JIM
SHOSHONE INDIAN
OVER ONE HUNDRED YEARS OLD
ERECTED BY THE ORDER OF
SEVENTY-NINERS.

History is the story of change, and its beauty and value are enhanced by perspective. Mike's story is meaningful when placed in context with his times in that it delineates the last struggle of a man, a race, a culture trying to remain pure and free. Where other Indians had been racially absorbed or had yielded to the reservation system, Mike was the last holdout, refusing to let his band capitulate to the white man's way. In time, he or any Indian like him was doomed to fail, for our society cannot tolerate men who are free and independent of it.

Without change he might have been successful, but there is no timeless land. However it comes, fast or slow, change is inevitable. In the Snake River Valley, where once Mike's band gathered wild food, a visionary named Ira Perrine dreamed up an irrigation system so staggering in its immensity that it turned a vast desert valley from a hunting ground of primitive people into one of the world's great garden spots.

Shoshone Falls rivaled Niagara for sheer spectacle, its rocky gorge a paradise of rainbows, the earth shaking with the crash of water, but as man bled the river into irrigation arteries, carrying life to a productive but demanding land, even the mighty Snake was tamed. In the valley men thought big, did big, and drowned out the sagebrush with their sweat.

Just as every rapid in the Snake had its backwater, so Rock Creek Canyon slumbered as progress passed it by and helped make Mike's holdout possible. But even there change came creeping. Carrie Crockett still lives in the old Crockett house, built in 1880, but the original logs cut from virgin forests in the canyon were soon covered over with siding. Fences march in thin brave lines up the face of hills no old-timer would have bothered fencing. In the canyon behind Charlotte Crockett's corrals sleeps a museum of dead car bodies and rusting machinery, bought, bragged on, used, worn out, cussed at, abandoned, and replaced by later models to be cherished in their turn.

Sagebrush grows through the spokes of old wooden wagon wheels, rims rusted through by time. Wagon beds swaybacked from the snows, wood gray with age, stand stationary. Mike knew them when they were more than scenery. In the brush rust hand-made sleds from an era when toys were made, not purchased, improvised by children for children and wheedled into being by the urchins pestering the hired man. Designed and cherished by youngsters now grown and gone, coming home only for holidays with husbands patient but busy with business thoughts of elsewhere.

Here and there along the canyon, Lombardy poplars stand in groves or lines where some settler, stopping for a few years, tried to make things nicer for a homesick wife, walked hand in hand with her amidst purpling evening sage, lived for a time and loved but failed, gave in to the realities of rural economics, then sold out to a neighbor and moved on. Near a stream on Charlotte's upper place, a throng of dancing daffodils grow wild in testimony to love or homesickness, planted by some long-forgotten woman's hand. Entwining a rotting balustrade is a matrimony vine, germinated perhaps in Illinois, taken by wagon train across the plains, and having graced a settler's porch and marriage until the last supporting pillar fell to leave it tumbling.

On a lone hillside, an apricot tree turns orange with fruit—unwatered, unloved, unpruned, unsprayed, bug-infested, sapsucker girdled, bird-thronged but stubbornly productive, grown perhaps from a cutting carried from Connecticut by prairie schooner or simply of a flung seed from a passing teamster's lunch. Mike's children lazed in its early shadow and filled each nut-brown chipmunk cheek with fruit, but now the old tree is hollow and gnarled with age. Some spring the leaves will fail to come.

Up in Mike's canyon, Forest Service signs shout silent disciplines at visitors who without them would not feel secure. At the sites where Mike once camped are throngs of campers, travel trailers, cars, tourists, and make-believe Indians, who build their fires of river birch that smokes and smoulders, polluting their canvas tipis and bringing a wash of tears.

Ravens still play, however, along the red rock rims, while magpies flash their black and white semaphore way across the canyons from one ridge top to another. From the thickets along Rock Creek, yellow-breasted chats mock startled fishermen with wild pure music from hidden bowers. Even along the rims there is change. The bunch grass of Mike's time has given in to cheat grass, a worthless invader brought in by sheep; the rocks are aflutter with common barn pigeons that pretend to be feral, but flock daily down the valley to a world of lush grain fields where Man's inefficiency of harvest is their bounty.

From Mike's hunting grounds atop the rounded mountains one sees everywhere the scars of roads drifting nowhere, as though built to function merely as raceways and dancing grounds for rabbits. On the hills too are wounds where motorcycles without conscience have hurried the eroding process of time. Here still are golden eagles, hiding from sheepmen paranoid about predators, indelicately whitewashing the tips of power poles and fence posts, nesting on lonely rims amidst boneyards of rodents. But each year takes its toll of their numbers.

In a few lonely canyons amidst grass and rose briars, a remnant population of huge white-tailed jacks hold out against the black-tailed invader. Sage grouse still strut ancestral courting grounds, though in diminished numbers. The mustangs, descendants of Spanish stock whose flinty hooves rang like bells amidst the devil's rock gardens of the desert, outlived the Indians who pursued them, but soon either followed the Indian to cultivated pastures to lose their identity or were harvested by mustangers for pet food, glue, and fertilizer. The prairie wolf is gone forever, and the cougar a passing shadow seldom seen, replaced by the more adaptable bobcat, which prowls the rims hunting mice, pack rats, and marmots, while the beneficial coyote goes his amiable way unmindful of the hatred some men have for him.

Even the small things belong to history—the apricot tree, the busted wagon rotting beside a corral of sleek, modern Hereford cattle, Carrie's house in a cathedral of ancient trees planted by settlers, the sod-roofed store at the Stricker ranch, and even the story of Mike's little mom and pop band of Indians, who, clinging to ancient ways, out of context with the times, made one last cultural stand against the white man's overwhelming way.

Seen in perspective, the white man seems a strange species —not yet mature, as savagely territorial as a robin; he is still the hunter, but with little more foresight or sense of history than an antelope. While his accomplishments in science cannot be denied, all the atomic wizardry of which he is capable cannot bring back Mike or his world. As a people we are the summation of our cultures, and with each cultural loss we too are diminished.

Time runs a course. Even the desert yields to change. The trails of covered wagon, Indian, and buffalo grow dim. Even the reservations designed to keep the Indian isolated and apart seem doomed to progress and the slow stress of time. Isolation could only delay what time must do inevitably, but it is the senseless loss of the Indian heritage for which we weep.

263

The Indians I played with as a boy are gone. Some fell prey to the neuroses of being Indian in a white world. Others were assimilated, became doctors, lawyers, teachers, merchants, leading citizens in their communities, but tragically they made white men of themselves to do it, their great traditions and rich cultural history forgotten.

Even my white goose vanished from my life. One morning when its pinion feathers had grown out, filled with cravings, it flew on creaky wings to battle the west winds out over the valley. Captivity had done it no favors. Somehow it could no longer cope with hardship, and, like the Indian of old, it vanished from the scene almost before I missed it, and it was seen no more.

I am left alone with memories fragile as a waking dream. Mike lives on now in memory alone, but as I wander the lonely wastelands of northern Nevada and southern Idaho, I feel his presence still, as though he rides the wind and guides my way over his lost domain to tell his story. From somewhere in the sage, a vesper sparrow lisps its silver song, and from the weathering rimrocks, Mike's friend the canyon wren pipes plaintively as though to ask where all the Indians have gone.